**THE DAVID GLENN HUNT
MEMORIAL LIBRARY**
Galveston College
Galveston, Texas

Classic Americans

Classic Americans

A Study of Eminent American Writers
from Irving to Whitman

with an Introductory Survey of the Colonial
Background of Our National Literature

By

Henry Seidel Canby, Ph.D., Litt.D.

NEW YORK / RUSSELL & RUSSELL

The Library of Congress has cataloged this book
as follows:

Canby, Henry Seidel, 1878–
    Classic Americans; a study of eminent American writers
from Irving to Whitman, with an introductory survey of
the colonial background of our national literature. ₍1st ed.₎
New York, Russell & Russell, 1959.

    371 p.   22 cm.

    1. American literature—19th cent. — Hist. & crit.   2. American
literature—Colonial period—Hist. & crit.   I. Title.

PS88.C35   1959   928.1   59–7257 ‡

Library of Congress

Preface

THIS book, which is the fruit of reading and study extending over ten years, was originally planned as a history of American literature studied in the light of its social and intellectual backgrounds. A busy editorial life has made such an ambitious project impracticable, but necessity has had its compensations, for the substitution of criticism for history has left me free to take up the congenial task of interpreting to the best of my ability the abundant material now at hand for the study of American literature, free, too, to concentrate upon the great writers who are the essences of their times. With a few exceptions, I have not attempted to go beyond the facts already accessible in embarrassing quantity to scholars, but have been content to confine originality to the interpretation and criticism of texts and biographies, which, for our eminent writers, are ample for satisfactory criticism, even if in some instances not by any means yet complete. An exception must be noted for Herman Melville, who has been discovered by scholars only in the last decades, though long known to good readers, and whose perplexing career and difficult books still need research and elucidation before the basis upon which a summary opinion must be erected is sure. I have confined my remarks upon him to a half chapter, and have used his work, not, I trust, in derogation, as a means of interpreting by contrast and comparison the writings of Hawthorne, while my estimate of his quality is confined to certain aspects that seem to me the most important. It is not as a compilation of new biographical or historical facts, but as a contribution to the better understanding of American literature and the American mind, that I offer this book.

The limits of the work require, I think, no apology. I should have liked to include Mark Twain, but he belongs clearly in the postbellum atmosphere after the end of a great period and in a society in many respects reconstructed. With James and Howells and Emily Dickinson, his place is in a second volume. But as apology or as explanation, it should be said that the chapters on the classic Americans from Irving to Whitman, as well as the briefer studies of colonial figures, do not purport to say all that can be said, or to tell all that can be told, of their subjects. The criticism in this book, like all criticism, is personal, and represents what have seemed to me the really important aspects of these men and their works, after all methods of approach—social, psychological, æsthetic—have been duly employed. I have written of Cooper or Thoreau what seemed to me both true and important for a reader of our generation.

Annotation has been kept to a minimum with due regard for evidence and reference. For broader reading the excellent bibliography of "The Cambridge History of American Literature" is available in any good library, but in order to cover important recent books, and to supply a

PREFACE

ready guide for readers, a selected bibliography of texts and authorities relevant to the authors discussed in this book has been prepared with the assistance of Professor Randall Stewart of Yale, and will be found in an appendix.

HENRY SEIDEL CANBY.

New Haven,
  May, 1931.

Contents

Introduction

American Literature

IN THE turbulent years at the dawn of the nineteenth century, the Hartford wits (who got their rhetoric and what wit they had at Yale) wrote epics, for only epics were worthy of the new era of republican institutions and republican art. At the end of the century Walt Whitman was still proclaiming that only a new literature could do justice to American democracy. And throughout that century, which is to be the main subject of this book, American literature has been subject to moods of patriotic inflation or violent reactions into self-conscious inferiority, with the natural result that it has been constantly overpraised or underprized. For sensitive patriotism, in a country made from a group of colonies and more conscious of its future than its past, has been ready with overstatement, and provincial critics have given attributes belonging to Shakespeare or Cervantes to authors differing from the great in kind as well as in degree. In sharp contrast, and for reasons which seemed to them good, more competent critics and scholars trained in universities have, until recently—with rare exceptions—slighted their own literature or condemned it because it was not what it could never be. In the early decades of the twentieth century the majority of American universities were still unwilling to admit that American literature was a fit subject for research leading to the doctorate, and professors of English, at home in narrow corners of the Renaissance or the Middle Ages, were grossly ignorant of all but the best advertised fruits of their own culture. They rightly held that the greatest names lay without the brief span of American writing, but were curiously unaware of the great social importance of our own literature. Doubting its absolute preëminence, they not only missed its relative importance, but were unable to appreciate the real æsthetic and intellectual value of our greatest writers.

We have histories of American literature, but very little historical criticism based upon a sound knowledge of the qualities that make American literature American. Vernon Louis Parrington's excellent "Main Currents in American Thought" * is the only thoroughgoing survey, and this is a history of the American mind rather than a study of American art, and an answer by a democrat to the egregious Federalism of previous American literary history rather than a balanced estimate. Our earlier histories were studies of English literature in America, which is only one way of looking at American literature. Our best criticism relates native writers to the great tradition of European literature, which is well enough, but slips over the very qualities that give them individuality. Poe was an American journalist as well as a figure in the romantic movement. Conservatism, natural to the scholars and critics of every race, has been made crusty in us by an instinctive dislike for every divergence between our own literature and the European tradition in which the erudite have been educated. The new duckling has been scolded for his strange uncouthness. American authors have been urged toward an artificial refinement as much out of place in vigorous American communities as chaps in London, and have been most heartily praised when they were most imitative. Irving was made a classic here, not so much because he wrote well of America as because he wrote as well

---

* The third volume was finished only in first draft and outline because of his untimely death.

INTRODUCTION

as Englishmen, and in their manner. If the native guardians of our culture had got their way, the American ideal of literary achievement would have been always the French or the English standards of about ten years earlier. The Federalist, with his idealization of European systems, lost his political power with the election of Thomas Jefferson, and many good things passed with him, but the Federalist mind has been self-perpetuating in American criticism. It has kept ideals high in a constantly vulgarizing republic, yet it has often, perhaps usually, set standards inapplicable to the living literature it has tried to dominate. This Federalist criticism has been too inclined to suggest that every ugly duckling, whether its name was Clemens or Whitman, should be trimmed to resemble a registered English fowl, and this is a more serious error than the popular opposite of believing every awkward drake to be the original American swan. As a result of such confusion of judgments we have had to revise our estimates of American excellence in every generation, not changing favorites as in France and England so much as reversing the table of merits altogether. Irving, Bryant, Longfellow, Lowell, Whittier, go down; Melville, Poe, Whitman, Mark Twain, come up.

American scholars have been supercilious toward their own, more supercilious than the English, whose worst fault has been a weakness for frontier authors with two-gallon hats and barbaric yawps. But the disease is deeper set. We have tried to assess the absolute value of our literature before understanding its significance as the expression of a complex and extraordinary national life. The Germans once approached Shakespeare that way, studying him in a vacuum in which all national and temporal characteristics were absent. Shakespeare has come off better under such treatment than Cooper or Mark Twain, for he has more that belongs to all the ages and is proportionately less bound to social history. But little success waits upon the endeavor to discuss Thoreau or Emerson without reference to the American scene. All literature in a nationalistic age is national as well as international, and the youth of the American experiment has been sufficiently extraordinary to make its impact felt.

Finally, our native literature has a value for Americans as an index to their emotional and intellectual life that is indisputable and holds even in default of absolute excellence. Yet even absolute excellence is better understood when the environmental forces that make the men that make the literature are not neglected. This is a task for American criticism, and a main purpose of this book.

American literature deserves to be studied in its American aspects, precisely as American history has recently been studied in the light of its chief native factor, the American frontier. If Whitman and Emerson belong to world literature, their eminence is not due to their quality as Americans, but to the excellence of their ideas and their art. Yet in order to assess these ideas and to comprehend this art, it is essential that they be interpreted in terms which include their native environment.

This environment is surely one of the most interesting in history. We can see now that the history of America is a narrative of moving peoples, subjecting themselves and the culture and character they bring with them to influences different both in degree and in kind from those of the old world, or of the European pale in the settled East. What literature and what ideas crossed the seas and the Appalachians we know with some accuracy. The subtle influences of environment, physical, intellectual, emotional, spiritual, all acting upon a vast and lengthy immigration, we begin to understand. So long as the question asked of American literature was, What have Americans written which is as good as the works of their European contemporaries? the answer was both difficult and unsatisfactory. But American literature becomes far more interesting and its study much more rewarding when not merely its excellence but also its essential nature is the problem to be faced.

A study of our eminent writers as men who were Americans as well as artists will reconcile many contradictions in opinion. It will explain the apparent opposition between Henry Adams's theory of our political precocity and Barrett Wendell's somewhat labored thesis that in literature we have lagged a generation or more behind English models.* It will illumine a perplexing time relationship between American and European literatures, by which the really original American author is usually both in advance of and behind his contemporaries overseas. It will explain the obstinate stepping aside from the æsthetic as such so characteristic of the American genius, and the dominance of ethics over two centuries of literature. It will throw light on the failure of the first-rate literary mind in America to express popular opinion, except at fortunate moments; and many minor developments such as our ardent cultivation of the short story.

There can be nothing mechanical in such a study, and the results can seldom be neatly demonstrable or logically complete. European influence cannot be eliminated and individual genius canceled in order to discover the pure Americanism. The American writer has undergone America without in any sense escaping from Europe. As a man he has been less sophisticated and often less subtle than the European, yet the influences to which he has been subjected have been quite as powerful and more numerous and more varied. No formula will explain his literature. The critic has no docile sand flea or obliging

* See his "A Literary History of America," and Henry Adams's "History of the United States of America," *passim*.

fruit fly in a controlled environment whose curves plot with ease. He must generalize on the race while never forgetting the personality; he must seek tendencies, influences, and national characteristics, yet remember that a sense of humor may stand out of relation to time, and that Cooper's wife, Poe's nerves, Whitman's vanity, or Mark Twain's training as a lecturer may be as important in the history of a given genius as the romantic movement or democracy. And his goal must be neither history nor biography but the interpretation of art.

Viewed with this discretion, American literary history becomes the adjustment of a European, and generally a British, culture by new men to a new environment. It may be likened to a tumult of waves from abroad sweeping inland, broken or moulded by that which they strike upon, and often re-formed in the returning wash of new waves from the West. The figure is inadequate, yet suggestive.

Perhaps it is too early to follow the complexity and reaction through three centuries of writing, much of it futile, still more of it grossly imitative. Certainly the writer of these preliminaries feels his own strength and competence too little for the task; believes, furthermore, that here at least criticism should precede orderly history, and prefers to focus the results of his reading and study upon the outstanding figures of our national history because in them the qualities that made both us and their work have taken form and artistic and spiritual significance. Against as broad a background as I can command I propose here to study with what penetration I possess, Irving, Cooper, Emerson, Hawthorne, Melville, Poe, Thoreau, and Whitman, stopping short of Mark Twain only because that tragic comedian raises all the questions of the second age of the United States which followed the Civil War. The choice of these individuals is not, I think, arbitrary; nevertheless, this is a critique, not a history, of

INTRODUCTION

American literature, and must be judged as such. These men would be meaningless as Americans, without a background as well as an environment, and hence I have begun by discussing in summary fashion the colonial literature in which the shaping influences of our national development, faintly sometimes, and sometimes with resounding emphasis, became articulate. The facts will be familiar to many readers, the interpretations of the outstanding figures have, I hope, some novelty, but the purpose is always to point the way to the chapters that follow, in which I have set down—too narrowly, I fear, but with honesty— the estimates of our great writers that are the fruits of my studies.

Classic Americans

CHAPTER ONE

The Colonial Background

THE sixteenth century is the age of discovery in northern America, the seventeenth that of discovery and first settlement; in the eighteenth, the English pale on the seaboard reaches its colonial maturity; at the end of that century colonial life disintegrates under the powerful influences of revolution; about 1800, when the political genius of America had reached, and perhaps passed, its peak, a consciously American belles lettres begins.

The literature of the first age of discovery is, naturally, not American at all. It is to be found in many languages, and is more often history and science than belles lettres. Shakespeare's "Tempest" is one of its few monuments of imaginative literature, for that play symbolizes the characteristic reaction of Renaissance man in first contact with a savage and yet romantic environment. The sequence of the literature of American discovery by no means ends with the seventeenth century. It has been unbroken from the "Journal" of Columbus to the "Alaska" of John Muir, and still continues.

The literature of the age of settlement, which was the true heroic age of America, is also in its early stages but vaguely American. Captain John Smith's "True Relation" of his Virginia experience is an English book, the prototype of a long series, some literary by intention, some literary without intention, most literature in the broad

3

modern sense of the word, but not literary at all. These narratives of settlement, a mine of extraordinary experiences, are written by Americans as soon as there are Americans to write them, continue down through Hamlin Garland's "Son of the Middle Border," and are not yet concluded.

Colonial belles lettres in the regions now part of the United States is in general precisely what it is named. It is British literature with a difference that was often mere inferiority, and at most a divergence in the kinds of topics chosen and the nature of the ideas expressed. Although the American type in physique and mental habit had certainly been born of the new environment by the mid-eighteenth century, really American literature had not. Virginia planters and New England divines of the sixteen hundreds were transplanted Britishers, and many of them, like the elder Mather, felt most at home in England. But Franklin, Edwards, Jefferson, Washington, even in their youth, were colony men. They thought of themselves as Pennsylvanians, Virginians, New Englanders, and they had unmistakably differentiated from the parent types in mental habits, and probably in physique. The men had grown further away from Europe than the books in which they recorded their ideas in the formality of literature, a characteristic of American writing that extends certainly to the twentieth century and was partly responsible for Whitman's violent reaction against conventional literary form.

The books themselves have small place in art; indeed, with a few exceptions, they have sunk below the reading level; and yet for a study of American literature, some of them at least are of great importance, since the ideas that dominate them are still powerful, if not dominant, in a later America. Jonathan Edwards's "Freedom of the Will" is sophisticated logic and John Woolman's "Journal" is naïve art, but both contain philosophies that, directly or indirectly, are of almost incalculable influence upon American culture. Franklin's "Autobiography" is a brief for common sense in nation-making, Crèvecœur's "Letters," a casual revelation of what the new environment was making of the European, Mather's "Journal" and "Magnalia," a revelation of New England intellectualism. As symbols, weathercocks, trail-markers, these outstanding books are of the greatest interest, and I shall briefly discuss them and their authors in that sense.

The new school of social history has emphasized the importance of the American frontier from its very beginnings. But in our colonial record this importance is greater for men than for books. Men changed rapidly in a few respects, slowly in others, and not at all in some, for they remained, and remain in essentials, Europeans. Such changes might have been recorded in imaginative literature but of this there was a minimum in the colonies. Indeed, pioneer and frontier experience had one chief effect upon literature, and that was to suppress it entirely, except for the unrecorded folk literature of the uneducated. Hence, in literary history and criticism, the powerful ideas in circulation in the colonies are of more importance than the physical and mental changes made in the first centuries by the new experience. The first are recorded, the second—except in politics, and in the social descriptions of Franklin and Crèvecœur—were inarticulate in literature. The powerful results of Calvinism, the subtler and the often unrecognized persuasions of Quakerism, can be traced to their source in the colonies, while the shaping of new manners and a new outlook can be discerned only by the testimony of description and comment, or deduced from the solidity of American types when they appear later in fiction, drama, and poetry. The Quaker influence, the Calvinistic dominance, like the later romantic movement, come out clear at the beginning of our intellectual history.

2.

THE settlement of America resulted from an excess of energy, backed—like all human energies—by a complex of motives, in which, however, intellectual and ethical cravings were more largely blended than is usually the case in great immigrations. Naturally, the desire of land-less men for land, and the wish of the servant to become his own master, were main factors in the settlement of the seaboard, as later of the West, and certainly the will to conquer material obstacles for material ends helped to shape American character. Most certainly, too, among those who came to seek religious liberty the knowledge that fines and confiscation would impoverish them at home, while overseas they might stay rich or grow so, was the older brother of resolution.* Yet to disregard the intellectual motive is to disregard the yeast in the bread. Ideas of the kind called abstract were at least one cause of migrating for a powerful minority, and the energy this minority brought over was intellectual energy. The exploiters of America—traders, planters, soldiers—were no more concerned with abstract ideas than the Indians, or the raw labor they brought with them, but intellectuals, and furthermore high-powered intellectuals, came also.†

* For the prosperous, middle-class Quaker particularly, Pennsylvania was a means of preserving his estate, which at home was subject to fines amounting to confiscation for his nonconformity.

† Increase Mather, in his "Relation of the Troubles which have hapned in New England, By reason of the Indians there: From the year 1614 to the year 1675," remarks upon the two sorts of men that settled New England: "Some that came thither on Account of Trade and worldly Interests, by whom the Indians have been scandalized," and "others that came hither on a religious and conscientious Account, having in their Eye the Conversion of the Heathen unto Christ." Quoted by Kenneth B. Murdock, in his "Life of Increase Mather." It was, according to Mather, the latter that prospered—certainly they held the dominance, and their leaders supplied the active thinking of the communities.

THE COLONIAL BACKGROUND

If those who so carefully controlled the nineteenth century immigration to New Zealand had been able to send professors, bishops, scientists, and leaders of social movements, they might have given us a rough parallel to the settlement of New England.

This intellectual energy was concentrated, not diffused among the mass of immigrants, which, in the beginning, was only a little better educated, and later even less so, than the illiterate or semiliterate left behind. New England in the late eighteenth and the early nineteenth century was to approximate an intellectual democracy, but it was an aristocracy of the intellect in the beginning, at least in the towns. In Virginia or South Carolina the occasional educated planter with his library was no more likely to be a radiant point of ideas than the college graduate today who settles in remote British Columbia; and indeed the crude Virginia of the pioneer period is much more truly presented in Defoe's "Moll Flanders" than in the glamour of such books as Mary Johnston's "To Have and to Hold." But in New England men of unusual intellectual force dominated communities that respected them for their ideas as much as for their political power, and which conformed to an ideology that they established for the general betterment. Kenneth B. Murdock's "Increase Mather," or L. H. Gipson's account of such a prosperous commercial town as New Haven, even after the great age of the New England clergy, in his "Jared Ingersoll," or G. S. Dickerman's "The Old Mount Carmel Parish," shows the religious intellectuals giving tone and character to a society that had its due share of wastrels, dare-devils, land-getters, traders, fighters, and dolts.

New York was a trading community absorbed in trade from the beginning. In Pennsylvania, a society made homogeneous at the beginning by a singularly humane ethics attracted gentle spirits, who lived sweetly but did

7

little thinking. In all the new American stock the natural selection that accompanies new settlement, plus the impact of an environment that bred self-reliance, produced an unusual average intelligence and exceptional vigor, or an even more rapid decay. Americans, as soon as they became Americans, were designated by observers, here and from abroad, either as shrewd and resourceful, or as dirty and degenerate. Nevertheless, in New England and Pennsylvania, where the leaders were consciously trying what they termed God's experiment in new living, a tiny but prepotent minority was whole-heartedly concerned with ideas as the common man never is and never can be. These leaders in Pennsylvania were dominant only at the beginning and with their lapse the intellectual influence of the Quakers lapsed also, and was continued only in a mild concern for better ethics that has been powerful in America because of its durability rather than its strength. In New England the Calvinist intellectuals kept a longer control and succeeded in implanting their conception of will deep in the American consciousness. Hence precisely as the New England stock has contributed a disproportionate number of men of eminence to American history,* so New England, from a very early period, began to exercise her own peculiar influence over intellectual exercise, including literature. Virginia also, favored by a somewhat different natural selection, produced great men, and Pennsylvania supplied common sense and practical energy, but New England became the school-teacher of the nation, and thus gained a certain control over the printed word.

There has been just complaint that New Englanders have written the history of American literature in terms of New England, and that undue importance has thus been attached to books that in their relativity to American achievement are of little significance. It is not the in-

---

* "Who's Who in America" still indicates that dominance.

fluence of New England that has been exaggerated, but the importance of specific New England writers, especially the group that made Boston a Main Street Athens in the mid-nineteenth century. If the subject for discussion is not politics, economics, or sociology, in which the most resounding American successes have been won and the most impressive American writing in the first two centuries accomplished, but specifically belles lettres, then the Puritan influence of New England, exercised through books, education, and the pulpit upon the whole later course of American literature, can scarcely be exaggerated, although this is no excuse for critics who neglect fine work because it was not done in Massachusetts, or for students of social forces who fail to discern the persuasive influences of the Quakers working in mild diffusion through and beyond the aggressiveness of Puritanism. There was no monopoly of Puritanism in New England, no exclusive experience in the shaping of energy into the will to improve, but these things were stamped upon the New Englander by a civilization as self-conscious and almost as prepotent as the culture of Greece.*

Jonathan Edwards

THE religious history of early New England has often been written, and those who have read it know that the dynasts of ministers who governed New England thinking in its formative period were trained intellectuals in the modern sense of the word, indeed in everything but celibacy a learned monastic order of Protestantism. If they did not practice, and did not often read, belles lettres, it was from

* The reader should consult in addition to the earlier standard works upon the New England Puritans, their literary history from a democratic angle in Parrington's already cited book, and the antagonistic but heavily documented survey in Charles Angoff's "A Literary History of the American People," Vol. I.

choice, not incapacity.* They undertook a definite experiment to establish a kingdom of God where grace might have free entrance, and their purpose was to make a community of minds trained to discriminate in theology, and disciplined to a power of decision between right and wrong. Their influence was as distinctly intellectual as the influence of the later Methodists was not, and Whitefield's emotionalism when he invaded America was a cause of pain to men trained in the logic of Calvinism and prepared to defend the ways of God with man by right reason, not by sentiment and orations. Often harsh, usually dogmatic, the protagonists of Calvinism, whose stronghold was New England, fought such a fight, and so early in American cultural history, as to set and determine a heritable type of will before the inrush of the romantic spirit in the eighteenth century, and before the pervasive influences of pioneer and frontier life had begun to work into articulate expression.

I choose Jonathan Edwards as a symbol of the dynamic force of New England intellectuality because, while he belongs to the last, not the first, period of Calvinist triumph, he is a first-rate Puritan mind in conflict with a society rapidly assuming the settled and complex character of a nation. I choose him not as a symbol of what New England was in the first half of the eighteenth century, but of what New England did to the American mind.† The intellectual may embody ruling ideas of a civilization as the artist may typify its ways of seeing and its sense of form, but neither represents everyday familiar living. Wood was hewn, water drawn, love and money made, in Puritan New England as elsewhere, and to an

---

* See T. G. Wright's "Literary Culture in Early New England, 1620-1730."
† In particular, the literary mind. In political and social thinking, that fine intellect, neither Calvinist nor man of letters, Roger Williams of Rhode Island, would deserve full consideration.

alien observer the customs of a life led still near the wilderness, and a few pious mannerisms of speech, would have been more noticeable than the Puritan idea.

Nor was Edwards a typical Puritan. He was abnormal and supernormal, as much so as his contemporaries of a different world, Laurence Sterne or Horace Walpole, more so than Dr. Johnson, who touched somewhere the characteristics of all normal men and typical Englishmen. Yet geniuses, like Jonathan Edwards, may be so dominated by their own physical and mental environment as to be its servant even at the cost of their own proper individuality, and may transmit and intensify its own especial energy. Such a man was Jonathan Edwards.

New England's great experiment in godliness under a theocracy was already overstrained when he was born in 1703. A succession of parson statesmen had taken their interpretation of the Old Testament as a perfect pattern of government and held the people too hard. Congregations were growing weary of being preached at in one vein, and that vein damnation, and men and women, no longer facing disaster or even rigor of living, could not be disciplined into making life an experiment in exact conduct with the satisfaction of a vengeful God and the faint hope of a happier hereafter as the only rewards. New England by now was reasonably safe, and quite prosperous. Even in Cotton Mather's day it was impossible to keep the popular mind upon a theology that demanded the sinner's whole attention. Yet the clergy, tasting power, had asked not only for the soul's attention, but for the control of politics and education. Edwards, who led the great revival of 1739-40, was at outs with the older clergy in his attempt to bring back a warmth of spirituality into the church, but he was one with them in exercising every intellectual influence to combat worldliness. New England for him, as for Cotton Mather, was no mere colony or trading set-

tlement but the visible evidence of great plans nobly conceived in spiritual minds. To be prosperous but ungodly
was not success but horrid failure.

Our standard literary histories of the older type fail to
grasp the significance of such an intellectual as Edwards
because they define him as a Puritan or Calvinist inhabiting an isolated tract of time sharply cut off from our own.*
We do not learn of him as a man, and we think of his work
as absurd variations played upon an extinct theological
formula. We know something of his theology, less of his
practice, much of what he was supposed to think, but
little of the real effect of that thinking. Edwards has been
dismissed as a preacher of hell-fire sermons by critics who
have clearly read no further in his writing, whereas the
weight of the New England will upon later American literature is better explained by his towering metaphysics,
or by the famous death speech of Richard Mather—"I
have not been in my study for several days; and is it not
a lamentable thing that I should lose so much time!"—
than by dozens of the too familiar quotations from sermons expressing beliefs that seem to us inhuman.

Edwards was very human, though a saint and a genius.
His mental strenuosity was excessive, but the famous
strips of paper pinned to his saddle at the end of a day's
ride, each recording the termination of a train of thought,
were simply a "visible index" contrived to suit his circumstances. The few bloody sermons that his quiet reading
voice hung like low thunder over his "loose" and backsliding congregations were the escapes of an inner struggle
to rationalize the relationships of God and sin and mind.
When his Northampton young folks took to "bundling"

---

* Recent studies of Edwards may be found in Parrington and Angoff, *op. cit.*,
and in a new biography, "Jonathan Edwards: The Fiery Puritan," by Henry
Bamford Parkes, written for the general reader. The standard biography is
still "Jonathan Edwards," by Alexander V. G. Allen.

and to reading improper books (not, in all probability, "Pamela" but less ethical and more worldly stories), when his intensity, rather than his hell-fire, wore them out, and his insistence upon too rigorous standards for church membership led to his exile as a missionary among the hopeless Indians and the "ignorant, stupid Dutch" of the Massachusetts frontier, his passions calmed and he began to write in the luminous fields of the pure intellect.

2.

EDWARDS had been a sensitive child, struggling for the experience of conversion, praying with two others in a "booth" they built in a swamp, and walking with prayer on his lips in woods and solitary places. At six he studied Latin, and precocious mental exercises opened a mind intensely curious in the processes of nature * and deeply susceptible to beauty. There is no lovelier bit of prose than his well-known description of Miss Pierrepont, his future wife. When she was young, she would "sometimes go about from place to place, singing sweetly; and seems to be always full of joy and pleasure; and no one knows for what." The images in his sermons have the fresh vividness that belongs to the born man of letters.

He was precocious but not a prig. He admits a part in the "carryings on" of the Wethersfield students when they were brought to join the infant Yale at New Haven. "Very immoral" they were "in their Conversation so that they became odious to the people of the Town," said Tutor Samuel Johnson. He was a man strained to the last degree in the pursuit of duty, but still lovable in private life. There is a letter to his recently married daughter in the unpublished Yale mss., written from Northampton

---

* His often-quoted letter on the floating spider shows not true scientific interest so much as the curiosity of a mind intensely sensitive to all evidences of creation.

13

June 3, 1743, which seems to bear out all descriptions of the New England Puritan as a dry stalk of rule and creed. Beginning "My dear child," it is a sermon on the duty of the converted, without one personal word unless it be the conclusion, "Your affectionate friend and servant in Jesus Christ." But this *is* a sermon, as pastors' letters often had to be. Beside it I find on a torn fragment, a real letter to "My dear Companion," his wife: "Our daughters have the headache and are beat out. . . . We got Hannah Root to help them." Providence is once mentioned! God not at all! Nor can the human import of his shrewd letters from the frontier in 1756 be doubted, in which the relative positions of the French and English in America at that dangerous moment are vividly described, the folly of neglecting the border Indians emphasized, and the British scolded for sending stupid officers instead of ammunition. Against the sordid exploitation of his own Indians by powerful interests he played a difficult part by intrigue and diplomacy, and won. The figure of a fanatic preaching damnation to his world must be put aside for Edwards and indeed for all the greater New Englanders.

I am not trying to reduce Edwards to common stature, nor to describe him as an apostle of tolerance. Thirteen hours in his study he regarded as a fitting day; his "Freedom of the Will" is one of the major feats of the pure intellect performed on this continent. Yet he lashed himself in his diary for "indulging of a horrible laziness." He grows "lifeless" because he has let himself anticipate ease and rest when they are not necessary if not expected. He examines his dreams to discover his prevailing inclinations, and resolves to be open-minded to new discoveries. He determines never to eat too much lest the process of digestion interfere with working, and is remorseful after backsliding dinners. In Yale in 1720 he began a set of extraordinary "Resolutions." He resolves (like Thoreau) "to live with all my might, while I do live," and does so, though he denies it. He resolves "to endeavor to my utmost to act as I can think I should do, if I had already seen the happiness of heaven, and hell torments," which is certainly a strenuous wish. No wonder that he had attacks of listlessness, which we should call fatigue or anæmia, some of which obscured the vividness of his living for days.*

A careful student of Jonathan Edwards, the late Williston Walker,† has noted the hardening of Edwards's creed as he grew older, until what had been almost mystical experience became more and more dogmatic and polemical. A rare spirit, a mystic and a saint with a curious and active mind, who in another age might have been an Emerson, a Thoreau, a Herbert, or a Browne, Edwards could write in his account of his conversion and youthful religious experiences, set down when he was about forty: ‡

"The soul of a true Christian, as I then wrote my meditations, appeared like such a little white flower as we see in the spring of the year; low and humble on the ground, opening its bosom to receive the pleasant beams of the sun's glory; rejoicing as it were in a calm rapture; diffusing around a sweet fragrancy; standing peacefully and lovingly, in the midst of other flowers round about; all in like manner opening their bosoms, to drink in the light of the sun. There was no part of creature holiness, that I had so great a sense of its loveliness, as humility, brokenness of heart, and poverty of spirit; and there was nothing that I so earnestly longed for. My heart panted after this, to lie low before God, as in the dust; that I might be nothing, and that God might be ALL, that I might become as a little child."

* See "The Works of President Edwards," edition of 1881, Vol. I, p. 3 ff.
† See his "Ten New England Leaders."
‡ "The Works of President Edwards," edition of 1881, Vol. I, p. 13 ff.

But this delicate, yet powerful, spirit was trapped by practical necessity. He believed that he had to use every ounce of energy to demonstrate the nature and the necessity of righteousness by cold and convincing logic. He had to take his place in the succession of God's ministers whose duty it was to make a holy land of New England. He felt the prophet's call as strongly as the heroes of the Old Testament who were his predecessors.

That call was sounded by the opportunities of a new land, whose inhabitants were to be saved by a logical scheme of salvation, as rational as the philosophy of Aquinas, which John Calvin had provided for the intellectual backbone of the Puritan church. New England, as the intellectuals saw it, was to be devoted to the triumphant working out of this orthodoxy, and Yale, in 1701, had been founded when Harvard, under secular influences, seemed to be wavering from the intellectual purity of the faith.

But Yale, when Edwards in his tender but brilliant youth was there as student and as tutor, was in turmoil. The rector and the chief tutors were infected with Arminianism, with its different conception of will and grace and predestination, and later seceded in a body to Episcopalianism. Among the dissenters was Samuel Johnson (afterward first president of what is now Columbia University), with whom Edwards had earlier come into conflict. In an atmosphere of bitter controversy, Edwards was forced by both necessity and inclination to choose a side. It is just possible that he was present at the famous debate in October of 1722, when the trustees and Governor Saltonstall, honest and godly men, but not subtle, were bewildered by the scholarship of the rebels.* Certainly he was in the midst of preliminary discussion, and acutely aware of the

---

* He probably left for his eight months' trial pastorate in New York in August or September, but may have returned.

need for trained minds for the defense in a controversy as sensational as if Harvard should turn to Bolshevism today, or the Princeton faculty become Roman Catholic en masse. And from that time the nascent man of letters and speculative philosopher, whose mind had been opened by Locke's "Human Understanding" in the Yale library, turned to the supreme duty of perfecting the Calvinist argument, met scholarship with scholarship, and (when his Stockbridge exile gave him leisure) poured his whole energy into this lifelong work. Gross intellects, like Saltonstall, might rest upon a formula, but Edwards, in his great defense of a God who determined but did not will evil, labored from point to point of argument back into metaphysics and philosophy, until his subtle intellect let go its intuitive sense of truth and its mystical union with God, and dared to rest upon pure reason for the satisfying of all doubts and the proof of the ultimate goodness of God. The change came, I believe, with his first contact with opposition. Before that it had been a question between himself and God. Thus the course and nature of his intellectual life was dominated by his epoch, and he expressed its intellectual problems more fully than his own soul.*

3.

THESE problems are best expressed in "An Inquiry into the Modern Prevailing Notions Respecting that Freedom of the Will Essential to a Moral Agency" (1754) and in his scarcely less remarkable "Dissertation concerning the Nature of True Virtue" (posthumously published). The famous monograph on the freedom of the will, written among the Stockbridge Indians where there were few savable souls to distract him and the pettier theological

* For the Yale controversy see Edwin Oviatt's "The Beginnings of Yale (1701-1726)." This theory of Edwards's intellectual development has not before been suggested, but I think the facts warrant its adoption.

squabbles of the seaboard were far away, is not a defense
of original sin, as Barrett Wendell described it, but rather
a pessimist's attempt to prove that the doctrine of free
will as held by the Church of England gave no relief to
the distractions of man. The Arminian philosophy held by
that church made man (so he argued) less than a machine,
for this philosophy of free will, which Dr. Johnson said
all men, in practice, must share, left the will in control of
blind contingence and accident. By a chain of arguments
irrefutable except in their premises, he destroys the Arminian logic, and leaves man not a mere machine (for he
grants him the use of reason and choice, and says his external acts are subject to his will), but at the best a
supermachine caught in the net of necessity. Although
man is free to choose his actions and therefore can be cen-
sured or praised, he is under a "moral necessity" to will
in a certain fashion. Yet the nature of his will, which is
predetermined by God, can be praised or blamed, and deserve reward or punishment. An ugly thing is ugly, and
sin is evil, irrespective of its cause. Will (says this meta-
physician) is pre- not self-determined, but once determined man is responsible for the use he makes of it.*

America (and Western culture in general) has been in
reaction ever since against this pessimistic philosophy,
which in effect destroys the happier idea that we are masters of our own souls, while by elaborate and not convincing arguments it forbids us to shift all responsibility upon
fate or to God. We have been in reaction against a realistic
philosophy determined to be logical at the cost of easy
thinking, but we have not thereby escaped from the net
of determinism. We have merely denied its existence or,
in the later scientific and industrial period, have accepted

---

* Of the many discussions of Edwards and the Edwardsian philosophy one
of the best brief statements is to be found in "The Encyclopædia Britannica,"
11th edition, by H. N. Gardiner and Richard Webster.

it on other grounds without worrying much about the result, as men will often do in a time of prosperity.

But although we have repudiated the harsh theology of Calvinism, and now read with amazement the infinite niceties of debate by which Edwards endeavored to reconcile the existence of sin and the nature of God (our minds being tuned to a different scale of importance), yet we have not escaped from the mental habits that were ground into the consciousness in these formative generations, and by no means only in New England. The chief legacy of Puritanism,* in this country at least, was neither theology nor even morals, but a habit of the mind. As with so many other great religious and philosophical movements, it left not a doctrine so much as an attitude. The ultimate of Calvinism, and of all those modifications of its orthodoxy which New England debated, was the absolute necessity of willing, and willing the right. God's grace was not extended to good works, but to a good will sprung from a nature elected by God for salvation. Only by a right exercise of the will was it possible to learn whether one belonged to the damned or the saved. The sermons from which hell fire played over the heads of a pallid congregation were at their worst hysterical attempts to rouse the will to be saved, at their best solemn reminders of the necessity upon every man to strive for salvation. The emphasis in the Puritan period is not upon doctrine except in the wranglings of the professionals; for the layman sus-

* I am well aware of the disputed meaning of Puritanism, and of the fact that the will toward individual salvation was a heritage from Protestantism in general. In this brief survey I am concerned not with the complicated and still not entirely unraveled religious history of the colonies, but with outstanding evidences of the intellectual influences that are most readily traceable in the great American writers of the national period. I have chosen Calvinism and Quakerism because these very different creeds were both especially prepotent and were both made articulate in colonial writing of unusual distinction. See for recent discussion "The Puritan Mind," by Herbert W. Schneider, and "The Religious Background of American Culture," by Thomas Cumming Hall.

ceptible to moral or religious ideas it was upon the need of willing the best. He felt a moral necessity, his community believed in a moral necessity, his children accepted moral necessity, or slyly escaped to the sea or the West. The result in New England was a civilization that, various in its components and its practices, was unusually sensitive to ethics, with the habit of conscious willing strongly implanted in its leaders, and this civilization, intellectually the strongest on the continent, and physically as vigorous and more expansive than any other, gave tone through its preachers and teachers to a good share of American intellectual life, and eventually influenced all of it.*

Jonathan Edwards, of course, is a symbol of this influence rather than a cause in himself, although his intellectual descendants were legion, his books were widespread, and even his doctrine was given a little longer life through his efforts. In the course of his "Travels in New York and New England," published in 1821-22, Timothy Dwight remarks that the destruction of Edwards's works would distress Christians more than the loss of half the ancient authors extant, which, from the ex-president of a college whose curriculum included the classics, was an impressive statement. Edwards is a prophet of that will to be saved, will to improve, will to succeed, which, through

* There were of course outposts of New England Puritanism like the colony at Newark, New Jersey, founded to preserve orthodoxy when the theocracy at home was crumbling, and there were Yankees everywhere along the seaboard teaching and preaching as well as trading. The influence of the French Huguenots, few in numbers but, like the New Englanders, strong in personnel, was also Puritanical, especially in the first generations. Charleston, although in Crèvecœur's day it was described as being as lavish as Lima, in 1724 was sending to Boston for a minister of Cotton Mather's ordination. The Scotch Irish, who spread down the Appalachian valleys into the far South, were Calvinists. So were the Dutch of New York and the Delaware. But the greatest extension of typical New England Puritanism in its later stages came just after the Revolution when the immigrants broke westward from New England across the lands of the Six Nations and into Ohio and the first Northwest.

the "relaxation" of the early eighteen hundreds when mercy was substituted for the austere justice of the Calvinist creed, on to Emerson and to the strenuous uplifters and go-getters of modern America, changed its direction, lost its aim, but did not alter its habit of purposeful energy.

4.

JONATHAN EDWARDS cannot be called a man of letters. In his youth he wrote passages of sensitive prose in which a poet's nature responded to beauty, whatever its source; but in his maturity his power resides in the colder realms of the pure intellect, his strength is expended upon the perfection of logical structure with concern only for a mathematical proof, and his style is sacrificed to the urgencies of exposition. In his "Journal" he regrets that he has paid so little attention to style, which was "not cultivated in the Colonies," but the regret is the not too humble apology of one for whom the call to salvation was a practical necessity asking for force, not beauty. His sermons are rich in images. He could write:

"When we go to form an idea of perfect nothing we must not suffer our thoughts to take sanctuary in a mathematical point, but we must think of the same that sleeping rocks do dream of"—

which is worthy of the great stylists of seventeenth century English. Yet these lovely passages are rare and incidental. His typical achievements lie in such a fabric of magnificent reasoning as one finds in Part II, Section 1, of "The Freedom of the Will," where he destroys the fallacy of the will's self-determination, or in his excellent analysis of vagueness in the use of terms in Part IV, Section 2, of the same book. There the man's full power develops, and there his style is uneven, careless, and often harsh. Like so many other early Americans of high potential in literature—like Jefferson, like Hamilton—he met

21

early a practical necessity of environment, suppressed (in Edwards's case powerfully suppressed) his literary instincts, and bent a first-rate talent to other ends. It is quite certain that he would have regarded a Sterne, or a Warburton, in New England much as a big business executive, who feels that the fate of industry is in his hands, might estimate the sonneteer who describes the skyscrapers of modern New York.

Cotton Mather

Colonial New England was crabbed as well as wilful, and it restrained as much as it inspired in the later American mind. Viewed one way, American literature might often be called the comment of a relaxing Puritanism upon an ever more complex life, viewed another, it is an attempt of the imagination to escape from the obsession of Puritanic will.

I do not refer to the failure of beauty in Puritan life, for there was more beauty in the life of the New Englander, Puritan or not Puritan, in the seventeen hundreds than in the nineteen hundreds. It is true that whatever lightened the spirits was generally distrusted—"Resolved," writes Jonathan Edwards, "never to utter anything that is sportive or matter of laughter, on a Lord's Day"—but then no people in the grip of a religious or ethical revival have been mirthful of spirit—there are no jokes in the Old Testament and no laughter in the New. Yet to say that the Puritan New Englander was arid in his social contacts and afraid, like the Quakers, of worldliness, is not to deprive him of beauty. Periods of settlement and exploitation are never eras of easy culture, and while life went more merrily in Charleston and more comfortably in Virginia than in Boston, there is no reason to suppose that it was richer in a sense of beauty. There was the beauty of holiness, which was more familiar in New England and Pennsylvania than among the traders of New York or the planters of the South. There was the beauty of structure, in which the New England farmhouse with its sweet proportions, and the New England village in its admirable decorum, where the inhabitants purposed to "sitt down there close togither,"* may enter in competition with the best manors of the South, and these manifest an æsthetics of environment incomparably superior to our own. The Puritan New Englander was ignorant of good music, and persuaded that he should resist all indulgence, whose further end was sin, and this made him narrow, but considering the moral condition of contemporary Europe, and a possibility of extravagance limited to lechery and rum, this can be regarded as restraint rather than mental defectiveness. It was a restraint with unfortunate consequences, yet it was but the shadow of his virtues.

By crabbedness I mean that self-consecration of the ego which so often results from excessive strains on the intellect. The Quaker escaped its harsher manifestations because he sought peace and not wrath in his self-examinings, and seldom overworked his mind. He stepped aside from life while the Puritan tried to bend it to his will. The constant questions, "Am I a sinner? Have I grace? Am I better than my brothers? How shall I bring them to salvation?" run through all Protestant literature, but were almost intolerably sharpened by Calvinistic Puritanism. Where, as with the unfortunate Cotton Mather, there was a congenital vanity, the results were distressing in the extreme, but through all New England the strain of Calvinism inflamed the ego and created a habit of mind, and even a manner of speech, that the "obnoxious" colonies—as Mather calls them—to the south and west felt

* Quoted by Lewis Mumford in "Sticks and Stones."

rightly to be highly objectionable. Like all habits it was passed on to later generations. The sententiousness that comes from constant introspection is marked in Emerson, who was anti-Calvinist to the core; the ready censure of others by a mind that keeps its own soul constantly at the bar, is a definitive quality in Thoreau, who would have loathed the Mathers and all their works. The unpopularity of the New Englanders in the Revolutionary armies was due to their manners quite as much as to the shrewdness developed by the will to succeed. The self-righteous and hypocritical Yankees in Cooper's novels show how long the type persisted, and how it was disliked beyond New England, and often misunderstood.

2.

No BETTER illustration of the ego warped by straining to be virtuous can be found than Cotton Mather, by no means one of the great minds of New England, but profusely articulate and representative, if not typical. Great influences can sometimes be best understood through their exaggerations.

Third in the line of great preachers who reigned over the "greatest church in the Colonies"—the Old North Meeting House in Boston—he gave the governor advice when he seemed to need it, he bore the sins of his entire community on his own conscience, he wrote two hundred and fifty books and pamphlets while he was still relatively young, and was one of the most virtuous prigs and well-meaning asses in history.

Here was a sheer intellectual, a scientist in his way, willing to risk his son's life to demonstrate the inoculation theory of smallpox, curious (as is shown in his "Magnalia," the "Ecclesiastical History of New England") as to the nature of the new American environment, but warped in every fibre by the dominance of obsession over character.

Professor Parrington, in his chapter on the Puritan divines in "The Cambridge History of American Literature," speaks of Mather's career as "incomprehensible to us." He means his admixture of credulity and wisdom, his violent self-righteousness, his constant meddling in the affairs of state, in everyone's affairs, his intolerable vanity. Given the vanity, the rest is but a natural result of a theology and a social and political environment that could make one man feel responsible for God's kingdom planted in New England. Edwards, a little later, also knew that the Great Experiment of grace to be obtained by a better life in a new England was declining, and the violent passion of his sermons expresses his soul's agony. He took refuge in the armor of pure reason; Cotton Mather could not escape because he was bound to the affairs of Boston and the success of its theocracy by the shackles of egoism and vanity.

It is hard to say whether his "Diary" is more pathetic or more comic. It is certainly the most human document extant from the American eighteenth century. When he woos the reluctant Mrs. George in servile pomposity; when she reluctantly marries him; and then in a fervor that he believed insanity and we suspect was the result of living with Cotton, hides or destroys the precious writings which (it is too clear) meant more to him than family, or even God, then it is high comedy. When he writes—

"I must watch against the Entertainment of too much Leaven in my Spirit against a People whose Behaviour towards me is very unrighteous and ungrateful. I must enjoy a sweet Satisfaction of mind if I find myself conformable unto Him, who was despised and rejected of men"; when he reflects how he shall "glorify my just, wise dear Saviour," on the "deplorable Occasion" of his "miserable Son Increase," who has brought himself, and his

father, under "public Trouble and Infamy by bearing a
Part in a Night-Riot, with some detestable Rakes in the
Town"; when after the usual succession of widows who
are to be comforted (his strong point), relatives whose
piety is to be investigated, and Indians who are to be
plagued into Christianity, he remembers "the poor young
Man, who is to dy this Week," and visits him to obtain
"an instrument of pertinent passages" (that is to say,
copy) to serve the interests of piety and "give to the
Bookseller"—

Why, after all this the affair begins to be tragic, for one
begins to understand how an upright and ambitious man
could be deviled by this obsession that the backslidings of
the world should be corrected, and would be, if only he
were energetic enough. When he is successful the flame of
God has uplifted him. When he fails, "the Town has become almost an Hell upon Earth, a City full of Lies, and
Murders, and Blasphemies, as far as Wishes and Speeches
can render it so." And this is Puritan Boston at its most
pious period, not contemporary Chicago or New York!

3.

ONE begins to understand the karma of doubt, perplexity,
and egoism that this self-willed religiosity made inevitable for men who were too intellectual to dodge its implications, but not great in spirit. For a half-dozen generations the spectacle of intellectual New England is of
an attempt at escape from self-accusation. The ancestral
leaders had pledged themselves pridefully to a literal transcription of God's will narrowly interpreted that was not
possible except for saints and madmen. Edwards was essentially a saint who nevertheless quieted his conscience
only by the consecration of a great intellect to the defense
of his God. Cotton Mather—and far better men than Cotton Mather—who could not take refuge in genius plagued

themselves their lives through with a sense of failure that was transmuted by their vanity into legions of enemies or the omnipresence of sin.

Less spiritual men escaped (like the later Quakers) into the comforts of material success, rebellious spirits struck by hundreds westward or to sea. Thousands of New Englanders, of course, were moved neither to good nor to ill by the winds of doctrine. Weariness overtook most of the debaters, the easy emotionalism of the Methodist revival relieved the intellectual strain, and the political controversies that began in the seventeen fifties drew off energy from the senescent Puritan Church. Nevertheless, the line of intellectuals, working out the karma of an undue sense of sin and a strained egoism, is unbroken from the Puritan divines through the ameliorators—Buckminster, Channing, and the Unitarians—down to Hawthorne, who carried the battle into art, Emerson who, looking westward, soared above it, Thoreau, who turned his back on the world to study duty, Alcott, who escaped from Calvinism into the lunar paradise, Longfellow, whose ethics were calm because they were meaningless, to the last twist of powerful Puritanism in Whitman himself.

New England, of course, was not America, and her intellectuals were only an aspect of New England. Irving, Cooper, Poe, Twain, are of primary importance in American literature with only a finger of influence from New England. That is another story. Nevertheless, it must be repeated that of the three greatest influences upon our national literature—Puritanism in its local New England sense, romantic European thinking, and the frontier—the first must be grasped first because of its immediate transmutation into ethical and psychological values spread by writing, preaching, teaching, and example throughout the colonies, and most of all when New England captured the Middle West.

Cotton Mather and Jonathan Edwards as symbols for their age explain the practical character, the ethical intensity, the overstrain, that for a century and a half appear in the majority of the really important writers in America, and are latent in the majority of the readers who bought their books. There is a direct line of influence between "The Freedom of the Will" and Cotton Mather, and "The Scarlet Letter" and "Moby Dick."

John Woolman and the Quakers

God's experiment in Pennsylvania, although it was never so egregiously named, was begun by William Penn and his associates with an idealism as lofty as the Puritans', but in a different temper, and with a more perfect blend of spirituality and common sense.

The Puritan leaders regarded their America as a place of preparation for successful dying, and their somewhat tyrannical grip upon manners and politics was excused by the exigencies of salvation. The Quakers were determined to have successful living first. The legacy of the Puritans was strong will in the modern sense; the Quaker legacy was good will in the Scriptural sense. The New England intellectual implanted in the national consciousness an obsession with ethics as a means to a divine end, which remained as an obsession when it descended through the generations, but lost sight of its original purposes. The Quaker discipline, as it slackened, left behind it a series of humane ideas that have retained their essential character and are powerful in their original form today.

That succession of strong-willed preachers, teachers, statesmen, writers, which came from the Puritan stock and has made the very name of Puritan both famous and infamous to our own day, has no parallel among the Friends. An inhibition of passion, more powerful because

28

more consistent in the Quaker than in the Puritan, a concern for simplicity that led John Woolman to take passage in the steerage because there was wood carving in the cabin, unfitted the Friends for pure literature, which succeeds by mastery, not by abstinence. There is no true Quaker literature comparable with Puritan poetry and Puritan prose. And the Quaker fear of that pride of intellect which obscures the God within us made the Friends distrustful of higher education, and intellectual aggressiveness in general. Nevertheless, the Quaker influence upon the American mind, though diffuse and mingled, is far greater than critics and historians have let us suppose. Advertising is not a Quaker gift. With less obvious psychological effects, the Quaker heritage has been more durable as a spiritual influence than the Puritan, and upon our philosophies of living has been only less powerful than Calvinism.

The Quaker aimed too broadly, as the Puritan aimed too high. He proposed to make all the world Friends, and there was a moment in the troubled seventeenth century when it seemed that he might be incredibly successful. If he has by no means succeeded, yet, especially in this country, he gave the widest diffusion to the optimistic humanitarianism that was the direct result of his theory of a beneficent inner light. Distrust of violence, a belief in the essential kinship of mankind, respect for the individual without reference to rank or estate, justice and mercy to prisoners and to slaves, dislike of pomp and circumstance, all these Quaker fundamentals have been American ideals also, held by many if by no means all, and strong enough to shape American history. In literature, Whitman among the greater names, Whittier among the less, are Quaker, entirely or in part, Cooper and Melville learned much from the Quakers, and one of the few books of colonial America still living, the "Journal" of John Woolman

(1720-1772), published in 1774, is also perhaps the best expression in English of the Quaker spirit.

2.

A COMPARISON between "A Journal of the Life and Travels of John Woolman in the Service of the Gospel," his "Considerations" on the Keeping of Negroes, on Human Policy, on Labor, on Schools, on The True Harmony of Mankind, on Loving Our Neighbors, and his "Caution to the Rich," with Edwards's nearly contemporary "Freedom of the Will," is as instructive in its way as a contrast between Shakespeare and Racine. Both men were saints, but it seems improbable that they will understand each other better in heaven than did their sects on earth. Edwards's terrific argument ignores the world save as a place in which men may gather strength to placate God; he is an Archimedes, busy with his logic while war and business go on without. The gentle Woolman would have believed such pride in reason sinful. One remembers how he feared to stay on in the Indian town of Wyalusing lest it prove to be his courage, not his God, that he was serving. Woolman and his Quakers love the world while fearing its enticements. Instead of essential depravity, they argue for an inner light that can clear the way toward righteousness. Their philosophy is instinctive, even though Barclay * (a second Paul) made it seem logical. It was as essentially optimistic as Calvinism was pessimistic. The brotherhood of man was for them more important than a search for the elect, since everyone who listens to the God within him can be saved. Greed, conflict, pride, injustice, egoist passion, and all "worldliness" are clogs upon the

---

* Robert Barclay, "An Apology for the True Christian Divinity as the Same is Held Forth and Preached by the People Called in Scorn Quakers," 1678. In his second Proposition he defines the inner light as an inspiration that, though not Christ himself, is the spirit of Christ.

indwelling spirit. The worldly cannot hear its voice because they are deafened by the clamor of their own desires; therefore the mind must be cleared of all the fogs that hide the inner light. Edwards and his colleagues, as we read them today, seem pessimistic rationalists debating an issue that no longer interests us because, while we may share their pessimism, we do not accept their premises. Woolman and his fellows still speak an intelligible humanitarianism, and represent causes coexistent with man. The "Journal" of John Woolman, in spite of its quaint pieties, is still a modern book.

His was, as is moderately well known, the first effective voice against slavery, and if his descriptions of the damage done to the mind of the slaveholder had been as often repeated as his arguments for the welfare of the slave, later Abolitionists might have been more successful in stirring the conscience of the South. His warning to the rich, whose luxuries breed wars, and whose tax upon property is a first cause of crime, is not so often quoted, though it was deeply read by the Friends, nor his remarkable vision of the price that a country growing richer pays in the morale of its youth. He lived much with sailormen and was "tender" toward them because of their depravity, which he traced, like the modern moralist, straight back to the economics of superfluity; would, indeed, have had men content themselves with the necessities of food and raiment for the common benefit of all. He was a spiritual communist who would have praised Russian equalitarianism and been aghast at the materialism of Marxist ends. Sugar he would not eat because slaves raised it, would not go to the West Indies because the fare was lower than would have been possible without the trade in slaves, would not drink from silver cups. It was a counsel of perfection, but more humane and more human than the Calvinists'. Here is a characteristic passage taken from his account of a journey into the Indian country of the upper Susquehanna. The scene is on the banks of the Lehigh, beyond Mauch Chunk:

"Near our tent, on the sides of large trees peeled for that purpose, were various representations of men going to, and returning from the wars, and of some killed in battle. This being a path heretofore used by warriors; and as I walked about viewing those Indian histories, which were painted mostly in red, but some in black, and thinking on the innumerable afflictions which the proud, fierce spirit produceth in the world; thinking on the toils and fatigues of warriors, travelling over mountains and deserts; thinking on their miseries and distresses when wounded far from home by their enemies; and of their bruises and great weariness in chasing one another over the rocks and mountains; and of their restless, unquiet state of mind, who live in this spirit; and of the hatred which mutually grows up in the minds of the children of those nations engaged in war with each other: during these meditations, the desire to cherish the spirit of love and peace amongst these people, arose very fresh in me."

Woolman belongs in literature with those sweet-spirited Anglicans of the seventeenth century, Herbert and Vaughan and Jeremy Taylor, whose radiant spirits clothed themselves in words far richer than he could use, but no more pure. He is more naïve than they, with no consciousness of the occasional beauty of his prose, and the constant loveliness of his spirit. His book, like "Pilgrim's Progress," is natural literature, yet it is noteworthy that one of the subtlest and most self-conscious of men of letters, Charles Lamb, loved it. Of all the vast library of tracts of which English has been more prolific than any other language, it is one of the most deserving of new and wider reading.

We shall see hints of what this Quaker spirit can do when touched by æstheticism in the idyllic letters of Crèvecœur. We shall see its passion for man, freed from fear of the senses, in Whitman, its mystic communions with a God that said Aye or Nay to the heart, in the struggles of Melville with Moby Dick.

3.

I HAVE written of the Quaker influence upon the American mind with little reference to William Penn, or his Pennsylvania, the first of liberal modern states, because essential Quakerism had much less reference to its geographical center in America than did New England Puritanism. It was a migratory, and especially a missionary, religion to a far greater extent than the orthodox Calvinist church, and in ethics, in spirituality, and in its conception of politics, operated by example as much as by precept. Men and women were its concern, wherever and however found. There was no contempt for the Dutch, no hatred of the Indian. The other colonies might often be dangerous for the Quakers, but they were never "obnoxious." In towns and in farms and along the frontier, the Friends colonized north and south and west of Pennsylvania. Nantucket became solely theirs, and strange things happened when the most peaceful of men sought profit by bloody adventure in whaling. Their gentle religion made its deep impression everywhere except among the rich, the gay, the lovers of sensuous beauty—and the Calvinists. The Holy Land of New England—tolerant Rhode Island excepted—shed them off like water. But the simple people to the westward of the seaboard, from New York to South Carolina, received them gladly; and although the Philadelphia Quaker grew rich and rigid, ideas of simplicity, of peace, of possible brotherhood, of communion with a spirit within, were borne west by thousands who were not even Quaker in name. In England the Quakers have remained a "peculiar people," a powerful but minute minority; in

33

America Quakerism has diffused into the national consciousness.

Benjamin Franklin

RELIGIOUS and ethical literature had a powerful and enduring effect in America, but this does not, of course, mean that the population of the colonies, even of the New England colonies, was a religious society, or susceptible in the mass to the influence of intellectual ideas. A study of a typical shipload of immigrants, even in the sixteen hundreds, or a moment's consideration of the denizens of a New York manor, a Pennsylvania county, or a New England town, would correct any false impressions gained from reading the list of titles in Increase Mather's library. Boston by 1760 had changed from a religious capital into a trading city, New York was never anything else, Philadelphia was like Boston, though more cultivated in a worldly sense, Charleston like New York, with more elegance. In all of these towns, and on a few of the great Southern plantations, in Annapolis, Williamsburg, and wherever there was wealth and civilization, polite literature, not dedicated to a vengeful God, nor intended to reveal the inner light of the spirit, was cultivated, poetry written, plays given—when there was leisure, which was not often. But this literature was seldom indigenous and still more seldom provocative, and its pallid imitations of fashions overseas were of no more significance for the later national literature than schoolbook exercises for real education. The best of it was vacation literature, like Sandys's early translation of Ovid, British writing done by chance on this side of the ocean. If Goldsmith and Burns had come, as they planned, to North America, they would have written much as they did write—or more probably, busy, like everyone else, in establishing themselves in a new country, would not have written at all.

34

THE COLONIAL BACKGROUND

Belles lettres in the colonies was imitative because the aristocracy and the professional groups that read it were imitative in their culture. They had come from the European middle class, or lower, and were much too engaged in getting rich to be particular in their intellectual recreations. The great political struggle into which the literate laymen in the colonies entered in the mid-eighteenth century kept them from provincialism, as the sectarian struggle of the seventeenth century kept the Puritan divines from provincialism, but in pure literature they were not even provincial. Belles lettres was imported, like good wine and the best furniture.

Third-rate plays and fourth-rate poetry, nobly reflecting a far-away Europe, are less significant than the powerful influences of Quaker mysticism and the Calvinist will, and less important in the history of a nascent American literature than the slightest indication of the effects of pioneer self-reliance and adaptation to a new environment. Every side of the new American was touched by these new experiences, and hence every man. For the vast majority of colonial Americans, the colonies were obviously neither God's experiment, nor a place of spiritual refuge, nor understudies of foreign culture, but a new country in which homes must be made. If this vital experience did not make literature, at least in the mid-eighteenth century it began to be articulate.

Benjamin Franklin, the apostle of American common sense, was the publicity agent of the new American. In spite of his flashes of scientific intuition, his genius for statesmanship, and his easy sexual morals, Franklin was a good representative of the average American man—devoid of mysticism, little interested in theology, but determined to learn how to live in America. Broadly considered, this last might be said to be the theme of the most characteristic American literature ever since Franklin stated the problem in terms that if they were the lowest were, in their application, the broadest also.

Franklin is the practical man of common sense, who goes on and on after enthusiasms are dead. He is the New England farmer on weekdays, the New York trader, the fur-purchaser opening new routes, the engineer, the employer of labor, the politician who keeps his eyes on earth. Yet unlike the thousands whose common sense told them that they must get a living whatever the preacher might say, he was enough of a philosopher to stand aside and look at his America with a speculative glance. Edwards, Mather, and Woolman deal with souls; he is concerned with the American man as man.

When the social history of America is written, the eighteenth century will provide probably its most interesting and certainly its most difficult chapters. The metabolism of customs and ideas has never been more active anywhere, and that burst of executive energy which preceded, accompanied, and followed the Revolution, with its astonishing crop of men whose attainments would have been regarded as unusual in any age, will find its explanation in the history of their predecessors as well as in the exigencies and opportunities of their excited times. The mental tension of New England was only one of many causes. Thousands of immigrants coming from societies still feudal in their structure were pouring into a new land where ideas, both of government and of social organization, were still definitely feudal, yet where most of the important circumstances of actual living struck, even in the South, at the aristocratic ideal, by providing opportunity for the poorest, and rewards for courage, endurance, physical strength even for rascals and degenerates. A European who was a ne'er-do-well, a beaten man, or an outcast, passed from immigrant to bond servant, to landholder. The impossibility of keeping a common laborer a common laborer, or a servant a servant (unless he were black), is a constant theme in colonial writing.

The result in terms of civilization was a fluctuating balance between degeneration and regeneration. Dr. Johnson and Lady Mary Wortley Montagu gave voice to an idea widespread among the English upper classes when they spoke of the degeneracy of the American colonists, and General Wolfe's well-known diatribe was probably colored by prejudice acquired at home. The English judgment was usually based upon hearsay, but it would have found plenty of first-hand evidence in America. Men escaped from oppression into lawlessness. There was a general relaxation of manners; frontier life was brutal; the hardships of the pioneer included lack of education for his children, and lack of decent comforts in his life. The restraints of civilization were often far behind, and the colonial record, like the history of the West, is only half read by those who fail to see that the white man in America was by thousands headed backward toward barbarism. It is not in accounts of Boston or Charleston, but in the tales of travelers, in the narratives of border wars, and in the records of morals in rural communities, that this inescapable aspect of American life is to be found. The frontier—first on the eastward slopes of the Appalachians, then along a broadening band moving westward to the Pacific—must be thought of from the beginning not as a place of epic adventure only, but also as a lawless region of debauchery, exploitation, and miscegenation, where those too weak to make a place for themselves in a settled civilization, and those too strong to be content with what they had, made a society of contrasts where filth, misery, and semisavagery were as common as hardihood. And yet change and chance sharpened intelligence and increased initiative. The Hessian officers (as their memoirs report) were impressed by the active minds of the common people in New

37

York and New England, and amazed to learn that the officers of the Revolutionary Army had trades or professions other than war. Franklin speaks of the alerter brains of the American workmen. And indeed, if opportunity to escape economic oppression made many barbarous, it gave self-respect and self-reliance to as many more, and sowed broadcast the idea that every man had a right to prove that he was as good as another. The grandchildren of bond servants came to live in manor houses and men whose life in Europe would never have reached beyond the plough or the shop endured those great unwritten sagas of exploration, adventure, and escape in the Indian lands which, if they had been written down, would have been the chief treasure of early American literature.

2.

FRANKLIN began his career as a man determined to find and use opportunity; no sooner was he established than he undertook the broader task of making Pennsylvania a model modern state; and he concluded his extraordinary career as a specialist in world politics and the leader of the new school of bourgeois philosophy. This is the reason for the absorbing interest of his "Autobiography." Written by one who had gained perspective by experience, it records the story of how an intelligent man was formed by, and reacted to, the new environment of America.

The Philadelphia in which he lived after 1723 was no citadel of the inner light, but the prosperous and somewhat cosmopolitan metropolis of the colonies, the center, if not of intellectuality except for some scientific thinking, certainly of liberal ideas on government and such worldly culture as was imported from abroad. In comparison, New England in the mid-century was provincial, and New York commercial. As a chief port of entry, with a broad stretch of fertile land between the sea and the higher mountains, the experiences of the immigrant were most evident here, and the note of thrift and promise, which was the prevailing tone of colonial America within the frontiers, was most sure to be struck. If Franklin became a political philosopher and a scientist, as a writer from the beginning to the end he was first of all a journalist, explaining first to Americans, and then to the nations of Europe, what American colonists must do in order to make themselves at home in their new environment.* He had a scientist's imagination that projected beyond his own epoch, a scrupulously cultivated gift for words, an experience of men and cities perhaps more varied than any other individual in either hemisphere in his time, a lucidity, shrewdness, and intellectual curiosity as transcendent as the intellectual strenuosity of the Puritan divines. Possessing a genius for normality in spite of his abnormal powers, he was, as Carlyle said, the father of all the Yankees—of all the self-dependent, inventive Yankees, those "practical idealists" who came after him and made a character type for America.† Franklin is still modern, whereas Edwards, and even Washington, need explanation.

His faculty of observation was fresh and original, and so was his scientific imagination, but his interest in ethics came with him from New England and his philosophy of life was strongly influenced by the Quakers among whom he lived. In this, as in other respects, the father of the Yankees was a good representative for America.

* See his "Information to Those Who Would Remove to America," c. 1785, with an introductory account of the new attitude toward work as a duty for everybody, so characteristic of the century to follow, and especially in the United States, a philosophy not to be seriously challenged by economists until the fourth decade of the twentieth century.

† See the "Autobiography," p. 97. "I could not, as it seemed to me, afford time to practice . . . in the common attendance on public worship." And he regretted the time spent, since he was not to be a clergyman, in his father's library of "polemic divinity." Yet his mind was filled, then as later, with projects for general betterment.

His ethics of common sense—implicit always, when not explicit, in "Poor Richard's Almanack"—are mere pragmatism in comparison with the Puritan code. "Honesty is the best policy" sums up his creed—and not a bad creed for a new country that could certainly not be conducted on the Quaker assumption that all its inhabitants were to become saints. His constant insistence upon the importance of doing right derives ultimately from his youth in New England, and the specific stimulus was apparently from Cotton Mather's book "Essays to Do Good," which Franklin, characteristically, liked because the title seemed to offset the Calvinists' belief that good works in themselves were without value for the soul. His later Deism merely rationalizes a habit of judgment already formed. And indeed, when set against Mather's bigoted theology, his shrewd reasoning to prove that the good man is sure to prosper seems a justifiable materialism. But if Franklin's morals and his religion were determined by expediency, nevertheless they did not strain human nature, especially they did not strain his own, which in its moral vagaries might have supplied an argument to Puritan preachers against the relaxations of common sense. They were reasonable if not elevated, and applied to ethics in the religious life in general the logic of facts as he observed them in this world, rather than a logic based upon premises established by metaphysics.

His ethical ideas seem more doubtful when compared with the only other religious doctrine he seems to have strongly felt. Whoever knows Quakerism detects in a hundred places in Franklin's works the results of living with the Friends in Philadelphia. There is no evidence that the reasonable, reconciling, tolerant spirit that made him so successful as a mediator, was born in him. His biographer, Smyth,* describes him as self-willed, opinionated,

* Albert Henry Smyth, "The Writings of Benjamin Franklin; . . . with a Life."

and defiant in youth. Strong-willed he certainly was throughout life, but the cardinal principle of his political philosophy was tolerance when possible at home and abroad, whether it was the Germans to be assimilated in Pennsylvania, or the Revolution to be satisfactorily concluded.* The Quaker principle of good will, the Quaker insistence upon the essential nobleness of right-minded man, are dominant principles with Franklin that made him popular in France and, aided by his shrewd amiability, set a fashion in a Europe growing tired of privilege and distrustful of rank. Yet the Quaker spiritual dependence, the Quaker mysticism, are utterly absent. In a very real sense, the moral ideas of Franklin represent Quakerism conventionalized, stylized, and Deicized, if the word may be permitted, in order to become immediately useful in the skeptical eighteenth century world. There is no reason for good will given in Franklin's writings except its success, no reason for loving one's fellow man except expediency. As the Quaker grew rich because of his unworldliness, which made him inevitably prudent in expenditure and reliable in business, and then grew worldly because he was rich, so the political ethics of Franklin, with its liberal, Quaker tinge, became the common-sense utilitarianism of American business ethics. If not the father of dollar philosophy and dollar diplomacy, he is at least the foster father—the American environment and Ameri-

* See Franklin's letter to Joseph Priestley, of Feb. 8, 1780: "The rapid Progress *true* science now makes, occasions my regretting sometimes that I was born so soon. It is impossible to imagine the Height to which may be carried, in a thousand years, the Power of Man over Matter. We may perhaps learn to deprive large Masses of their Gravity, and give them absolute Levity, for the sake of easy Transport. Agriculture may diminish its Labors and double its Produce; all Diseases may by sure means be prevented or cured, not excepting even that of Old Age, and our Lives lengthened at pleasure even beyond the antediluvian Standard. O that moral Science were in as fair a way of Improvement, that Men would cease to be Wolves to one another, and that human Beings could at length learn what they now improperly call Humanity."

can circumstance, which he so shrewdly and prophetically viewed, being presumably the ultimate cause.

His practical mind made Franklin an extraordinarily keen observer of the actual business of living in the colonies, and one of the wisest of commentators upon how to adjust oneself to the new environment, or indeed to any environment. A collection of his more important essays and letters not devoted to immediate political problems would show a series of advisory articles telling how to light streets, how to avoid colds by air baths, how to get ready to immigrate, how to provide for universal peace.* The spirit of the logical, inquisitive eighteenth century is strong in all this, and indeed Franklin, even before his diplomatic residence abroad, was a citizen of the world— yet it is constantly evident how strongly his keen and lucid mind was stimulated by the needs and possibilities of a new state where nature had to be conquered, and where experiments in new and better human relationships could be hopefully inaugurated. A journalist by taste and talent, he became, as they say now, a specialist in public relations. His science was always applied science,† his great diplomatic achievements were gained by carefully applied publicity—if he could not speak, he wrote. It is questionable whether any pen did more to influence practical thinking in the latter eighteenth century than his, and this without any masterpiece of philosophical thought or literary expression. He was a first-class working intellect, smoothing the way by speech and writing, even more than by deeds, for the new republic.

3.

IF HIS place in American literature is as an influence

* Note in his "Autobiography" a project for a "United Party for Virtue"—a League of Virtue for all nations, to be governed by rules.

† See in his "Autobiography" the sections on the standardizing of shipbuilding and sailing, and on the motives for his electrical experiments.

rather than as a master, that is because he was a great statesman and a most articulate philosopher, but in no way a great artist, even in words. His style is trenchant, and carefully formed and imitated from models drawn from an earlier English period. The "Autobiography" is solid eighteenth century prose, cogent, luminous, strong, reflecting a remarkable mind. But the "Autobiography" is not quoted for its style, nor were the sententious epigrams of "Poor Richard's Almanack" borrowed everywhere because of their wit or form. School readers inevitably reprint the episode of the poor boy with the rolls under his arm while his future wife watched him from a doorway, because it is the typical narrative of successful men in America, and several generations drew from "Poor Richard" because his thrift was a keynote for a country still empty of capital, and "Do it yourself," "You can be what you will," "Try and see," were slogans for initiative and hope. The physical and political development of the United States is implicit in the writings of Franklin.

Cotton Mather, a generation behind him, seems insane by comparison, Edwards, only three years older, a man of another world. Franklin, a far more capacious intellect than Mather, and intellectually more flexible if not more powerful than Edwards, is the expected voice to say that America is by no means an experiment of the Puritan God, but a great economic proposition, to be conducted ethically, sensibly, with freedom for initiative, hard work, and every resource of invention in a community where every variety of human nature is to have its chance.

Regarded as a man of letters—and in his capacity of prime journalist for the colonies, he must be so regarded—Franklin is, indeed, an excellent example of a phenomenon peculiarly American. In his social ideas he was ahead of his time, in his literary expression behind it. As Edwards's style belongs to the seventeenth rather than to the eighteenth century, so Franklin in his style and in his forms of address belongs with Addison, Steele, and especially Defoe rather than with his own English decades. Yet his social philosophy is abreast of the early eighteen hundreds, and if the French, always intuitive in such matters, felt in him the exponent of a new order, it was because in what they called his simplicity (he was never simple) they saw the idea of a new community where intelligence, industry, and common sense would break through privilege into success. H. G. Wells has the same almost romantic faith in science, today.

It was his cool, practical advice, favorable to sensible living in a country poor in means but rich in ends, that gave prestige to worldly affairs (including science) in communities where eloquence had always belonged to the theologians. The brand of idealistic common sense that he stamped with his name has been staple in the United States ever since, and no philosophy was so thoroughly rubbed into the minds of youth in the young republic. Henry Adams praises it in the Pennsylvania of a century later, as the stabilizer of the Union. Never again after Franklin did it come so near literature as in his essays and his "Autobiography," but it has been the substance of the best American journalism, and in its decadence has provided a solid philistinism from which indignant literary genius has rebounded into art.

Evil is evil, says Franklin in one oft-quoted passage of the "Autobiography," not because it is forbidden, but because it is evil it is forbidden, the ugliness of evil and the advantage of virtue being proved by their results. As a proposition, this is not very different from Edwards's belief that the nature of evil is more important than its cause in predestination, yet the emphasis is entirely different. Edwards is concerned with the necessity of willing evil or good, Franklin with the results. And it might be added that Woolman's concern was neither with the practical results in this world nor with a practical necessity to prepare for the next by right willing, but with goodness itself, which must be apprehended before any attitude or course became of the slightest importance. These are the three strains of ethics, the three kinds of temperament that appear, reappear, blend, confuse, and create in the later American imagination, where they are further complicated by pioneer temperament and pioneer morals. Played upon by immense forces generated by immigration, settlement, and the establishment of a political and economic society under new circumstances and upon an unexploited continent, in a very real sense they condition the scope and ethical character of the literature of the first national century.

Michel Guillaume St. Jean de Crèvecœur

OF THE moulding influences slowly shaping the American mind and preparing for an American literature, those most obvious in the printed records, as has been said before, are not necessarily the most important. Quakerism and Puritanism are readily definable in our intellectual life, yet certainly the uninterrupted immigration of every variety of European man and the increasing play of new environmental conditions upon all and sundry constitute the central motive of our literary as of our social history. What they brought here can be known in general outline, but the subtle sea and land changes of a new and heterogeneous nation, and the still subtler accents placed by difference upon literary expression are difficult to determine. Our ethics, our conceptions of government, of law, of literary form, were imported, but the men who used these ideas soon changed.

There were hundreds to write of American circumstance,

but few whose observations, like Franklin's, were philosophical, fewer still who knew more than their own colonial corner, and yet fewer who on the frontier, away from the obsessions of theology or politics and away from the European atmosphere of the towns, could see with detachment and accuracy what America was doing to the immigrant.

This is the value of the appealing "Letters from an American Farmer" of the Norman emigrant Crèvecœur, first published under the name of J. Hector St. John in London in 1782, which, with the recently discovered additional essays,* give a picture of colonial life in the back country as seen by an intelligent man.

Crèvecœur, who had traveled widely in the colonies, was an intellectual inspired with that French curiosity as to the nature of society which was the hall mark of the *philosophe* who made the revolution. He himself was neither a profound philosopher nor a radical desiring change. The Quakers, with whom he had much contact, had given him a concern for a peaceful life, and Rousseau had kindled a sensitive interest in primitive nature not to be blunted even by a first-hand contact with Indians and the rough forest. He disliked busybodies, soldiers, Yankees (when they left New England to stir up rebellion), race prejudice, and violence. Our Revolution ended his idyllic dream of a new world untroubled by the ambitions and oppressions of the old. Become an American in his devotion to the soil, yet unwilling to take part in what he regarded as rebellion, he was driven into the British lines, and finally back to France.† He loved his country but

---

* See "Sketches of Eighteenth Century America," edited by H. Q. Bourdin, R. H. Gabriel, and S. T. Williams, and for other items the bibliography in the "Dictionary of American Biography."

† He proposed, if we may believe his "Letters," to retire into the Indian country to the westward, but was fearful for the results upon the education of his children. Separated from his family, he had no news of them until his return

hated violence still more—and there was no mercy for the moderate in 1779. His accounts of the hardships and the character of the Loyalists in the early Revolutionary period are important, but to their trials others are witness. Crève-cœur has a stronger claim to a place in literary history.

Not, however, as a stylist. The "Letters from an American Farmer" were carefully edited in England before their publication. His later letters, unedited, show that he was a better journalist than man of letters, and his imperfectly mastered English is that of a man who wrote because he had something to say, not to make literature. And what he had to say was this—that out of English, Dutch, Germans, Irish, Scotch, and French, America was making a new man. Dogs, he said, when imported, soon became a native breed; so it was with men.

Urged by a variety of motives the poor of Europe, landless, oppressed, starved, unplaced, came to America. "Everything has tended to regenerate them, new laws, a new mode of living, a new social system," Crèvecœur wrote in Letter III of the first series. "Here they are become men. In Europe they were so many useless plants, wanting vegetative mould and refreshing showers. They withered, and were mowed down by want, hunger, and war; but now, by the power of transplantation, like all other plants, they have taken root and flourished! Formerly they were not numbered in any civil lists of their country, except in those of the poor; here they rank as citizens. . . . The laws . . . protect them as they arrive: . . . they receive ample rewards for their labors: these . . . procure them lands: those lands confer on them the title of freemen, and to that title every benefit is affixed which men can possibly require. . . ." What then is the American, this new man? He is one "who,

as a French consul in 1783. His wife was dead, but after a search he found his children.

leaving behind him all his ancient prejudices and manners, receives new ones from the mode of life he has embraced, the new government he obeys, and the new rank he holds. . . . Here individuals of all nations are melted into a new race of men. . . . The American is a new man, who acts on new principles; he must therefore entertain new ideas and form new opinions. From involuntary idleness, servile dependence, penury, and useless labor, he has passed to toils of a very different nature, rewarded by ample subsistence."

The last lines of this letter show how thoroughly Crèvecœur shared the doctrinaire tendencies of his class, and in fact, though elsewhere he indicates a perfect knowledge of the difficulties and injustices of colonial life, he was essentially an optimist. Indeed his fervid descriptions of the bondman become independent are said to have led to the destruction in the malarial swamps of Ohio, of five hundred Norman families induced to emigrate by the French translation of his letters. This may or may not be true, nevertheless the optimists, so far, have usually been nearer right than the pessimists in America. His glowing generalizations do represent a typical process that in its effect upon the whole man must have been far more powerful than creeds or political theories, and of which our national independence was only one result. The theme, of course, is common in eighteenth century American literature. I have already noted it in Franklin, and it is repeated again and again in the century following, and until the deep changes that began in the early nineteen hundreds.

But Crèvecœur's interest in the new society did not stop with men. On his farm in Orange County, New York, he wrote of what hundreds felt, but lacked the romantic impulse to describe—the charms of wild nature, and the characteristics of the American background. His descriptions of the hummingbird and of the battle of the snakes have often been quoted; the newly recovered account of a snowstorm on the frontier deserves equal repetition. There is more. Man in the new continent had gained free access to unspoiled nature. It was his, not the estate of a nobleman, and it was a new nature, not yet a part of familiar knowledge. The wild bee, the tall primitive forest, the high skies of American weather, the wilderness to the north and west, the new flowers, the swamp where wildness still lingered even on the cleared farm—his descriptions of all these are inspired, no doubt, by his philosophic curiosity as to the making of a new man in a new environment, but he precedes nevertheless a succession of nature writers who, like him, endeavor to assimilate the new environment. Audubon was on his travels before the century closed, Bartram had preceded him, Thoreau in a half century would be seeking in American nature a spiritual outlet for American man.

The thing of course was inevitable, with romanticism in the air and sensitive spirits touched by new sensations, yet the value of Crèvecœur is not lessened because he described phenomena that to thousands were too familiar to suggest recording. The hardships of the frontier, the demoralization of Indians become half white and whites become half Indian, quarrels, theft, degeneration, and debauchery—these disillusioned many a romantic pioneer, just as the disorders of the revolutionary period burned Crèvecœur's home and wrecked the harmony of the pleasant existence he had made for himself. But the faith remained, the experience was repeated, and American literature gains thence some of its most characteristic traits.

Revolution

THE American Revolution was political, economic, military; it was fought by both sword and pen—but not in

49

literary criticism. Minds were changed by it, but not literary tastes, and indeed the colonial literature of the end of the eighteenth century and the first so-called national literature are completely imitative of European models, in spite of trumpetings to the contrary. There was no cultural break with England; no native belles lettres worthy of the name followed. The immediate results, indeed, for belles lettres, were naturally negative. A colonial English literature was nipped in its budding; the vigorous intellectual energy of the colonies was directed by necessity into politics, governmental theory, and executive management; and the struggle toward democracy that accompanied the struggle for independence, and went on after it was gained, was long to be inimical to the fine arts.

"What do we mean by the revolution?" wrote John Adams to Thomas Jefferson in 1815. "The war? That was no part of the revolution; it was only an effect and consequence of it. The revolution was in the minds of the people, and this was effected from 1760 to 1775, in the course of fifteen years, before a drop of blood was drawn at Lexington." *

When the new imperial system of Great Britain began to threaten the American tradesman with an increase of trade restrictions, and the American pioneer with limitations westward, the first battles were fought in type. The stream of pamphlets, best recorded in Moses Coit Tyler's "Literary History of the American Revolution," † is evidence of the virility of intellectual training in the colonies. It is notable that the debate ranges chiefly from Boston on the north to Philadelphia at the south, with Samuel Adams (for independence), Samuel Seabury (for

* "Correspondence of John Adams and Thomas Jefferson: 1812-1826." See Paul Wilstach's "Selections," p. 116.

† See also a convenient manual, "Prose and Poetry of the Revolution," by F. C. Prescott and J. H. Nelson, 1925; the discussion in Parrington, *op. cit.*, and Vol. II of Charles Angoff, *op. cit.*

conciliation with England)—both New Englanders—and John Dickinson of Pennsylvania (for the rights but not the independence of the colonies) as the most notable writers; followed in the second or revolutionary phase by Thomas Paine and Thomas Jefferson. The American state papers amazed Chatham by their excellence. Tyler thinks their force and clarity were due to the training of the American colleges, especially in New England. They were due even more to the growing self-sufficiency of the American mind, which found the sudden release of necessity in the great argument. And the high level of logic and the pertinacity in debate must be attributed very largely to the shift into political thinking of minds accustomed to constant wrestling with the politics of religion, and familiar with the technique of self-government. The lawyer class, as Crèvecœur notes, was supreme in the colonies in the last half of the century, and they had been educated in schools or colleges dominated by the religious intellectuals.

From 1760 to 1787, with intermissions for the exigencies of war, the debate over the nature and the rights of government continued, until the best minds in America, like the Roman intellectual leaders, were absorbed in the business of political persuasion. Much of their prose is dreary reading now, and in the whole pamphlet series perhaps only Thomas Paine (in his two famous works, "Common Sense" and "The Crisis"), Jefferson, and Hamilton, rise into literature. But a tradition of effective rhetoric was established that stretches with only a few breaks to Woodrow Wilson, while the groundwork of political and social ideas upon which so much of later American literature was built, is first laid down by these controversialists. The remarkable generation that was in control through the quarter century in which the republic was conceived, enforced, and organized, was still colonial in its esthetic culture, but original, independent, mature, and prepotent in its mastery of social science, theoretical and applied.*

2.

THE precocious achievements of American politics are abundantly recorded in history, although too much credit is usually given to patriotism and too little to the good judgment and imagination of men by no means committed in advance to the courses that were followed. The Revolution, however, not only made men, it lost them. The tradition of close dependence upon English culture was not broken; much of it, however, was literally carried away.

The Revolution when it reached the stage of active rebellion was a radical movement, in which men of property and education joined with extreme reluctance. The failure of conciliation came as a surprise and a calamity to all but propagandists, trouble-makers, and the turbulent among the lower classes who had little to lose and something to gain. When the decision was forced, it was men of light and leading who became the most ardent patriots and who nursed, defended, and established the republic. Nevertheless, the polite world, the Anglicans, and most of those free from the prejudices of Puritans and Quakers against "polite literature," were chiefly Loyalist, at least in their sympathies. Boston, New York, Philadelphia, Charleston, the colonial centers of such literary culture as existed in the revolutionary period and the depots for the importation of European books, were in British control through much or all of the war. The Tories who remained in these ports, or took refuge there, were not the brainiest of Americans, but they were a heavy majority

* See David Ramsay's "History of the American Revolution," 1789, Vol. II, p. 401. "It was found that the talents for great stations did not differ in kind, but only in degree, from those which were necessary for the proper discharge of the ordinary business of civil society."

of the educated world that read books, saw plays, wrote poetry, and had lived abroad. Many remained in America, changing their opinions successfully at the end of the war, but they lost both social and intellectual prestige; yet so many went into exile in Nova Scotia, Nassau, and England as to alter profoundly the complexion of cultivated American society. We bled away our inherited culture and conservatism, though much was left. There are no old Boston families, says a story told today; the Boston aristocracy came from Salem after the Revolution, the old families went to Halifax. The American society which produced an Irving and a Cooper differed from the colonial culture not merely because it had become national and was obsessed with economic and political problems all its own, it differed in personnel. The Federalists, who became the conservative party in the early years of the nation, were colonial liberals, reacting toward conservatism—republicans, not democrats. But they were not strong enough to nourish such an English literature in America as might have come from the rich colonial soil if the growth had been unchecked. Until the War of 1812 brought deeper rancor between the two countries, the young United States was still a literary colony seeking education from the mother country, but there were fewer desiring such education. The most English among cultivated Americans had been driven out.*

The Tory exodus is a factor of first-rate importance in explaining the subsequent growth of American literature. It changed the American mind by subtracting quantitatively certain elements; the barren decades at the end of

---

* The immensely important fact of language made these transatlantic dependences largely between the colonies and England. The cultivated Frenchman or German who emigrated in the eighteenth century, Americanized with such rapidity, that, like Crèvecœur, his cultural activities were inevitably merged in the English tradition. French and German were read and spoken in colonial America, but the cultural framework was English.

the old and the beginning of the new century are barren because no audience for belles lettres had reassembled; even Washington Irving wrote for English as well as for American readers. And this exodus of the cultivated conservative sharpened the conflict between aristocracy and democracy of which the Revolution was only a phase and brought its inevitable conclusion nearer by half a century. The war found three classes: Tories, moderates, radicals; it left two: organizers and lovers of unlimited freedom.

In the conflict between the aristocratic and the democratic principle lies the chief literary importance of the revolutionary period, which, in this sense, began with the first republican stirrings in 1760. It was inaugurated, indeed, when the back-country men, who had tasted liberty and self-reliance, began to struggle for power in every colonial government. It was reflected in the arguments of the pamphleteers over the rights of man. The forces of conservatism and aristocracy rallied after the disastrous experiences of the Confederation, securing reorganization by a constitution the purpose of which was to establish a liberal republic controlled by responsible men. But maintaining that the fruits of revolution were being taken from the people, Jefferson defeated the Federalists in 1800. The struggle continued until in 1828 Jackson marched his muddy boots into the Capitol and the plain democratic man seized the government.

Upon this great struggle the American mind was bent, and literature, so far as literature was made, was its servant. Even Knickerbocker's "History of New York" is as much a political satire upon Jefferson and Jeffersonian democracy as a burlesque upon the colonial Dutch.* The war pamphlets argue political and economic rights more

* Many of Irving's figures and incidents are easily identifiable, and new parallels are undoubtedly to be discovered.

than British oppression. In one verse satire that deserves to live from prerevolutionary days, John Trumbull's "M'Fingall," a free and very skilful imitation of "Hudibras," the Tory squire takes the hated place of the Puritan original. Philip Freneau, the only other poet of the period of real promise, has left only a few fragile lyrics to pure literature, his energies being thrown into journalism and Jeffersonian propaganda. And the rhetoric of Thomas Paine's "Common Sense" and of Patrick Henry's famous speech, derives what excellence it possesses from the intensity of a cause that was quite as much the plain man's against aristocracy as America's against England.

The cause itself shifts. Liberal becomes conservative, as the people encroach upon government.* When independence is a fact, the conflict opens between Alexander Hamilton and Thomas Jefferson, each a mind of the first order intellectually (and in practical affairs also), each representative of an American attitude still strongly held and deeply influential upon American thought.

3.

JEFFERSON was essentially a scholar and a scientist, with a gift for political leadership that determined his career. He might have been a writer of social and philosophic criticism in a less exigent period, as his correspondence and his intelligent "Notes on the State of Virginia" prove.

* The voters described in H. H. Brackenridge's "Modern Chivalry" would not vote for the weaver because he did not represent the people. Says one of them, "It is a very strange thing, that, having conquered Burgoyne and Cornwallis, and got a government of our own, we cannot put in it whom we please." Compare this with the Letter of Submission of the Constitution, signed by Washington and dated Sept. 17, 1787: "It is obviously impracticable in the federal government of these States, to secure all rights of independent sovereignty to each, and yet provide for the interest and safety of all. Individuals entering into society must give up a share of liberty to preserve the rest. The magnitude of the sacrifice must depend as well upon the situation and circumstance as on the object to be obtained." Here is the irrepressible conflict, in essence.

He was not a man of letters; rather, in American thought he is to be regarded as a philosophic force, equivalent in many respects to Locke in the eighteenth or Darwin in the nineteenth century. The conception of Jeffersonian democracy, which rightly bears his name, is fundamental in American history.

There is still much argument as to the influence of French ideas upon Jefferson. That they increased a native political radicalism is unquestionable. More important, however, is the nature of his own ideas, whatever their source, as he imposed them in a long series of writings—of which the Declaration of Independence is chief—upon a country where he came to be regarded as either devil or hero, with little shading between. He is the idealist of democracy and at the same time a political scientist who believed, with all the fervor of the Puritan's belief that New England was God's opportunity, that the United States was the world's experiment in new social and political relationships. New England after the Revolution had had enough radicalism, but Jefferson wanted to go on after she was ready to stop. Men were created to be free and equal as regards opportunity, hence privilege must be abolished so that the common man might become fit. Government had been an instrument for subjecting the many to the will of the privileged few, therefore the less government the better, which meant decentralization and anti-imperialism. War was against reason, and against policy because by war tyrants grew strong, therefore a virgin republic in a new world would maintain its rights by economic pressure and keep out of war by staying at home. In these policies, which Jefferson supported in practice with a varying consistency but with an undying belief, one sees the background of a characteristic type of American thinking. He ruined his own Virginia by the embargo, which, nevertheless, was the first experiment in that economic pressure which statesmen are now urging as a substitute for war. "Manifest destiny" and a turn of chance made him our greatest expansionist when he consummated the Louisiana Purchase, but did not alter his belief in anti-imperialism. In his faith in the common man as the ultimate authority for government, he spoke equally for the rapidly growing West, whence he himself came, and for new philosophical ideas as to the natural rights of man. A scholar and a gentleman himself, and allied through his mother to the aristocracy, his policy of rights for all led into the tumultuous government by the largely uneducated of the Jacksonian era, and produced finally such anomalies as a party led by both Woodrow Wilson and William Jennings Bryan. Yet as an ideal, his program has by no means exhausted its power in the United States.

Alexander Hamilton, the organizer of capital, the centralist, the prime Federalist, is also a symbol and a force in American thinking, most of all through the success of his organization, but also by the fruits of his pen. "The Federalist," to which he was the chief contributor, was one of those transcendent efforts in journalism that are prime factors in political change. It was an important agency in the adopting of the Constitution, and became immediately a source book for American political thinking. It was a part of the regular curriculum at Harvard in Emerson's day.

Jefferson, like the New England divines, was willing to defer—and perhaps to sacrifice—prosperity, security, growth, in order to make surer the attainment of an ultimate ideal. He would risk a weak government in spite of the challenging militarism of Europe, and was willing to trust to the ignorant energy of the West. But Hamilton, an efficiency expert of the first order, saw that the American experiment was bound to fail unless the anarchic independence of the members could be curbed by a central purpose. A central purpose cannot be formulated by democratic impulse, but must come from the uncommon man who has enough intelligence to build a complex machine and then run it. The Federalist party, of which he was the genius, was essentially an aristocracy, in which education and property (in which responsibility inheres, and where ability is most likely to be found) took the place of birth and privilege. Franklin was on his side; Edwards would have agreed with him. It is the principle upon which American business is organized today.

And it supplies inevitably a term to literary criticism. In literature, Irving, Cooper (in spite of his political affiliations), Bryant, Lowell, Longfellow, are Federalists. Emerson (mildly), Thoreau (in his own fashion), Mark Twain, Whitman, are Jeffersonians.

Hamilton in his moment of power was certainly right, and as certainly the savior, as much as Washington, of his adopted country. Jefferson, who triumphed over him, was as surely the spokesman of an American instinct so strong that more than a hundred years later it found expression in almost identical terms by the voice of Wilson, and aroused an equal popular enthusiasm, and a like scornful opposition among "practical" men. Federalist and anti-Federalist are terms that, with changing content but much the same general significance, go through American social experience, and are valid descriptions of states of mind long after the Jacksonian revolution had eaten up the immediate followers of Jefferson and Hamilton alike. The West won in the political struggle, the West has always won in the end, for the frontier and the advance of democracy are factors that steadily gain in influence, at least until 1898. Yet victory always renews the old conflict between tradition and revolt, between privilege and opportunity, between the plain and the polished man. Here is a key by which one of the doors that leads to an

THE COLONIAL BACKGROUND

understanding of American literature may be unlocked.

In one respect the rival intellectual leaders of the young republic were alike: the creation and definition of government absorbed the best energies of their lives. They were members of that remarkable generation to which reference has already been made, in which ability was stimulated by circumstance and irresistibly attracted toward politics. The scientific interests of an Audubon, of a Bartram, of Jefferson himself, were sporadic phenomena. The country itself, problems of government excepted, was in no intellectual mood; Washington at the turn of the century, a sprawling village, its bucolic atmosphere scorned by foreign diplomats exiled to its muddy streets and dirty taverns, is an amazing instance of great ideas at work in a petty environment. And though intensely energetic, the population as a whole was immersed for twenty years after 1783 in post-war relaxation and grossness. Morality had declined; * travelers and historians unite in describing an era of absorbed commercialism, with crudity in social life except in the Federalist society of the few cities, and on some but not many of the plantations, and a decline in ideals of living except in such favored communities as one found in rural New England. This was natural after a long and devastating war, a vast change in property ownership, unlimited opportunities for money-making with little capital to pursue them, while the Napoleonic wars were raising the premium on American exports, speculation was rife, the West was rapidly opening, and everything was to do and make and get ready for the prosperity that had not yet come. The nation was but just created—literally created, for if self-government was an old story, the ideas put into practice in 1787 represented

* See J. D. Schöpf's, "Travels in the Confederation, 1783-1784," H. H. Brackenridge's "Modern Chivalry," and David Ramsay's "History of the American Revolution," of 1789. Vol. II, p. 412.

a unity new to the science of politics. It was scarcely a favorable moment for the creation of a national literature. Irving, our first successful man of letters, had no such ambitious expectation when he began to write. But this was not the advice of the poets and panegyrists whose false dawn deserves another section.

False Dawn

HAMILTON and Jefferson met an immediate need for government by means which, whatever their sources, were highly original in their application. But there was no pressing need for a national literature at the beginning of the republic, and certainly no popular demand. The idea that a new United States should produce a new American literature as a natural function of independence was only a theory of the intellectuals. When the statesmen applied political ideas drawn from the eighteenth century in Europe to American conditions a new creation, the United States, resulted, but when poets and novelists borrowed eighteenth century styles in literature for their quasi-American themes they never got beyond imitation, presumably because the themes they chose were not vitally American. Indeed the more the first writers in our national history asserted their Americanism the more flatly imitative they became. Constitutions were indispensable, epics, especially second-hand epics, one could for a while do without.

It is true that Charles Brockden Brown, who has the doubtful honor of being the first man in America to try to live by his pen, was more interested in writing books that could sell than in presenting a literature to the new country. His failure came from lack of ability and the colonial habit of mind, not from an attempt to celebrate a nation that was politically precocious but socially adolescent, and in its esthetic infancy.* He failed because his servile talent could only copy Godwin in ideas and the Gothic romance in plot and atmosphere, and if he is to be read at all, it will only be for his curious perversions of the American scene. He gets space in literary histories that might better be devoted to the state papers, the political controversies, the correspondence, of the really great Americans of his times, and to the faint records of a commencing popular literature of the frontier.

2.

MORE worthy, more interesting historically, were the so-called Hartford wits.† They would have expected (alas, for the vain hopes of ambition!) a chapter to themselves in any work on the literature of the United States.

That group of Yale graduates had some reason to anticipate literary greatness. They were men of exceptional versatility in a period when exceptional and unexpected ability in war, diplomacy, and government was common. They were themselves soldiers, diplomats, college presidents, as well as poets (their most solid man, Timothy Dwight, was called the Pope of the Federalist party), yet it was from poetry that they expected their fame. But their ponderous epics have been read (when read) by later generations with scant reverence. The epic aspirations of Joel Barlow are scarcely borne out by his "Columbiad," even though the god of the Delaware presides over Washington's crossing, and all concludes in "one confederate, condependent sway which binds all regions in the leagues of peace." He thought that "This is the moment in America to give . . . direction to poetry, painting, etc.

---

* Yet he wrote under some influence from his intellectual superiors, the Hartford wits, and undoubtedly hoped to make Philadelphia and Connecticut as romantic as Italy. See F. L. Pattee's Introduction to his "Wieland."

† See for a general discussion, Henry Beers, "The Connecticut Wits."

that true . . . ideas of glory may be implanted . . . to take the place of false ones . . . that have degraded the species in other countries," * but the will was more than the deed. Dwight, raised above his sober New England self by the blood and fire of the Revolution, turned the conquest of Canaan into another epic, bearing that title but reflecting the Puritan patriot as much as his Old Testament sources. In his leisure hours as pastor of the Greenfield church, near Fairfield in Connecticut, he wrote still another epic in seven books, each one of which was intended to be an exercise in the manner of a famous British predecessor, the whole a historical pæan upon his beloved Connecticut. The real theme is always the same in all these long-winded utterances of commonplace verse: the fortunate (and moral) promise of America, the unhappy degeneracy of Europe, the importance of thrift, simplicity, and virtuous living. Or, as Dwight sings in "Greenfield Hill" (1794):

> Ah then, thou favoured land, thyself revere!
> Look not to Europe, for examples just
> Of order, manners, customs, doctrines, laws,
> Of happiness, or virtue. Cast around
> The eye of searching reason, and declare
> What Europe proffers, but a patchwork sway;
> The garment Gothic, worn to fritter'd shreds,
> And eked from every loom of following times. . . .
>
> See too, in countless herds, the mistress vile,
> Even to the teeth of matron sanctity,
> Lift up her shameless bronze, and elbow out
> The pure, the chaste, the lovely angel-form
> Of female excellence. . . .
> See the foul theatre, with Apaz steams,
> Impoisoning half mankind!

* Preface to "The Columbiad," 1st edition, 1787, enlarged under its present title, 1801.

THE COLONIAL BACKGROUND

Here is shocked New England, pale with conscious virtue, exulting in the "sacred institutions" of the native land. Continue to elect, says this staunch Federalist, "the virtuous and wise; men tried, and prov'd, of steady virtue," and heaven shall bless America.

These monuments to the influence of Pope and Thompson, Goldsmith and Gray, and other imitations of equal mediocrity, will never be read by lovers of poetry, yet historians and critics might profitably peruse them. The Hartford wits (of whom only one was really witty) were not small men imitating the great; they were intellects of unusual ability, functioning in a medium where their talent was small. They were the poet laureates of a new nation, who wrote not because they could, but because they felt that the occasion demanded nothing less than great and resounding verse.

> For pleasing Arts behold her matchless charms
> The first in letters, as the first in arms. . . .
> Sublime the Muse shall lift her eagle wings,

orated young John Trumbull at Yale in 1770, but the genius of America upon which they descanted so interminably was not yet ripe for poetry, or for that matter, for literary prose. The republicanism that triumphed in the Revolution did not pause long enough to become epical, but under the guidance not of the Muse but of Jefferson hastened on toward a most unpoetical democracy. These eulogists were successful in imparting a heroic flavor to the achievements of the Revolution, and the glamour that has hung over its protagonists ever since, concealing the great struggle between democrat and aristocrat in a mist of glory, is due in no small part to the high dignity of their stilted praises. But where they dealt in futures—and they dealt largely in futures—they reckoned without their America, and especially without the new

West and the surge of democracy. Their grandiloquent echoes of classicism bear much the same relation to American nationalism in its actual development as the Græco-Roman busts of early Western senators in the Capitol at Washington to their most unclassical originals. Yale, always the most conservative of American institutions, had hatched a brood that sang too loftily and too soon.

Yet this poetical apotheosis of Columbia shows the magnitude of expectation felt by every American in the last decades of the old century and the first of the new; cruder boasting in prose followed and became the commonplace of Americans abroad. These epics, which have their fine passages (Dwight was the first to give the American thunderstorm an adequate description), show that to create a nation is not necessarily to create a literature. The Yale conception of America was rhetorical, and the poems that embodied it, naturally, were rhetoric. In their magniloquence, inflated by great events, they represent not the first of our national literature, but the last of colonial English in America, celebrating unconsciously its end. In literature, in spite of boastings, there had been as yet no revolution.

3.

ONLY one of this group that tried to make literature follow the flag shows sparks of real genius. John Trumbull was a satirist in his own right, and satire could fruit in an age when epic only leafed. His best poem, "M'Fingall," already referred to, written in part in 1775, concluded in 1782, belongs to the period of revolutionary controversy, but in style, method, and expectations he is one of the Yale wits, the only real wit among them. This still famous satire on the Tories is described by Timothy Dwight in his "Travels in New England and New York" as "not inferior in wit and humor to Hudibras, and in every other

respect . . . superior." It is, indeed, inferior to "Hudibras" only in pith and originality. One of its couplets still
sparkles—

> No man e'er felt the halter draw
> With good opinion of the law—

and the whole (to tell truth) is a good deal more readable
than "Hudibras," once Butler has discharged his epigrams in the first canto.

Trumbull had what was to be rare for many years in
this continent, a detachment from his provincial environment that marked a man trained as a gentleman as well
as a scholar. His little known "Progress of Dulness, or the
Rare Adventures of Tom Brainless" (1772-1773), begins
with a cogent attack upon the educational system of Yale,
his alma mater ("And nonsense long, with serious air,
Has wander'd unmolested there"), which, as satire, is by
no means out of date, at Yale or any other university. In
the history of a foolish parson bred by "the quackeries of
learning" he signifies the decay of that class of religious
intellectual leaders whose eminence in brains and executive skill had passed to statesmen and soldiers.

Trumbull was a man of the world even when condemn-
ing its fopperies. His companions were more heavy-handed
because they were more provincial. In his work one sees
colonial literature in the best sense, a generation to a century behind its models, but applied with vigor in a new
milieu. If the anthologists seek eighteenth century verse
from America, let them find it in him as well as in the less
skilful Freneau. And colonial literature, in a worse sense,
are the far more pretentious efforts of Barlow and Dwight
and their school. They made history, helped to sustain
the dignity of literature in a country growing rapidly commercialized, but proved by the very emptiness of their
rhetoric that they understood the classics better than the

nation which they had ably assisted to create and now proposed to sing.

4.

So MUCH for a general survey of the progenitors of American literature, and the forces, some subtle, some broad, that by 1800 were durable in the national memory and constantly emergent in American experience. With no pretense of having covered all of the complex movements that were focusing toward a national existence, I hope nevertheless to have described the influences most prepotent in the background of the great Americans of the first half century of the nation, which I propose now to discuss individually and in greater detail.

CHAPTER TWO

Washington Irving

IT was a sound instinct that led our forefathers to celebrate Washington Irving as the first American man
of letters, although they were far from discriminating
in their literary judgment of his work. By comparison
with Edwards or Franklin or Hamilton, Irving, in intellect, is a pigmy; beside that factory of ideas and energy,
Thomas Jefferson, he seems vacuous and imitative; yet
as a mere "belles lettres writer," as he deprecatingly
called himself in a letter to Brevoort of March 10, 1821,
he was the first American success, the first American to
win a place on the shelves dedicated to posterity. He had,
indeed, no rivals. The archprophet of orthodoxy and author of two epics, Timothy Dwight, president of Yale in
Irving's youth, and the prime intellectual of Connecticut,
was a stronger man but a much weaker writer, who believed that the only purpose of literature was to strengthen
the morals of New England. The other Hartford wits were
equally blown with didactism and pretentious rhetoric.
Charles Brockden Brown, Irving's senior by a few years,
was a good formal critic, but, as said before, a wretched
novelist who succeeded in debasing even the Gothic romance. With more justice than usually can be counted
upon in literary history, he was never successful.

The early eighteen hundreds were, indeed, in America,
a time most unpropitious to pure literature. A new political and moral fabric was in process of creation and first-
rate minds carried their charge of new ideas directly into

action. The Shelleys, the Keatses, the Wordsworths, the Coleridges, of America are the statesmen of the early republic. Furthermore, it was a period of aroused and absorbing commerce, and of pioneering over a front as long as the Appalachians. "I never knew," wrote Dwight in 1812, "half a dozen persons who here made writing books their business for life"—and without doubt these few wrote history or theology. "Works of the imagination," wrote Jefferson to Brown, apropos of his "Wieland," "have this advantage over history that the incidents of the former may be dressed in the most interesting form, while those of the latter must be confined to fact: they cannot therefore present virtue in the best and vice in the worst forms possible, as the former may." It was the most he could say for a trivial art in stirring times. "The cause why the intellectual soil of America is so comparatively sterile," said Brown himself in an announcement of *The American Review and Literary Journal*,* "is obvious. We do not cultivate it." No soil had ever grown a more abundant crop of social and political ideals than America between 1763 and the date of the novelist's words, but by "intellectual" Brown, like most literary men, meant "literary," and within his definition he was right. "We do not cultivate it." Barlow, Dwight, and Humphreys may be said to have cleared more than they could plough, Brown to have planted tares with his wheat, but for Irving "cultivated" is the right word. It is just what he did. Irving alone before the third decade of the new century had written enduring books of belles lettres, for Irving alone achieved a style. The amazing cerebration of the Federalist papers, the amazing erudition (and pedantry) for so young a country of "The Columbiad" and "The Conquest of Canaan," the astonishing verbosity of Brown's own novels, where, drunk with Godwinism and Gothic

* *Medical Repository*, Vol. 4, pp. 1–7.

romance, he turned Philadelphia into phantasmagoria, and the intellectualism of Jefferson, all reached varying degrees of importance—the least literary the highest—but none of them could boast of a literary style. Irving, though an American, had, as all Europe admitted, a style.

2.

I FEAR that for his contemporaries it was the European recognition that really counted. There is a little bitterness in his Introduction to "Bracebridge Hall": "It has been a matter of marvel to my European readers, that a man from the wilds of America should express himself in tolerable English. I was looked upon as something new and strange in literature." The reference is to the applause that greeted "The Sketch Book" of 1819-1820, which certainly was not the first tolerable English to cross the water, since Franklin's memoranda, the Declaration of Independence at which George III swore so heartily, and many a state paper of great excellence had preceded it. But this was the first literary book to be praised abroad as such. Young republics about to grow strong and wealthy wish to be told that they are civilized, and it was Irving's English reputation that gave tone to his American popularity.

Europe, indeed, was a little relieved. The distrust of this new American state was vast. Dr. Johnson and Mrs. Montagu had not hesitated to assert, what many thought, that in the new world men degenerated. Buffon believed that he had proved the case for animals until Jefferson at considerable expense procured for him the gigantic remains of a New England moose. As for men, the contrast between great talk of freedom and opportunity for all, and the actual commercialism of the seaboard, and the brutality or demoralization of the frontier, shocked European travelers.* There was power indubitably in the new continent, but it was power wielded sometimes by barbarians, sometimes by visionaries. The New England theologians were forgotten or outmoded, the Hartford wits were local celebrities, and their pretentious verse, if it had reached Europe, would not for an instant have stood the test of a great creative and critical generation. Barlow *vs.* Byron! Dwight (or Bryant) and Wordsworth! Brown and Coleridge! It was a relief to the polite of the old world to find, sprung from the new, an urbane writer, only mildly assertive of his republicanism, who spoke the language of universal culture in a charming and humorous style. America (they felt) began to be understandable at last. They were mistaken, for in Irving they learned about only one kind of American, but they were right as to the style.

Indeed Irving's reputation is the remarkable achievement of a style that sometimes rests upon little else than its own suavity. It was formed upon the prose of Goldsmith, Sterne, Swift, Steele, and Addison, with romantic coloring from Mrs. Radcliffe, and as early as the Mustapha letters † in those good-natured Salmagundi papers of 1807, which proclaimed the civilization of New York by making fun of it, was elegant, harmonious, and incisive. He sharp-

* An excellent discussion of this point is to be found in Chapter VI of Henry Adams's "History of the United States of America," Vol. I. Adams quotes appositely from Wordsworth:—

Long-wished-for sight, the Western World appeared;
And when the ship was moored, I leaped ashore
Indignantly,—resolved to be a man,
Who, having o'er the past no power, would live
No longer in subjection to the past, . . .
On nearer view, a motley spectacle
Appeared, of high pretentions—unreproved
But by the obstreperous voice of higher still;
Big passions strutting on a petty stage.

† The best of which were Irving's. See Pierre Irving's "Life and Letters."

ened its edge in the Knickerbocker "History" of 1810, sweetened it by 1819 in the best of the "Sketch Book" stories, brought it to full ripeness in "The Alhambra" of 1832, wrote it by second nature in his "Life of Gold-smith" of 1849, and did not relinquish it until the halting of old age appears in the very last page of the "Life of Washington" in 1858. It was a perfect instrument which, in spite of the terms of increase that I have used, changes very little from youth to age, varies scarcely at all in works of very different character, became, as a style should, the very accent of the man, but was and is a patina upon the metal of his thought rather than the flexible soul of the thought itself. Style with Irving was finish, polish, and when he took old chronicles of Granada, gave them romantic coloring, and then translated them into his personal diction, it is clear that he felt he was about the chief business of literature.

Irving, in fact, was not a man of letters who wrote history, he was a chronicler-historian who wrote like a man of letters. He was not creative, a fact that has been obscured by his successful use of legend and anecdote. He was more dependent upon his style than his famous predecessors, to whom he gladly admitted his debt, because the congenial task he chose for himself was to illumine history, myth, and character that appealed to him, by romance and wit gracefully expressed. In his authentic history—of Columbus and his companions, of Granada, of George Washington—he merely adds color * to an assemblage of facts, which he brings together in a skilful narrative order without the slightest evidence of a trained historian's power of criticism and interpretation. Myth, anecdote, and picturesque historical incident he suffuses with his own romantic sentiment or with ironic humor, according to the subject and his mood, and with real

* See the Preface to "The Conquest of Granada."

imagination builds into charming edifices of style. The Knickerbocker "History," "The Alhambra," and "Rip Van Winkle" are masterpieces of this kind. Real life he sometimes quite literally transcribed, as in the "Tour on the Prairies," sometimes suffused with sentiment and handled freely as in the feudal scenes of "Bracebridge Hall." When he tells stories of contemporary life, as in "The Wife" and that one-time favorite, "The Broken Heart" in "The Sketch Book," he is an arrant sentimentalist and conventional also, with no compensation for his lachrymosity except the unfailing suavity of his style.

To sum up, with no real power of character analysis, with no originality of thought, with no sense either of horror or pathos (his battles are usually humorous), quite immune to the great ideas sweeping through his world, Washington Irving relied upon a humorous, romantic temperament that mirrored with a difference the scenes that attracted such a mind—and upon a style. He was right, and he knew that he was right. The self-criticism in his oft-quoted letter to Brevoort of December 11, 1824, has more than rhetorical significance: "I consider a story merely as a frame on which I stretch my materials. It is the play of thought, and sentiment and language; . . . characters lightly yet expressively delineated; . . . faithful exhibitions of scenes in common life; and the half concealed vein of humour— . . . these are among what I aim at. . . . A constant activity of thought and a nicety of execution [are] required in writings of the kind." A novel may be allowed "pages and pages of careless writing," but in a tale the author may get "credit for his touches of pathos or humour; his points of wit or turns of language."

These are the words of a virtuoso, not of a creator of great fiction, of a stylist, not those of a man bursting with ideas demanding expression. "My achievements, tastes and habits are just such as to adapt me for the kind of literary execution I contemplate. It is only in this way that I have any chance of acquiring real reputation," he wrote again in the year of "The Sketch Book" to Brevoort, whose sympathetic nature called forth his most intelligent self-examinings, and meant that a lazy, dreamy observer of life, with nothing passionate in him but the desire to write well, must wait upon the happy arrival of a theme, and that for excellence this theme must not be stretched to weariness. It was only when his style became as easy as penmanship that Irving attempted long books—and they were formal, second-hand histories.

These histories, which Irving attempted in the hope that large, solid books would bring him in a steady income, did little for his reputation, which rests as he foresaw upon his miniatures and vignettes. Even the famous chapters in the Knickerbocker "History" scarcely exceed a long short story. He gambled upon belles lettres and won. The enormous achievements of his elder contemporaries, Jefferson and Hamilton, are at the very base of American life, political, social, economic, but who reads their works? And who ever read "Rip" without pleasure, or missed a word! It is as fresh as the day it was written, and as indisputably a work of genius as it is certainly in thought and subject the "bagatelle" that Irving called it. "The Alhambra" deserves the word "charming" as richly as the essays of Lamb. I can think of few books of prose that in this attribute excel it. If Irving is often *vox et præterea nihil*, and never more sonorous in the literary orchestra than his own favorite flute, yet in the earthy paradise of Sleepy Hollow, or the martial romance of the Moors, or the humors of Bracebridge Hall, he is a master of lovely rhythm. If his style gilds fustian, it can ornament the occasional nuggets of gold, and if it is monotonous, it is the monotony of fair weather. There is more than rhetoric in it.

3.

STYLE always has its secret, and the secret of Irving's suavity is well hidden in that native environment which through all his years abroad he professed to love, and did love, best. The student of sources has had his say, and it has not been enough. Irving is more than Goldsmith served cold, and far more than German romanticism brought overseas. He owes much to Goldsmith, but he is not cold. He is a romantic, but very definitely not German. The psychoanalytic school of biographers will get more, but little more, from their researches. Already the familiar tale of a heart broken by the death of Matilda Hoffman and a gentle melancholy transfused into his style (which thereby became excellent!) through a lifetime of regret, has been proved a romantic dream of critics too much influenced by the sentiment of his nephew and biographer Pierre Irving. Irving's full account of his relations with Matilda leaves no such impression of a blighted life, and his long and later devotion to Emily Foster, his letters, and his work itself disprove the fiction.* Irving was always moved by women, and often moving for them. They did well by him, and he never lacked for female affection. If he did not marry it was because his passionate desire from early youth was to lead the life of a gentlemanly dreamer, write when he felt like it, and when he wrote, write well.

Until the financial difficulties of the family firm in 1816-1818, he not only cherished this ambition but in some measure realized it, yet it was upon the sufferance of his brothers, an easy family, two of them literary also, and willing to give genius its chance. Strange fact in the land of what Irving was the first to call the almighty dollar!

* See the forthcoming "Life of Washington Irving," by Stanley T. Williams, and his "Washington Irving and Matilda Hoffman," *American Speech*, Vol. I, No. 9, also "Washington Irving, Esquire," by George S. Hellman.

WASHINGTON IRVING

"It is with delight we share the world with you," wrote William when they sent him abroad in 1804. Yet for an American, who was to write for a land where native books did not sell, and editorships were short-lived, this meant only economic parisitism, with the goal of independence far ahead. In the black years of family failure, the prop was rudely removed. The author of the Knickerbocker "History," who had patterned his life as an amateur of the arts, gracefully reflecting a world of his own choosing in careful prose, the elegant youth who now as later felt, as he wrote to Brevoort in 1827, that "publication lets in the noisy rabble of the world and there is an end to our dreaming," and who in 1819 was thankful that his writings had been so put in circulation as "to give the whole an independent and gentlemanlike air," now felt in danger of sinking to a clerkship in England or some humdrum office at home.* "I have no wife nor children, good or bad, to provide for. A mere spectator of other men's fortunes and adventures," he quotes from Burton on the flyleaf of "The Sketch Book." "A desultory writer," with "no command of his talents," unfitted for any "periodically recurring task," who has to "watch the varying of my minds," so he describes himself in the Preface to the 1848 edition. Even after the deep depression mixed with terror of the bankruptcy had passed, when he had made money from "The Sketch Book," and, though he had lost most of it in his brother Peter's speculations, had always a ready market for his pen, he could still write to Brevoort—"With all my exertions I seem always to keep about up to my chin in troubled waters, while the world, I suppose, thinks I am sailing smoothly." The world did. The jealous Cooper grumbled to his wife that Irving was a successful wire-

* He declined in 1817 a position on the Navy Board of $2400 a year so as not "to prevent my attending to literary pursuits." Letter to his brother Ebenezer quoted by Pierre Irving.

puller with an instinct for gold.* The facts were otherwise and they were all against matrimony, except with riches in the stocking—and Irving was both fastidious and no purse-hunter. The free-lance writer has always lived precariously. Let his pen go dry, his book fail, and he is penniless. Nor could men marry upon diplomatic appointments then any more than now.

It was thus no blighted heart but something much more common that made Irving a ready victim of the fashionable melancholy of the period and touched with the grace of sincerity the gentle sadness of his prose. It is clear that he was homesick, in the literal sense of the word. In all his books there is a longing for stability, for ease in surroundings to his taste, and for a home, which he never possessed until well into middle age. He makes the Alhambra domestic, and has drawn the classic picture of home life in the English country. Yet both ambitious poverty and the exigencies of his career compelled him to wander, and to wander single. The lands that supplied his sketch books, and hence his bread and butter, lay in Europe. "Food for observation," as he wrote his brothers, was to be found there, when the Knickerbocker vein was exhausted. "It was a pity he came back," he said to Pierre Irving in 1858, speaking of the friend of his youth, Washington Allston, the painter; "he could have risen to the head of his art." That was his own fear, that he would have to come back to commerce or a clerkship. And I think that the pathos, the loneliness, the love, the tragedy in Irving's books reflect the emotions of a wandering bachelor deprived of an ideal domesticity, which he first dared not attempt lest something he valued more should be lost, then could not find. His sufferings were real and were reflected in his melancholy, but it was scarcely because of them that he wrote so well.

* "Correspondence of James Fenimore Cooper," March 22, 1842, and elsewhere.

IF ANY outside influence is to account for Washington Irving's really remarkable success with only a humorous temperament and a sensitive soul to go on, then that influence will be found in American Federalism. For Irving, so far as his instrument permitted, represented the Federalist spirit in American literature, and this relationship is the key to much that is otherwise puzzling in a man at the same time so gentle and so famous. Not that Irving was ever interested in politics. He loathed them consistently through a long life in which he owed more to politics than most men, he was disgusted with his single electioneering experience as a Federalist,* found Republicans and Federalists equally agreeable and equally absurd when he met them socially, and made some of his closest friends in New York among that faction of the Republican party which, though aristocratic in feeling, yet used the masses for its own advantage against the Federalists, the faction of Judge Van Ness and Aaron Burr; nor can his attacks upon Jefferson and his supporters in "Salmagundi" and the Knickerbocker "History" be regarded as purely political. Jefferson to him was a fanatical hustler and bustler who would give authority to greasy mechanics. He was a disturbing factor in the settled, easy world that Irving loved, an antiromantic like the full-feeding, big-bottomed Dutch that Irving made fun of with a little less animus.

And yet, if Federalism as an ideal of living was to find literary expression, it was bound in that age of the romantic movement to have its Irving. For Federalism was essentially an aristocratic ideal struggling to adapt itself to the conditions of a republic and the equalities of a new country. The men who made the Constitution were neither

* See Pierre Irving, *op. cit.*, Letter to Mary Fairlee, of May 2, 1807, when "my forlorn brethren," the Federalists, were defeated.

dreamers like Irving nor prophets like Jefferson. They proposed, as has been many times made clear, to achieve a stable government by enlisting the monied interests in its defense. Privilege, in theory at least, had been abolished by the Revolution, but money remained, and not merely the provisions of the Constitution but the assumption of State debts and the redemption of depreciated currency were calculated to make speculators and capitalists friends of the existing order. Against the rising wave of democracy the Federalists set the barrier of class interests, and before it began to give way in 1800 (when Irving was seventeen) they had organized a government that, in its emphasis upon property, has remained the same ever since. On the other side was Jefferson, a landholder always short (like all landholders) of ready money, a practical idealist, as doubtful as the Federalists of democracy, but determined that in this new government the man who produced, whether laborer or landowner, should have political power, and be able to protect himself from militarists, speculators, bureaucrats, and all the parasites belonging to the capitalist system of a plutocracy. He was, if you please, an intellectual aristocrat, but more intellectual than aristocratic. The rise of democratic opportunism that swept away both Federalist and Republican in Jackson's days would have appalled him. But he looked backward toward the dangers of monarchy, not forward to the inevitable result of his policy of opportunity for the common man in America. He was determined to save the fruits of the Revolution, the Federalists were resolved to check the upheaval that accompanied it before the pleasant world they had made should be overwhelmed. Not again, with the exception of the decade of the Civil War, have such strong and diverse political and social emotions been aroused in America.

Irving was not interested in the political aims of either

78

party. In his letters and occasional writings he calls a plague on both their houses every time an election stirs the muddy minds of the populace. His New York did not take politics seriously except as a means of aggrandizement. Indeed, the modern Tammany Hall was already implicit in the factions of the Republican party headed by Burr and Clinton, and a young wit and beau, pretending to read law in a worldly little seaport where polite affiliations were almost as much European as American, could not be expected to sympathize either with ward politics, or with the moral intensities of a Dwight who believed that God had given America into the government of respectable church members, or with that Virginia idealism which proposed to erect a newfangled state utterly different from anything in the romances of Sir Walter Scott. In the England of Coleridge, Shelley, Byron, Wordsworth —to cite literary names merely—he was to see nothing but the picturesque, and the relics of Moorish Spain were to mean far more to him than Germany in its golden age. The ideas, great and small, of the formative period of the United States naturally passed over his head.

Indeed, when he does defend the American system he is a little absurd. In 1831, attacking European monarchies, he speaks of "these vile systems of falsehood . . . that have been woven on the human mind and . . . held it down in despicable thralldom." * All Americans were republican, in principle at least, after 1800! But an urbane New Yorker could scarcely be expected to side with a political party that existed to give tradesmen and farmers their rights, or to be vitally interested in the economic ideals of the Federalists, when he hated making money

* Letter to Brevoort, March 31, 1831. Philip Hone in his "Diary" for May 24, 1833, says that Irving on his return after seventeen years abroad "came out a Jackson man," with "warmth and enthusiasm," evidently a part of the same reaction, although not unaffected by Jackson's concurrence in 1829 in his appointment abroad.

and could not keep it. It was not merely old age that led him to end the "Life of Washington" at the moment when a heroic life of glory became involved in questions of domestic politics and a great career was used by partisans for their not very creditable purposes. Politics, for Irving, were New York politics, which meant a squabble between the ins and the outs.

And yet Irving, in spite of his indifference to party, was more Federalist than the Federalists, more Federalist essentially than the Hartford wits, who adumbrated in their vast poems a government by moral didacticism that was New Englandism rather than aristocracy. He was keenly aware of the deeper struggle of which the brawls of politicians and the ideology of statesmen were only symptoms. Like Talleyrand, he felt the old world slipping, and to him, an American, it was fresh and infinitely desirable, not stale and doomed. He felt, with the sensitiveness of a dreamer, the raucousness of a trading, manufacturing, exploiting society. Sprung from trade himself, and hating it, spending his youth in an illusion of a gay gentleman's world of the arts and conversation in a commercial town, he did not rationalize his desires, yet clearly lived and wrote them. "Salmagundi," like the "Spectator," and still more curiously like the "columns" of modern New York papers, is an onslaught upon manners, an attempt to give detachment, gaiety, civility, to a sodden town. Diedrich Knickerbocker's "History of New York" in its purely Dutch aspects is a satire upon a thoroughly bourgeois civilization, in its attacks upon the Yankees a satire on the ideals of traders and business men. The life of the gentleman, as the eighteenth century understood that word, is praised and chronicled through a long series of Irving's books, in which tradesmen, demagogues, innovators, upstarts (like the village poet in "The Sketch Book"), are the butts of ridicule, and feudal squires, however eccentric, noble adventurers like Columbus, heroes of lost causes, such as Boabdil, are the pets of his imagination. Half of Irving's heart is in "Rip Van Winkle," where the picturesque Rip and his cronies, so full of humor and honest if stupid happiness, are set in contrast to the shabby pretentiousness of the village twenty years later. And the other half is in "Bracebridge Hall" and "The Alhambra," for in each is a life tinged with the melancholy of departing, yet rich in loyalty, solidity, and human worth instead of human rights.

The struggle between the new and old world, however confused in its apparent issues, was uppermost in the American mind of the early eighteen hundreds. The West, removed in space and time, did not, it is true, count heavily in the contest, for it was scarcely America, yet the influence of that vast region so rapidly filling up with the rebel and the discontented who had lost the sense of respect for their betters, was already beginning.* More immediate in men's minds were the dangers from the common people who were determined not to stay common. Immorality, as has been noted before, had increased in the social demoralization that followed the long years of the Revolution. There was that sharp increase in acquisitiveness to be expected in a people diverted for almost a generation from the free pursuit of their private business. There was the example of France in turbulent democracy, and the opposite influence of aristocratic England, curiously dear to the aristocracy of the new world. Indeed the America of the early eighteen hundreds was alive in all its parts, perhaps more so than the standardized and accomplished America of the twentieth century. Pathetic, from this point of view, is the young Irving's illusion that he and the few like him could create and keep a milieu of

---

* Reflections of this are to be found in the Knickerbocker "History," with its descriptions of the upland Dutch.

taste in hustling young New York, but strong the pressure, far stronger than if he had lived in contemporary Europe, to do something, be something, that expressed his loves and his hates. Hence the sense of futility that is mentioned again and again in Irving's letters and implied in his prefaces from early manhood on. What could he do? I will not say, What could he do that was needed? for such a question, so familiar in New England, and later in a puritanized West, was not likely to be raised in New York! But what could he do that he wanted? The answer was to write, to write like an aristocrat, like a gentleman, like a Federalist.

For Federalism, as even the sinuous Walcott and the vehement Ames and certainly as Hamilton understood it, was much more than a political and economic system. It was a government by the best, the ideal to which all philosophic statesmen have aspired. It was, more specifically, an aristocracy, not of birth or of privilege, but of achievement, with the entrance door always open but a censor of manners, of morals, of capability, at the threshold.* The idea was never better expressed than in the provisions made by the New Haven colony (later the heart of Federalism) for the settlement of the wild lands in the parish of Mt. Carmel.† Land and the authority that went with it were to be taken up in quantity only by such as had means and character for its proper development with due reference to the religious nurture, the education, and the prosperity of those who were to inhabit it. To him who hath shall be given, provided that he deserves what he has, was the motto of Federalism. This was an ideal

* Josiah Quincy said that it took a half century after the Declaration of Independence "to reach a vital belief that the people and not gentlemen are to govern this country." (Quoted by Max Farrand in "The Development of the United States.") This vital belief was reached only over the dead body of the Federalist party.

† See "The Old Mount Carmel Parish," by George Sherwood Dickerman.

well worth fighting for—we may well regret that we have lost it through the greed and the tyranny of Federalist politicians and capitalists, and the rise of a democratic spirit that was oblivious to such subtleties and would not be denied.

It was to this intangible spirit of Federalism that Irving owed allegiance, a spirit deeper than economic theory, deeper than the struggle for power, a spirit which outlived the party that professed to represent it, so that it is still possible to call a man or a book Federalist in the United States. Irving shared the Federalist respect for the tried, its distrust of the new, its hatred of the vulgar, of "the beast," as Hamilton called the crowd. He was Anglophile as the Federalists were, and for the same reason. England, even in wartime, meant "the good old times" for Federalism. But Irving's feeling for England was magnified by his love for English literature, which was the basis of his education. What reading he did later in the literature of France, Spain, and Germany only served to turn his already active romanticism toward such veneration of the old as would fit him more than ever to play his part as the spokesman of Federalist culture. Indeed, if George Washington was an English country gentleman, with a difference, Irving was an English man of letters, with a difference, who turned in disgust from the sprawlings for food and water of the gigantic infant, his country, and in protest against the crude and new sought to write as elegantly as he could. Yearning for civilized urbanity in a continent designed to be great in quite another fashion, he perfected a style, and only then ceased to feel beaten, discouraged, and futile.

Irving as the arch-Federalist of American literature is much more interesting than Irving as a custodian of the romantic movement in America. In the latter function he had many colleagues, some, like Hawthorne, Poe, and

Emerson, far more powerful, both intellectually and emotionally, than himself. It is true that the romantic haze that still hangs over the noble estuary of the Hudson rose from his pen, and the romantic past of that least romantic of American cities, New York, is his contriving. True, too, that he made Europe picturesque for Americans. England was not picturesque to Richard Mather, or to Benjamin Franklin, but Irving imbued it with all that the rest of us have ever since felt of romantic veneration. Yet, although as a maker of glamour he was a pupil of Walter Scott, his inspiration was not all literary. He spoke for the nostalgia of the Federalists, for the decorum, the stability, of colonial days, for the richness of living of the mother country. He was a divided soul, like that stout old rebel, John Adams, with his agonies over the proper ritual for the first Federal government. He belongs with the Philadelphia society that was so gay and exclusive at the Binghams' when Congress met in Philadelphia. He explains the truckling to English visitors, the imitation in town house and countryseat of life in Britain, the intense sensitiveness to British criticism, which he voiced himself in "English Writers on America"—all of which betrayed a passionate reverence for the old land. The best of all this, and very little of the worst, is in Irving. As a romantic among the greater romantics of Europe he is humble and usually derivative, but as an American and as a Federalist he speaks in his own right, and had a motive to speak well.

5.

To READ Irving's works again with these facts in mind is to form a new estimate of the man as a writer. When he was young and heady, when, fresh from his first and idle ramblings over Europe in 1806, the Federalist conception of an aristocratic America caught his imagination (rebel as he was from a hardware store), there was more edge than sentiment in his romance. Though he said in his Preface of 1848 that his desire in the Knickerbocker "History" had been "to clothe home scenes and places with imaginative and whimsical associations, which live like charms about the cities of the old world," yet that really remarkable book was as much contemporary satire as whimsical chronicle of the picturesque old times. Does anyone read it from beginning to end? Certainly there is infrequent reference to the opening burlesque of world history in the manner of Sterne and Swift, adorned, like their work, with mock erudition, but far less excellent. It is only when the Dutch come to New Amsterdam that the book takes life, and why? Because these stupid Dutch with their sluggish bourgeoisity, their absurd parodies of courage, the "happy equality" of their intellects, their lack of fire, energy, grace, are perfect symbols of that sodden materialism which Irving found ridiculous in others and hated for himself. In spite of its comforts, which he did not disdain, it was the very opposite of all qualities of romance.* Because, again, the shrewd, invading Yankees of the "History," with the "duty to go right" constantly sounding in their ears and making hypocrites of them, with their ungainly manners and their shady tricks, represent the trading class and trading manners triumphant and odious.† And what a chance to take pot shots at absurd great ones of the opposition! If under the pseudonym

* His youthful impression of the Dutch when he visited Holland on his first trip abroad is not forgotten in the Knickerbocker "History." They were unromantic traders, in sharp contrast to the French with their imperial fervor and to his venerated England. He writes to Peter Irving on October 20, 1805, of the "monotonous uniformity prevailing over the whole country," which reminds one of the "happy equality" of the stolid New Amsterdamers.

† Note, for his general attitude, his letter to Brevoort apropos of the War of 1812 (January 12, 1813)—"If this war continues and a regular be raised instead of depending on volunteers and militia, I believe we shall have the Commissions sought . . . by young gentlemen of education and good breeding, and our army will be infinitely more respectable and infinitely more successful."

of Wouter the Doubter, the apoplectic little John Adams escaped with a few digs that his enemies in New York could not have missed, he at least was a Federalist. But William the Testy, who undertakes to conquer by proclamation and arms his ramparts with windmills, was no merciful portrait of Jefferson of the embargo and the wars waged by words against England and France, while the drunken meetings and windy discontent of the Dutch democracy, and their panic at the arrival of the British fleet, reflect with perfect clarity what gentlemen like Irving thought of his democratic clubs and his propaganda for the rights of man. Indeed, if the "History" is, as I believe, the meatiest of Irving's books, and excelled in style only by a few of the best of his later sketches, the reason is that never again did he have so much of his own observation, his own prejudice and rooted dislike, to add to the documents he drew upon. Never again were his spirits so high, never again was he so close in experience as well as in imagination to his subject. When, later, he began to conceive of his task as the romantic rendering of the European scene for Federalist consumption,* the reverence of the new world for the old or his concern with what to him was picturesque in England, Scotland, or Spain suppressed the satiric vein, or rather, his own detachment from the scenes he described reduced irony and humor to a consideration of general, and often very abstract, human nature. Instead of Jefferson and the commercial New Yorker one gets Spanish rascals and English eccentrics. When he returned to his symbolic Dutch, as he did from time to time throughout his career, he was always fresh and humorous.

The Knickerbocker "History," erudite, polished, suave, antibourgeois, a satire upon the unromantic, an attack upon democracy, a challenge to all ideologues, pedants,

* See Irving to Brevoort, March 10, 1821.

moralists, fanatics, a lampoon on besotted commercialism, stands at the head of Federalist literature. Poe and Lowell could understand it, though not each other; Whitman could not.

In later years, when Irving worked *con amore* it was not upon the continuous writing necessary for a complete book, but in bursts of energy upon the occasional sketches which he felt rightly to best represent his genius. His histories are admirable for style, but they are not literature, though often more literature than history. Indeed, Irving if he had lived in the twentieth century would have been a magazine writer, if not a columnist. His best work, after "Knickerbocker," consisted of essays and short stories, produced when time and mood were propitious and collected when the market was ready. Yet "The Sketch Book," which in 1819 won him international fame, is not a good book. It was arranged with the tact of an American who sought British recognition as eagerly as the British novelist today seeks an American sale,* but its texture lacks the homogeneity of either "The Alhambra" or the Dutch part of the Knickerbocker "History." As a book it displays, in its two Introductions, first Irving the humorist, then Irving the man of sentiment who "traversed England a grown-up child." It contains Irving at his humorous best in "Rip Van Winkle" and "The Legend of Sleepy Hollow," Irving at his shrewdest in "John Bull," at his manliest in "English Writers on America," † at the full stretch of his romantic veneration in the series of papers on English life, of which the famous "Westminster Abbey" is the most rhetorical and the less known "Country Church," "Rural Life in England," and the "Bracebridge

---

* I am aware that Pierre Irving thinks that he had only an American market in mind, but do not believe it.

† An essay that says all that has been resaid a dozen times since on English condescension, in spite of its typically Federalist inference that all Americans were once English.

Hall" sketches are far the best. But it is padded also with perfunctory Indian sketches, and with stories in the worst romantic taste of the time, full of false pathos and strained sentiment. "The Sketch Book" is a miscellany, a travel book, sweetened to the taste of the times by romantic sugarplums, and rising to literature only when Irving was more Federalist than romanticist, or more story-teller and essayist than an adorner of sentiment by style.

There was of course some truth, and a good deal of insight, in the romanticizing of jolly old England that makes up so much of "The Sketch Book." And it is Irving, not Dickens, who is chiefly responsible for the glamour that ever since his day has hung about Christmas in the old hall, the stagecoach, the waits, the loyal tenantry, and all the paraphernalia of merry England. It is only romantic truth, as can readily be ascertained by reading in order from "The Sketch Book" and from the contemporary pages of Jane Austen. Nevertheless, the literary symbolism that he found for the picturesque as he saw it at Abbotsford and Newstead Abbey took such hold on his readers on both sides of the water that it became to them history, and is as vivid in the imagination of the American tourist as manor houses and crumbling castles to his eye. With such an England, Irving was quite sure to please both the Federalist at home and John Bull in his romantic mood, and it had much to do with the book's success.

Without the two Dutch stories, however, "The Sketch Book" would not have worn so well. They are perfect examples of what Irving best loved to do, and naturally he did them well. "Rip Van Winkle" and "The Legend of Sleepy Hollow" are history of that legendary character which he fed upon—history that preserves, with little care for too minute reality, the memories of a period. "The Alhambra" is full of such stories, whose plots are old tales, whose characters are fireside companions, the scenes in those golden ages before hustle and bustle were invented, the subjects such as to arouse that humorous irony which was Irving's reaction to wiseacres, busybodies, scolds, gluttons, fanatics, the whole imbued in the mist of romance. He himself, in "The Sketch Book," was Rip, gentle, pleasure-loving, inadaptable to the crudities of business and family support. He loved the rascal because he was as Irving might have been without brothers and friends. Dame Rip was the urge of hustling, unsubtle America that threatened to drive him away from the pleasant loafing that he loved into a mode of life he most philosophically disapproved of. The Catskills were those hills of romantic dreaming in which he wandered seeking the future—and the harsh disillusion of the bustling ugly village of twenty years afterward, where no one knew Rip, or wanted him, was no bad similitude of the future in those depressing years from 1816 to 1819 when the failure of his brother's business roused in his imagination the spectre of a return, *auctor ignotus*, to job-hunting in New York. No such symbolism, I suppose, was in Irving's consciousness, but he wrote these humorous idylls of picturesque living from his heart, and told them superbly in a prose so pure and harmonious as to speak of a master at his best.

Reviewers and readers, however, praised "The Sketch Book" and Irving most often, not for the narrative, but for the style, the source of which I have already put in question. The sense for style in 1819-20 had not yet been sicklied by the welter of romanticism. Houses were still being built with that easy mastery of form and proportion which was the gift of the eighteenth century, and if the crisp outlines of English prose were blurring under the pen of a Walter Scott, and if the quaintness of Charles Lamb and the profuseness of De Quincey were beginning to be preferred to the cool clarity of Goldsmith, the conception of measure, harmony, restraint, was to last as long as good architecture. Indeed, it is perhaps not altogether a coincidence that Irving and good architecture died in the same decade in America. A delightful temperament, a pleasing play of sentiment and humor upon fortunate themes, and a triumph of style—this was the current estimate of "The Sketch Book." And it remains our estimate, except that the "sob stories," as they would be called in the modern vernacular, can no longer be regarded as fortunate.

The rest of Irving that really matters is implicit in the books I have already discussed. "The Alhambra," that romance of history mellowed in a style that is too pure and clear to permit of turgid extravagance, is of course another "Sketch Book," with the single theme of a lost and beautiful civilization. The earlier "Tales of a Traveller" are less admirable because, paradoxically, they are more original. Here Irving trusted too much to invention, and when he left legend and history and scenes that he knew by deep experience he fell almost invariably into mawkishness or into rhetorical display. Irving could write well on any theme, but rhetoric alone never turned a bad theme into literature. "Bracebridge Hall," written because of the success of his earlier narratives of the romantic last stand of English feudal life, was also a miscellany, successful this time because the book flowed from the romantic reverence that was Irving's second rich reaction to life. "A Tour of the Prairies," a work that deserves more reputation, was conceived as another "Sketch Book," with included stories, and, like "The Alhambra," with a single romantic theme—the march of the Rangers through the Indian country. But here Irving was too close to his subject. The Indian stories were not in his vein, the companions of his voyage did not project their shadows against historic backgrounds. There is a camp scene, firelight flickering on wild faces, psalm-singing, alarms, rough humor of the frontier, which is Irving at his best, but he could not sustain it. The material that Cooper found so rich was, for him, too thin. Edward Everett, reviewing the book in *The North American Review*, thanked Mr. Irving for "turning these poor barbarian *steppes* into classical land." That was the trouble: they would not turn, ought not to be turned, and Everett was ridiculous in thinking that they could be turned into the kind of romance that Irving practised. Nor were they poor either to the right imagination, as Cooper showed in his admirable "Prairie," but Irving was not the man. He was, after all, a bookish writer, and the life he best interpreted was seen through books or under their influence. For the frontier he had no books with the flavor of history and hence no perspective.

6.

SOME of the current estimates of Irving must be altered after such an analysis. He did little to illumine American life and character although so much to enrich the American romantic imagination. He endowed the Hudson Valley with a past of legend and fable borrowed from the old world, but his Dutch are quite false, except as satire, his Yankees no more true than Yankee Doodle, his New Amsterdam a land of Cocaigne, which has bequeathed to posterity an idea that New Netherlands was the comic relief of colonial history.

He was not a great romantic, if Scott and Byron and Shelley be taken as models of romanticism. His gentle melancholy is more akin to Collins, and his humor to Goldsmith. In truth, where Irving was most eighteenth century in manner he has best survived, for his humor, his sense for the quaint, and his admirable feeling for proportion are more valuable than his attempts at pathos, terror, and grandeur in the style of the Teutonized romance of his own period. Revolt, that great theme of his

English contemporaries, never moved him, for, like his fellow Federalists, he had had enough of rebellion. In pure romance he is never excellent except in that minor category where the light of fancy is made to play over the vanishing scene—there he is superb.

Yet many a more pretentious author of his age has died utterly, while Irving, in spite of his modern detractors, lives. Stylists do not die if they are fortunate enough to find even a few themes that summon all their powers. The romanticist in Irving powerfully influenced a century of American writers ("The Sketch Book" was Longfellow's first school of literature) and usually to their hurt. They sucked sentiment from him and left the humor behind. But equally strong, and much more fortunate, has been the ideal of excellence set up by his style. Every American writer who has cherished the Federalist hope of urbanity and a counsel of perfection in the midst of democratic leveling may claim Irving as his spiritual father.

The textbooks call him the first ambassador of the new world to the old. That is to look at him through English eyes and is in fact a repetition of his first authentic praising, which came from abroad. He proved that the barbarous American could write as the captains of 1812 had proved that Americans could fight on the sea, he tickled John Bull's romantic rib, but his true ambassadorship (and his real importance) was all the other way, and his oft-repeated arguments for his residence abroad show that he knew what he was about. Call him rather an American Marco Polo, bringing home the romance of other countries, bearing their gifts of suavity, detachment, ease, and beauty to a raw country dependent upon its vulgar strength, stronger in brains than in manners, yet not devoid of a craving for civility. He was in this always a good republican, but a better Federalist.

In 1860 William Cullen Bryant published "A Discourse

WASHINGTON IRVING

on the Life, Character, and Genius of Washington Irving,"
which he had previously delivered at a meeting in com-
memoration of the dead author. Bryant also was a Federalist in spirit, a Federalist in American literature whose
very respectable poetical talents were diverted into a lifetime of struggle as editor of Alexander Hamilton's *Evening
Post*, which long after the death of the Federalist party
kept its ideals alive. In his early promise, in his absorption
by a commercial, political régime, in the decline of his
writing, and the lessening reputation, as time goes on, of
even his best, he is a picture of what Irving might have
been had he come home to an office or an editorship.
Irving, Bryant said, was the first to make Americans believe in the possibility of financial success for a native
author. Our American fiction, poetry, history, so he maintained, should be dated from the publication of "The
Sketch Book" in 1819-20. Undoubtedly, as the literary
criticism of the time pathetically indicates, the United
States was suffering from an inferiority complex, made
more grievous by the competition of English books, which
could be pirated and sold at a price that the native product
naturally could not touch. And undoubtedly Irving's triumph over handicaps * and his recognition abroad spurred
on Cooper, Prescott, Parkman, Hawthorne, and his many
other successors. He may be said to have indicated the
possibility of a literature not merely didactic or utilitarian in America.

And yet it is more noteworthy, I think, that he gave it
dignity. In 1832, Irving, then in London, addressed to
Samuel Rogers a Preface to the Poems of Bryant, which
he thereby introduced to English readers. What he admired, what he expected Rogers to admire, in Bryant was
the "purity of moral, and elevation and refinement of

* There was a complaint of the $.75 price set upon the first number of "The
Sketch Book."

thought, and a terseness and elegance of diction" that belong to "the best school of English poetry." Irving might well have written, for his own epitaph, that his writing belonged to the best school of English prose, that his style also was terse and elegant, that the "persuasive grace," which he maintained was shed over Bryant's descriptions, was his in larger measure, and that he too was "imbued" with the "buoyant aspiration incident to a youthful, a free, and a rising country." He praised, as so often happens, those qualities in the work of another which were most certainly his own. They were precisely what England expected of America, still regarded as a colony, and what the American who wished reunion with the culture and grace of the old country most desired. This was not the American ambition that burned in Jefferson, or John Adams, or Daniel Boone, nor certainly the American desires of an Aaron Burr or an Andrew Jackson, but it was a voice of America. Great American themes, native to our development, were later to find both prose and verse; they are not in Irving. He was the type of that American, always commoner than Europe believes, whose nostalgia in the midst of prosperity, strenuosity, and progress is genuine and enduring. Federalist that he was, he longed for types of character and achievement alien to the United States of his own days, and was blind to romance of a far different order, which, with axes and rifles and hopes for the common man instead of banners and swords, was a living presence in the forests of his own land, forests that he loved only because they were solitary and vast. Cooper and Parkman succeeded where Irving trod half-heartedly because his heart was elsewhere.

And yet his theme is as genuine as theirs and he was more perfect in the voicing of his romantic melancholy than Cooper in his romance of the pioneer. The America of the early eighteen hundreds was profoundly different

WASHINGTON IRVING

from Europe, in spite of an external resemblance in all that concerned culture and the ordinary practice of living. Its economic outlook was different, its spiritual and ethical emphasis was different. It was committed to a different theory of the future. Nevertheless, it was bound to Europe by the strongest ties. The social history of America is a history of straining at the bonds, straining toward the West. At the points of juncture and of binding—the seaports most of all—a profound tension of the spirit resulted. Every man looked two ways, and wished to go in two directions. There was that genuine emotional lesion which gives rise to literature. One sees it in Crèvecœur, in some of the discourses of Franklin, but the medium was imperfect. Irving, the first to make his pen a perfect instrument, took the side of regret. He wrote like a European, but with the desires, the mentality, the outlook (already defined), of an American. His style is English, but made in America, for an American need.

And because in order to speak for Federalist America he learned to write with a vanishing grace and a suavity not again to be attained on this side of the Atlantic, his future is more secure than that of his successors in the historical vein, Motley and Prescott and Parkman, better historians than he, who transcended the "Washington" and the "Columbus," but could not write an "Alhambra." Cooper, crabbed republican aristocrat, came nearer the ruling passions of his country, but his loosely held romance of the frontier has already suffered from its slovenly diction and uneven texture. Hawthorne's didactic obsession stiffens the sombre beauty of his work, but Irving's lighter craft is well trimmed for the shifting gales of fame. He had a style, he had a temperament, he had an eye for the humors, he was born a New Yorker, he could say, as New Englanders would not say, as Philadelphians and Virginians and Carolinians could not say effectively: While we create

95

a new society in a new republic, let us not forget the mellowness of the age we have left behind us overseas, let us not forget the graces of life, let us not forget to be gentlemen. And if this was all he said, it was put admirably, in a time of need, and with apposite and succinct example. He made Spain glamorous, England picturesque, and his own land conscious of values not to be found in industry, morals, or politics. A slight achievement beside Wordsworth's, a modest ambition by comparison with Byron's, but enough. Not a great man, not even a great author, though a good chronicler, an excellent story-teller, a skilful essayist, an adept in romantic coloring; not in accord with progress in America but the most winning spokesman for the Federalist hope; a musician with few themes, and the minor ones the best, and many played perfectly—that is Washington Irving.

CHAPTER THREE

James Fenimore Cooper

COOPER is the fighting Quaker of American literature. While Irving, the æsthetic Federalist, tidied
his garden plots and built Dutch Alhambras,
humorously romantic, on the Hudson, Cooper swung toward democracy, colored his social philosophy with the
ideas of Jefferson, and took the continent and the oceans
for his theme. He is a pound American where Irving is an
ounce, yet more propagandist than artist; a maker of
national epics (almost our only ones) who never achieved
a style, a man on a scale as great as the popularity of his
books, which exceeded that of any other American writer
and equaled Byron's and Scott's, with faults on a scale as
great also. He alone was able to make literary use of that
passion for what his compatriots called so vaguely freedom which inspired the political and social achievements
of the young United States. Not creative in his ideas like
Emerson and Thoreau, not a humanist and artist like
Poe and Hawthorne, he belongs with Melville and Whitman, men borne upon the surge of the American flood and
torn by its conflicts, incoherent like them sometimes and
sometimes eloquent and expressive.

It is impossible to discuss Cooper merely as a man of
letters, for he was artistic by instinct only and a writer
by compulsion rather than determined choice. To write of
him, as has been the custom, solely in terms of the romantic movement, as if Rousseau and Scott plus a forest made

97

Leatherstocking inevitable, is to reduce one of the most revealing figures of the early century to the dimensions of a second-rate imitator. Cooper's sins against art were sometimes monstrous, and when he wrote in what he regarded as a literary tradition, he could be insufferable; but when he was his own man he was a world figure.

The panoply and trappings of the romantic movement have, indeed, gone stale in Cooper's books. The Unknowns who stalk through his novels and at the end are little more than gestures, the chivalrous gentlemen always proposing to die for some one, the rebels against tyranny, the blighted souls, the too modest women who would burn to death rather than remove their petticoats, are all imitated from the fashionable romance of the day or his favorite Shakespeare, and are usually tiresome and sometimes impossible. Nothing could be less like the direct force of Cooper's correspondence than this folderol. He was fascinated by it, as we are fascinated by realism, but it was not the man himself nor his real "gift" in writing. Like most unliterary writers, he picked up the vices of a contemporary style and thought they made literature. More of this later. It was the inner spirit of romanticism, its expansiveness, its passionate cult of the ego, its rush back from artifice to the vast simplicities of nature, that touched his heart and moved his pen to its best writing, perhaps because one hope of romance was a fresh world where man could be reformed in the image of desire, and Cooper knew the wilderness (and the sea also) when (for a moment) it was, in this sense, romantic.

The influence of Rousseau was as great, though less direct, upon Cooper as upon Jefferson. The rights of man (when he likes the men) are to him indisputable, the primitive draws him like a magnet, he distrusts every convention that interferes with free development, provided his prejudices allow him to call it a convention. It is he and not Scott who describes the wild landscapes in which Rousseau's ideal man might return to nature. The Trossachs are mere stage scenery beside the Adirondacks, or the plains and the forests of the Oswego. Scott's primitives are by-characters merely, while with Cooper they become protagonists of the stories. Cooper gave to his country and to Europe, particularly to restless Europe, the concrete figures of noble savage, simple-hearted woodsman, and the conception of free opportunity in a boundless West that called like Alps to Jura to fervid imaginations fed on Rousseau's philosophy. After the disillusionment of the Napoleonic wars, here courage, innocence, generosity, skill, might all adventure upward in romantic air.

The happy union of history and romance that Scott had effected for two continents was undoubtedly a factor in Cooper's success. An imitator thus far, he borrowed and worsened not merely the romantic trappings of Scott's novels but their stiffening of historical incident, and so profited by the path round the world that they had made. Yet he realized his essential independence. "Americans," he wrote in "The Travelling Bachelor," "have too much common sense to make good subjects for literature. Descriptions of society on the borders have positive though no very poetical interest. History and romance have not been successfully blended in America." His "gift" lay elsewhere, and nothing disgusted him more than to be called, as he so often was, the American Scott.* Their provinces were different, and where they overlapped, he was an imitator, and often a bungling one. To help the imagination to escape from a cramped or a petty life is a function of romance that both men shared. To let man return to nature and the unspoiled virtues of a wide but not un-

---

* See "The Correspondence of James Fenimore Cooper," edited by his grandson, James Fenimore Cooper, p. 227.

friendly wilderness was a function of romance also, in which Cooper was Rousseau's disciple and a scout in the new continent for the powerful romantic ideas of Europe. Hence his easy popularity. But to stop with such a definition is to miss the qualities that make Cooper unique. If there were only Rousseau and Scott to account for Cooper, we should have added one more to the long list of American literary parasites upon European fashions who still fill our libraries with volumes that nobody reads.

European literature formed Irving, but European literature (beyond the primary urge of romantic ideas and political philosophy) was Cooper's bane. His Americanism was a raging lifelong combat which engendered such heat that his books are hot with the fire and clogged with the ashes of the conflagration. Irving was a man of letters who knew how to profit by his borrowings: Cooper was a hard-headed romantic who used literature as the handiest means of gaining ends that often had little reference to art. He was best when most self-reliant. More than Irving, he must be seen as an American before the fruits of his genius and the qualities of his romance can be appraised.

The scene for both men was that turbulent America of the early 1800's (Irving was born in 1783, Cooper in 1789) in which the Federalist plutocracy was in disastrous combat with the advocates of the rights of man and with republican principles logically carried out. Both men were brought up Federalists, but while Irving gave up the real world of American struggle for a Utopia of his own imaginings and warmed his blood at the dying fires of European feudalism, Cooper never ceased striving to find a medium between democracy and aristocracy. Both men fled to Europe. Irving returned with his English reputation, and letting politics and his fellow countrymen go their own way, was almost forgotten, but loved and respected. Cooper, the patriot, who for five years had de-

fended republicanism in Europe, came home, still angry
with Europe, to a commercialized, equalitarian America
—and never to his dying day knew clearly what had happened to him or to America. Irving's art was minor,
though excellent, because only minor impulses, negative
chiefly, went into it. Cooper's was major in scope and
most imperfect in execution, because most of the great impulses of his age in murky confusion crowded upon his pen.

2.

THERE was no official biography of Cooper. His family
was one of those fortunate ones in which perfect harmony
and mutual adoration prevail. The source of all authority
was Cooper himself, who submitted his career to no influence whatsoever except his dearly beloved wife. It was
not to be expected that his daughter Susan, in spite of her
youthful literary ambitions, should violate the will of her
revered parent, who, still smarting (one supposes) from
his battles with a libelous press, ordered, shortly before
his death, that no biography should be authorized. She
outdid his commands, destroyed what material she could
lay her hands upon, and had his most interesting journals
buried with her. Those that remain are so dull that her
zeal seems excessive.

Yet few men need a biography less than Cooper. The
study that Thomas R. Lounsbury wrote in the eighties
still sparkles with epigram and is a satisfactory record of
all but those important formative years when Cooper was
in the forest and at sea. This study has been supplemented
by two volumes of correspondence and other papers,
edited by the third generation, a recent "Life" by H. W.
Boynton, and annotated editions of Cooper's "Gleanings
in Europe," by R. E. Spiller. Nevertheless, Cooper's
best biography is still in his books, and they are the
only record of his childhood in the wilderness and his

youth in the merchant marine and the navy, the substance from which was built the elaborate fabric of his best romance. Never, indeed, was there a more personal writer than Cooper. His ideas on general and particular burst out on every occasion, sometimes obscuring the narrative they are supposed to adorn. His memories are woven in and out of his stories, and his friends and acquaintances sometimes, at least, supply the outlines for characters in his novels. "The Spy" and "The Pilot" recall the traditions and probably some of the personalities of his wife's family, the Tory De Lanceys, "The Pioneers" is a detailed portrait of Cooperstown in his youth, "Afloat and Ashore" and "Miles Wallingford" tell in free fantasy his own story of a love divided between a career on the ocean and Cooperstown (here Clawbonny) and the wife of wealth and station who wins him, as his own wife did, for the land. "Homeward Bound" and "Home as Found" are Cooper and family returning from Europe with uplifted noses to what shocks and disillusionments! "The Travelling Bachelor" is Cooper himself.

Indeed, like many men who live in an adoring family circle, Cooper talks too much of himself. He is most interesting and best reveals his genius when he is less communicative, when from his memories he erects magnificent combats and escapes, or lengthens his childhood trails to savage pursuits and marvelous escapes in the forest.

Yet the picture of the man is clear, for Cooper is as vigorous in his books as in his life: a dominant man physically and mentally, aggressive, active, who could argue with eloquence before the courts and spoke, as Bryant recalled, with a frankness not always agreeable to mild men; a man bound to attract attention in speech or writing by his courage and truculence, deeply pious, intensely patriotic, sure to make mistakes, but a felt personality and a force.

JAMES FENIMORE COOPER

Judge Cooper, his father, and the Judge Temple of "The Pioneers," was a birthright Friend from the still lovely town of Burlington in New Jersey, who kept an affection for his Quaker memories while (like so many others in that expansive period) he broke through the Quaker quietism, and became a better business man than Friend. One of the great land entrepreneurs of his day, his dearest exploit was the settling of the great tract about Cooperstown on the borders of the old empire of the Six Nations. Here he became by necessity a feudal proprietor, half landlord, half chief, the great man of a million acres. In such an environment, where ideas of simplicity, notions of the aristocrat, and the democracy of the frontier incongruously mingled, Cooper spent his boyhood, with unbroken forests around and beyond. As a child of one he was brought there in 1790.

Like most rich men in the Quaker tradition, Judge Cooper was a Federalist (he died, in such a paradox as often waits upon the descendants of Quakers, from a blow on the head in a political brawl) and Cooper was given a Federalist education—tutoring by an English rector, and residence in Yale College under the Pope of the Federalists, Timothy Dwight. It did not take. Like other geniuses who have gone to college, he was expelled before he completed his course,* and entered the merchant marine in preparation for the navy. On a trading ship and in the navy until 1811, he knew the humiliations of that period of ambiguous independence when the new nation was scorned and insulted by the mighty opposites of the Napoleonic wars.

* And yet he pays a handsome tribute in "The Crater" to his impatient alma mater. "The three years of his college life, . . . filling his mind with the germs of ideas that were destined afterward to become extremely useful to him." The reference is clearly to himself. I doubt Lounsbury's opinion that the slovenly construction of his novels is due to his deficiencies in formal education. The man was educating himself all his life, as his books show. It was lack of artistic conscience that made the trouble.

He came back to land (I judge from the outspoken opinions of his books, for there are few records of his early years) indignant with the Federalists who fawned upon anything English, and afire with a lifelong patriotism that made him more sympathetic with the democratic ideals of Jefferson than with the Federalist hope of another England in America. Then he fell in love with the De Lancey heiress, married her, and retired from the sea. In 1810-11, the United States offered little to naval heroes; it is not surprising that he reverted to the family instinct for land, and set out to become a gentleman farmer. It is a bluff, salty letter that he writes his brother, telling of the match, "I loved her like a man and told her of it like a sailor," * and a fine figure of a man Cooper must have been then, for his letters suggest not merely a salt bluffness, but some of the ornate dignity of the eighteenth century that so often stilts the dialogue of his romances. His wife must have been a rare woman, for she was able to turn this active spirit into the backwater of a country estate. But then he wished it so. Like his Miles Wallingford, he enjoyed adventure, but sought it only for definite ends—an income, an establishment, domestic bliss. Like him, too, he reached his objectives early. At twenty-one he was, so he thought, provided for life with a home, means, and happiness. It will be remembered that most of Cooper's romantic heroes conclude their active careers in the twenties. Afterwards there is only to live happily. He was a realist in his ambitions, and a romantic in his hopes.

Here then was a man content, in all seeming, to become a squire of Westchester or Cooperstown. Fortunately he needed money.

The story of how Cooper began to write has been misinterpreted. His daughter tells it. "Precaution," she says,†

* "Correspondence," Vol. I, p. 82.
† "Correspondence," Vol. I, p. 38.

was written to prove that he could write as good books as the English fiction they read aloud in the evenings at Angevine, the Westchester farm; a story of Mrs. Opie's (the Quaker romanticist) was what set him off. But "Precaution," in spite of its absurd snobbishness and utterly unreal life of an English aristocracy that Cooper knew only by hearsay, is too elaborately constructed, has too much hard work in it, to be the result merely of a dare. The truth is that Cooper was energetic, idle, and dependent. Thanks to his uxoriousness, the sea was closed to him, trade he detested, his wife disapproved of pioneering, and could not at this time be reconciled to Cooperstown. Yet her fortune, for some reason not clear from the documents, was declining, and his own share of a much subdivided estate in land mostly wild, was by no means sufficient for his ideas of an American gentleman proprietor. He was a voracious reader of history. If he began to write by apparent accident, it is significant that he imitated (then and later) not history, but current, sellable romances.

"Precaution" was approved beyond his expectation and even had an English edition. Immediately he turned to his own memory, packed with anecdotes and reminiscences of his wife's family, and drawing upon the legend and history of the county in which he was then living, produced —with little hope, to be sure, but with great energy of writing—"The Spy," which made a reverberating success. It made money. And now, with equal energy, he drew upon his own experience, first of childhood in "The Pioneers," where the vividness of the memory makes realism dominate romance, then from the sea in "The Pilot," then, after an experiment in documented historical romance à la Scott in "Lionel Lincoln," from the wilderness of the last of the Mohicans, with a sudden lifting of the narrative and release of joy in a subject truly found at last.

There is not the slightest indication in the prefaces of

these books, or in the correspondence saved from this period of his thirties, that Cooper felt the most meagre interest in "art" or "self-expression" or "beauty," or even in literary reputation. What moved Irving did not move him. He regarded his work, and often spoke of it in deprecation, as "light literature" in contrast to politics or history that could inform as well as amuse. He wrote to make money. His letters to his wife about his books are long lists of expenses and royalty figures. He had found a means of support compatible with his taste, his honor, and his domestic responsibilities. He could write at home. One other motive soon entered his work, to tell the world how to be republican, and America how to be American. This Cooper regarded as his patriotic duty, and he spoiled many good romances by conscientious scolding. But when he wrote just for money (after the prentice step of "Precaution") he wrote well. And in 1831, he could say to Caroline De Lancey that his income for the year from his books was expected to be about twenty thousand dollars, a fortune in itself for an American in those days.*

Yet the making of money is of course no final explanation of the burst into voluminous writing, rising sometimes into greatness, of a practical, unliterary man, whose sole remaining private journal reads like the records of a retired banker. The mounting energy of his stories of adventure must rather be charged to an ardent mind escaping from enforced inactivity into a hurricane of imagined deeds; and the criticism that constantly breaks in upon his narrative and changes in a moment a great romanticist into a truculent scold, may probably be attributed to the suppression of an instinct for leadership not to be satisfied in a life spent among European resorts, printing offices, and the family circle. Stopped short in the flush of his active youth, where he had been a woodsman, a sailor, a

* "Correspondence."

trained fighter before twenty, captured and domesticated, the husband who reached home and stayed there soared on and upward in his imagination. Deprived of command outside the home circle, unfitted by his independence for political life, with a personality strong enough to dominate the rather distinguished assembly of the Bread and Cheese Club that he founded in New York (and which died without him), he very naturally made a forum of his books where he argued with satisfying dogmatism every topic of contemporary discussion.

Yet if Cooper is what the psychologists call a "case," not much literary criticism can be squeezed from his complex. If he suffered from suppression, the pain was small, and the results for literature more good than bad. He was an eminently practical man. He had had his fling, and not even the War of 1812 tempted him to sea again, nor the westward rush of the twenties and thirties into the far forests. In his books he gave himself more adventures than he could have hoped for at sea or in the woods—and kept his happy home. As for leadership, his furious indignation with those who refused to take his advice suggests the humiliations that would have awaited him in public life. His wife ruled him, but it was a fortunate rule that left him a sense of absolute mastery. Like Emerson, he was a happy man, who got the most of what he wanted. To be active in youth, and tell about it afterward, is not that a desire of all the world? And is it not more agreeable to remind the age of its faults than to lead unwilling cattle toward a destination they will never reach? And so he stayed at home and wrote stories in which Anglophile snobs, rude democrats, self-seeking traders, and corrupt aristocrats all come to grief, while the bold sailor (or woodsman), who relies on his own "gift," goes on to happy success.

This is why he wrote—why he wrote so effectively is

the challenging question: why his romance, like Scott's, became robust and freed itself from the unreality of his contemporaries, why he captured the imagination of Europe,* gave an ideal picture of the frontiersman that has become a symbol, romanticized the Indian more justly than anyone else, and was read halfway round the world, while committing nearly every sin against good writing except impotence!

Here is a man of irregular but commanding intellect, not subtle, not learned, not original, powerful in concrete imagination, but quite without artistic conscience, obsessed by the American experiment, which went invariably wrong according to his thinking. This is no man of letters, like Irving, gently winging from the tumult, nor a professional author, such as Charles Brockden Brown, feebly trying to cultivate the muse while the rude current of American life sweeps past him. Cooper belongs with, not beside, the group of great Americans developed by circumstance at the moment when a new nation was being made. He has the energy, the scope, the courage of Jefferson, Hamilton, Jackson, and when he fails it is because energy, scope, and courage are not enough in literature. His books succeed, not by charm as with Irving, but by a sweep of novelty and power, as did the ideas of the new Republic. If they are less original than the idea of the United States, they are as vigorous and as fresh. He liberates the western imagination by his vast scenes of unconquered wilderness, gives the romantic ego a continent to dwell in, and establishes a new ideal of the simple life. And whereas Irving in his Federalist straining became more polished than the Europeans, more impeccable than his sources, Cooper is like the young republic which, two generations ahead in political theory, was a generation behind in the arts.

* "My clients are in Europe and long have been," he wrote somewhat biliously in 1847, but it was true enough. "Correspondence."

Supremely skilful in the technique of rapid action, he can yet be as awkward on occasions as a Western senator in the White House of the 1830's, and his constant scolding is the dogmatism of a strong but uncultured man.

3.

IT IS difficult indeed to grasp Cooper from the accounts usually given of him. Lounsbury, whose history of the reception of his books can scarcely be excelled, was too engaged in carrying on the Cooperian vendetta against a supercilious England to be much concerned with subtle analyses of the man. D. H. Lawrence, in his epic chapter,* neglects the patent fact that Cooper's perfect domesticity makes him a bad theme for an essay upon blighted lives, and does not see that his intense virility is poor evidence for a revival of the eighteenth century thesis that man degenerates in America. American critics have discussed him chiefly as a child of the romantic movement or an offspring of the frontier. But the unique quality of Cooper's romance at its best cannot be explained by either Rousseau in Europe or the forest at home. It comes from deeper levels than his truculence or his hard-headed desire for an income, and the escape of energy suppressed is merely its vehicle. It is based upon predispositions deeply bred in the man. It is characterized by two strong emotions of which one, a fierce republicanism, is obvious, and can be left for later discussion. But the other is not obvious. Cooper, in one part of his soul, was and always remained a Quaker. As a Quaker he judged human nature, and created character when he could create at all. To call Cooper the Quaker romanticist is to put too much in a term, but without his Quakerism he would have been much nearer to a merely American Scott. Without this imprint of a peculiar culture he would never have made Natty

* "Studies in Classic American Literature," Chapter V.

Bumppo or Long Tom Coffin, never in short have been Cooper. Lounsbury calls him a Puritan, forgetting for the moment that his dislike of New England Yankees was so strong that even Boston biscuits kept him awake at night. He was Puritan when he scolded, but at his moral best a Quaker. The distinction is important.

The Quaker doctrine of the inner light and the Quaker discipline of simplicity, so widely spread in early America, have seldom survived in the conflict with more noisy or more adaptable religions, and have ever given way before an increase in luxury and self-gratification, or hot blood demanding the active life. Yet where youth has been exposed to their sweet austerities there is seldom complete escape. The intellect may seek a more measured approach to the Deity, yet a sense of fortifying spiritual presence will remain. Gusto for living, a will and a means to sharpen taste and savor experience, may make impossible for the Quaker's child that plan of simple living, self-restrained, which keeps the soul in readiness for the inner voice, yet a belief that simplicity of heart is more valuable than cleverness will persist, and the conception of a spiritual democracy, in which the pure of soul are equal in the sight of God, remains as a social philosophy that is overlaid but seldom entirely forgotten. Tolerance, respect for the good wherever found, non-aggression, a readiness to trust human nature, distrust of all mere worldliness, these traits have been carried out of Quakerism by thousands once subjected to its discipline, and woven deep into the fabric of American idealism. Some of the threads have quietly rotted away, but many are still strong although they have long since lost the name of Quaker.

Curiously enough, but not so curiously after all, the rebels from Quakerism who covered their hearts with the shields and armor of the world, have, with remarkable frequency, gone to the further extreme of Protestantism.

JAMES FENIMORE COOPER

The Episcopal Church, with its decorous ritual, its traditional discipline, its language attuned to lovely communication with God, received the too worldly Quaker, and gave him a spiritual home and a creed and authority to stiffen the faith that his sophisticated soul could no longer find for itself. Simplicity and ritual, authority and self-discipline, are akin in this, that both escape disorder; and tradition is but self-dependence at a long remove.

Cooper is a perfect example of the Quaker transformed. His truculent, militant spirit, his willingness to fight (but not to seek combat), whether imaginatively at sea or in the forest, or actually in courts of law, his dogmatism, his violent energy always seeking deeds (though after youth seldom achieving them), seem little fitted to Quakerism. Yet George Fox was truculent. The Nantucket Quakers sought the whale in gory combats around the world, and the practical energy of the Friends made Pennsylvania the model community in prosperity as well as government in the middle eighteenth century. That Cooper could have remained a Friend in any circumstance short of persecution, where he would have shone, is improbable. He was too full-blooded for such a faith except in its creative youth. He was not the Quaker type, and he was never consciously Quaker in his professions.

But no man can escape his youth, especially the child of a Quaker. His mother, so I judge from her portrait made in Cooperstown shortly before her death in 1817, was a good Quaker until the end, for she wears the "plain clothing," sure sign of an unwavering adherence to the "discipline." Quakers from the South (which means presumably New Jersey) visited Cooperstown "by fifties" in those early days. Judge Temple, in "The Pioneers," Cooper's study of his father, is just such a Quaker as I have been describing, forced by temperament and his own ambition into a pioneer world where the already stiffening

Quakerism of Burlington was too ideal and too rigid to live by. It is rumored that the real Judge had been "put out of meeting." Yet in his ethics and his deeper purposes, Judge Temple seems Quaker still. He smiles with the author at the attempt to foist high church upon the New England immigrants, laughs at the pretentious worldliness of Richard, despises the pious legalism of Hiram Doolittle, and yet responds to good wine, good living, and good adventure as such hearty men will but Quakers should not. In strong emotion he drops constantly to the "thou" and "thee" of his upbringing, and Cooper says of him that "he retained them [the habits and language impressed upon his youth by the traits of a mild religion] in some degree to the hour of his death." His dress is described as plain neat black. Thus did Cooper depict his father in the Judge, and thus, with qualifications and a deeper self-analysis, he might have described himself.

From this influence Cooper never entirely departed. There are numerous references to Quakers and Quakerism in his books, most abundant naturally in the early volumes, but all respectful and sometimes affectionate. "A sect," he says in "The Crater," written toward the end of his life, "whose practice was generally as perfect as its theory is imperfect." Long Tom Coffin is a Nantucket whaler, and therefore a Quaker by inference, and his simple religion is essentially Quaker, as anyone who reads over the chapter that records his death in the wreck may see. When Natty Bumppo in "The Pathfinder" is urged to join the Church of England: "The 'arth is the temple of the Lord, and I wait on him hourly, daily, without ceasing, I humbly hope," he says. "No—no—I'll not deny my blood and color, but am Christian born, and shall die in the same faith. The Moravians tried me hard . . . but I've had one answer for them all—I'm a Christian already." This is naïveté, but it is not difficult for the reader of the "Leatherstocking Tales" to discover that Natty's Christianity is rudimentary Quakerism, with its sense of the immanence of the Creator, its non-aggression, its distrust of the intellect, its intense self-respect, its tolerance: "Each color has its gifts," says Natty, "and one is not to condemn another because he does not exactly comprehend it." This was the first Christianity that Cooper knew, the simple and persuasive religion of his youth.

In spite of Miss Cooper's indignant denials, old Shipman, who supplied them with fish and venison at Cooperstown, was undoubtedly the prototype of Natty ("a very prosaic old hunter," she calls him, who wore leather stockings but was otherwise not the noble scout of the books). Miss Cooper was thinking of the transmogrified Natty of the later romances. Natty in "The Pioneers," scrawny, simple, a little dull, is presumably a free portrait, like the others in that group, most of whom can be identified with the figures of Cooper's youth. But in a moral sense even the unromantic woodsman of "The Pioneers" is a new creation. "In a moral sense," Cooper says in his Preface to the "Leatherstocking Tales," * "the man of the forest is purely a creation," and he adds in the Preface to "The Pioneers," "a creation rendered probable by such auxiliaries as were necessary to create that effect." At first this moral conception is expressed in simple terms of loyalty and an intuitive sense for the right. But later the moral nature of Natty gets a sharper definition. He becomes a philosopher who talks garrulously of his relations to the universe. Indeed, once past "The Pioneers," Cooper never wavered in his conception, which was, as he says in the general Preface already quoted from, "a character who possessed little of civilization but its highest principles as they are exhibited in the uneducated, and all of savage life compatible with these great rules of conduct."

* I quote from the edition of 1861.

It was into Natty Bumppo that Cooper put his Quaker heart; indeed, his description of the old scout as "a character, in which excessive energy and the most meek submission to the will of Providence were oddly enough combined," * might have been self-portraiture of his best moments. But Cooper made of him a symbol of romantic escape, a figure ever retreating from the crash of falling timber and the smoke of clearings, on into the unspoiled West. And next, an incarnation of ideal man in a definite limitation of circumstances. He is a primitive Christian who holds "little discourse except with one, and then chiefly of my own affairs." He depends for inspiration upon no book, for he cannot read, and upon no man, for he sees few who are spiritual, but only upon the inner light. He is tolerant. If the Indian scalps, it is because he is Indian, not because he is wicked. He is humble, and yet self-respectful as one who reverences God in himself. He defers to differences in worldly station, but only as of the world. He kills only where he must, and in needful killing is mindful of a concession to necessity that puzzles him. It is the one compromise the wilderness forces upon him. He is proud only of his "gifts" of white blood and a sure aim, his "nature" he takes from God and is true to it by simple inevitability. Strip him of his romance and he sinks to such a figure of a daring frontiersman as Simms, in Cooper's own time, has drawn; then, on broader view, rises again by his ethical qualities to a figure of literary importance. The moral study of the naïve Hawk-eye is in many respects more interesting than the far subtler but turgid analyses of "The Scarlet Letter." And it is his moral nature that gives him distinction among other brave and loyal figures of romance.

It is Quaker morality, Quaker spirituality, and Natty is the best Quaker in American literature. His reliance

* "The Prairie."

upon the inner light, his inflexible simplicity, are Quaker traits that led him to choose an environment where, as he says in "The Deerslayer," he can meditate, where he can live with loyal natures in accord with his "gifts." And indeed his love for the forest is far closer to the Quakers' withdrawal from the world than to Rousseau's conception of primitive environment. George Fox, who himself wore leather breeches, and, more pertinently, urged men to forsake whatever cramped their spirits, would have heard his own words echoed by Natty, and been far more comprehensible to the scout than were the Moravians.

The Quaker has been unfortunate in fiction and drama. Prosperous Friends, turning to the world, have been proper subjects for satire, the humble Quakers in their communities have been too prosaic, too dull (the fire of martyrdom having long since departed) for literature, which turns from the mediocre. Quaker writers have been too single-minded to do justice to the characters moulded by their faith. Milton could remain Puritan yet write a "Paradise Lost," but the æsthetics of the Quaker was burnt up in his inner fire; or his distrust of the world and its intellectualizing inhibited him from art. One had to be a bad Quaker in order to be a good poet or romanticist. Yet the Quaker ideal, as the seventeenth century created it, is winning and powerful. Cooper followed it to an environment where its principles synchronized with the simplicity of the wilderness and the theory of the natural dignity of man. Hence the power of Natty Bumppo.

But Quakerism for Cooper was a faith of naïfs, lovely but lowly. He had long since overlaid the simple religion of John Woolman (also from New Jersey) with sea experience and what he regarded as a more reasonable faith. Although he did not join its communion until just before his death (a fact in itself striking) he was a lifelong Episcopalian, and if his novels are rich in Quaker principles, they are even richer in Anglican arguments. The Quakers of his own day and association were "plain people" in the literal sense of the term, and indeed this was a common appellation of derogatory intent for the smug, comfortable folk who had profited by the inhibitions of Quakerism and lost its spiritual intensity. Once the inner fire is quenched, the limitations of the simple life result in a barren experience and cold and petty minds. For Cooper, Quakerism was a religion of the plain people, and in its place he loved it. He himself was no longer simple, thought himself indeed far less simple than he was.

Natty, therefore, in so far as he is Quaker, is a symbol of the faith of Cooper's ancestry, a faith that seemed to him still lovely in uneducated men, and appropriate to naïve characters in a primitive environment. It was his plain intention in "The Pioneers" to make his Quaker naïfs lovable but quaint. But the beauty of the Quaker ideal was more to him than he knew. Natty became its spokesman, and his estimates of human values, when translated into philosophic English, represent a system, lucid and complete in its own sphere, that has been deeply influential upon the American mind. Nor has Natty himself been without deep influence upon the readers of Cooper.

It is an influence sharpened by tragedy. The philosophy of the wilderness was a protest against the onswelling rush of industrialism. Natty was driven before it, Quakerism was drowned in it. It was Cooper's tragedy too. Neither his religion nor his country would stand still for him, and it was fortunate that in embracing the tradition and the authority of Anglicanism he found a stay upon which to rest his spirit as his love rested upon his wife, while the America he had defended so passionately whirled on into what he believed was debasement and confusion.

"My longing is for a wilderness," he wrote to his nephew

Richard, from Paris in 1831; "it is my intention to plunge somewhere into the forest, for six months of the year at my return." Such romantic longings were deep in Cooper's hidden feelings, and seldom expressed except in his books; his religious ideas were vividly conscious, even when he did not fully grasp their import. Natty Bumppo is the child of their happy union.

4.

FOR all his Quakerism and his Jeffersonian principles, Cooper was an aristocrat, and sometimes a snobbish aristocrat. In his youth, Cooperstown was as near to a feudal community as the backwoods could come, his sea service ingrained the idea of rank, his first book is a record of English aristocracy and a satire on social climbers, he won a bet by knowing who was the premier baron of England (a highly technical question), his favorite characters, if they are not naïfs or family servants, are invariably Indian chiefs of high lineage, heirs to great estates, officers of rank and distinction, or, at the least, gentlemen and ladies. Chingachgook, says Natty, would disdain to look into the open lodge of a chief, for that would imply that another sagamore was great enough to excite his curiosity. "There resided formerly near this village," says the Travelling Bachelor, writing of Cooperstown, "a gentleman who is the reputed author of a series of tales," with this illuminating footnote, "The Americans, like the English, rarely put their names to any light works." One remembers Congreve and Voltaire! In "The Crater," the scene is a South Sea Utopia that is wrecked by the arrival of a lawyer, a printer (who becomes an editor), and four dissenting ministers, bearing with them the coils of democracy. Cooper has organized the Utopian government according to his own beliefs. Place and power inhere by right in the original proprietor, whose daring labors had made settlement possible. He was to be ruler for life. The judiciary were appointed by him; only the legislative was subject to representative control. Government was to be by ability and ownership, not by the majority. Social distinctions were to create themselves by the good manners of the best. His Federalist father would have approved of such a constitution.

It is easy to pile up instances of Cooper's hatred of mass rule. His famous series of libel suits against an ill-mannered press was intended to protect the private rights of a gentleman. What he thought of democratic editors is made clear in "Homeward Bound." The rights of property against the rabble was a favorite, almost a lifelong, theme. "The people" he disliked as heartily as did Hamilton. "Every hour I stay at home convinces me that society has had a summerset, and that the *élite* is at the bottom." * New York was full of "rum folk, rum fashionables, and rum punch." † In his diary for 1848, he writes that he would as soon confide in "the people" as in convicts. And it is Cooper who almost alone celebrates and regrets the Tory gentleman who chose the wrong side in the Revolution and left America poorer in civility for his loss.

And yet Cooper was a lifelong republican, and in politics a democrat, and not afraid of the word. The stimulation of intelligence and prosperity by the democratic spirit in New England is the theme of whole chapters in his "Travelling Bachelor." He supported Jefferson, admired Jackson, and was a foe to privilege, as he saw privilege, always and forever. While his romances breathe aristocracy, advocate the division of society into classes, exalt the great name, whether sagamore or baron, are anti-democratic, anti-equalitarian, they are at the same time vivid with proclamations of liberty and intensely devoted to a republican state. "Heidenmauer" and "The Bravo"

* "Correspondence," 1834.
† "Correspondence," 1834.

118

were written as attacks upon the European political and social system. "We will lift up our voice against the Humbugs [meaning aristocrats]," William Dunlap writes to him of the latter book, "who have kept this goodly world in a turmoil since the time of Nimrod." * "You hate aristocrats," wrote his dear friend, Peter Jay (son of the Federalist Chief Justice), "and therefore should not complain that they hate you. . . . Your publications are intended to do them harm." † "All but the extreme aristocrats like it," he quotes Bryant as saying of his "Sketches of Switzerland." "They complain of its democracy." ‡ "Social distinctions exist," he says in "Afloat and Ashore," "but not by primogeniture." § And Natty's simple philosophy is constantly turned toward pride of place.

Here is a contradiction worthy of a man who could both love and be hated by his country, be popular in his romances and unpopular when he grew serious, praise action and be content himself to be writer and country squire. But there was no more contradiction than was inevitable in America, where practice and theory were in inextricable conflict and both in vigorous growth.

Like his Miles Wallingford, Cooper belonged to the landowning class, but not to the descendants of a colonial aristocracy. By his marriage he was allied to them, yet he kept his sympathies in strict control. As a seafaring youth, and still earlier in the study of his tutor at Albany, he had encountered the superciliousness of the British toward an ex-colonial, and the experience rankled for life. The truckling to England and the denial of human rights, common in the best New York society of the first decades of the century, enraged him. He was a republican, not what he calls in "Homeward Bound" an English Federalist. He was a republican, but not a democrat.

* "Correspondence," 1831.
† "Correspondence," 1832.
‡ "Correspondence," 1836.
§ P. 388, edition of 1861.

He was a republican made up of several strains where politics, as such, entered scarcely at all. In the backwoods, amidst the peculiar conditions of the frontier, with the best and worst of savagery in contact with the white man stripped to his "nature" and dependent upon such "gifts" as he might apply there, Cooper knew that it was possible for an unprivileged, uneducated man to take his place beside kings and leaders of old-time romance. Richard, the fine gentleman of "The Pioneers," makes an ass of his amiable self whenever action is required of him. Natty, the symbol of natural man seeking his level, rises to heroism, a logical result of Rousseau's theory worked out in American practice—where it could work out. This is not political democracy, not social democracy, it is spiritual democracy; and Natty himself defines its bases for Judith in "The Deerslayer." There is "nature," which in all men of a civilization is alike, and "gifts," which are different and must be so accounted. By his nature and his gifts man earns his place in society. Thus, on Cooper's ocean, the poor negro in many instances proves to be worth two white men; but his gifts are not white gifts—he remains a good negro. And these fruits of youthful experience were given a philosophic justification by the Quaker estimate of values, which lauded spirituality without insisting that it should be rich or have a vote.

The rights of man were accepted by Cooper only in this qualified sense. However, his predisposition to liberty and fraternity, though not to equality, was strengthened by the American struggle for intellectual independence into which he entered like a crusader. "Her mental independence," he wrote of his country in 1831,* "is my object, and if I can go down to the grave with the reflection that I have done a little toward it, I shall have the consolation of knowing that I have not been useless in my generation."

* "Correspondence." To the editor of *The New Monthly*.

And in the same year to Caroline De Lancey: "It is biting to find that accident has given me a country which has not manliness to maintain its own opinions." * By "opinions" he meant, as the context shows, the republican institutions he had defended, institutions that represented his conception of the idea of the United States.

This republicanism was not likely to make him popular, for he was explicit in his statement that government by the best was precisely what no party was giving his country. Thousands of men of course agreed with him in hating both demagoguery and snobbishness, but these thousands did not pour out a stream of romances read half round the world, in which every chink was filled with defense, attack, and invective. It is not surprising that when Cooper began to criticize his own country for her backslidings from pure republicanism, as he understood it, he had few public friends to approve. Only a partisan can be safely critical of his home, and he must criticize the other party!

Hence Cooper is as valuable in studying American opinion as Emerson in understanding it, and the American situation at the watershed between republicanism and industrial democracy is essential to an understanding of Cooper. He seemed a bundle of inconsistencies to his contemporaries—a patriot attacking his country, a lover of freedom despising the masses, an aristocrat disliking his class, a romancer always scolding. But to us he is a single-minded gentleman who unifies in himself tendencies that would have been contradictory anywhere but in America. The inherited respect of the Quaker for spiritual excellence blends with the pioneer's admiration for self-dependence, making a hate of mediocrity not incompatible with a love for the simple heart. A ringing belief in freedom for the individual comports with a distrust of equality among those not equal. Rank by merit and by breeding excludes

* "Correspondence."

121

rank by privilege and by name. The rights of the governed admit of neither demagogues nor tyrants. Here is the type republican, a rarity in Europe, where there was no background which could make republicanism seem inevitable, a passing type in America, soon swept over by democracy, yet the creative principle in our institutions.

Unfortunately for Cooper he was too typical and too consistent. There may have been a moment in time when some part of the United States was liberal enough in its policies and conservative enough in its choice of men to meet with Cooper's ideal, but it could only be for a moment. He asked for the simplicity of the Quaker, the decorum of the Church of England, the opportunity of the frontier, the manners of Europe, the professional attitude of a gentleman, the patriotism of a soldier, perfect honesty, deference to real superiors, an independent spirit —and this is too much to ask of any civilization, especially of a nation in tumultuous development. The social thinker —and Cooper, intellectually regarded, was always a social thinker—makes a pattern for his world that is good or not according to the breadth of his experience and the lucidity of his thinking. But good or not, if the community persistently slides away from it he, perforce, turns critic and scolds. So with Cooper. In political life he was ineffective because he fought the current always. In written criticism, where he pictured in his books the vulgarity and money-madness of his country, or the intolerance of foreigners, he was not very effective, although at this distance it is hard to be sure. Such a sound and shrewd analysis of the value of republican institutions as one finds in "The Travelling Bachelor" seems to have made little impact, "Homeward Bound" and "Home as Found" roused only wrath,* his friends regretted his violence, and Horace

* Which may be measured by the publication of "The Effinghams" in two volumes, a weak parody designed to show how good were good Americans.

JAMES FENIMORE COOPER

Greeley spoke for many when he begged him to drop social politics and begin again to write the romance that charmed the world. A hustling community, more and more commercial and more and more democratic, found Cooper's ideas of a republic of gentlemen and lovers of real freedom stale and out of date. It was only when the same ideas were transfused in romance that they caught the imaginations of two generations.

The romances that held these ideas lacked homogeneity, and so were human. Cooper chose for them aspects of the good old and the desirable new and made these social traits lie down together, a characteristic of all social states that appeal to the imagination—and are never realized. The aristocratic virtues—generosity, loyalty, courage, disdain for the mean, honor in all its senses—are incarnate in those noble Delawares, Chingachgook and Uncas, who, if much more Indian than Cooper's later critics were willing to believe, are also much more imbued with the theory and practice of aristocracy than Cooper realized. Beside them, respecting their essential aristocracy, but stating its limitations for use in a Christian world, is Natty, who, on his part, advocates the value of spirit, the rights of the common man, and the universal tolerance of democracy. Thus in the "Leatherstocking Tales" one gets it both ways —the ideals of the old world, the ideals of the new, both romantically successful in a no man's frontier between Europe of the past and America of the future. Alas, in the real world of America, it was not, it could not be, so except for the happy moment, and he who stirred the imagination with tales of noble adventure and sacrifice, when he left his frontier fairyland for his actual country could only scold. Natty flying westward is, symbolically, Cooper himself, in search of Utopia.

And now to recapitulate and focus this criticism upon Cooper's literary art.

123

At the bar of heaven Cooper would have answered: first, I am a gentleman, next, I was a sailor, third, I am a patriot, and fourth, and with some derogation, I am a maker of light literature. He is the great amateur of novel-writing, beside whom Trollope is a professional and H. G. Wells a self-conscious artist. He is, furthermore, an enduring example of what may be called the American idea, that anyone can do anything, if it happens to be his "gift." His father became a judge without studying law, and Cooper a novelist without serious study of literature. He began to write because writing fiction did not seem to be difficult, and continued because he had nothing else to do, and fiction made money. There is no record of a correspondence of a writer of his reputation that contains so little reference to literature, including his own. And in all the numerous questions that his characters discuss, sometimes at moments of the greatest danger, literature and the taste for literature are almost never present.

Hence there is no design in Cooper's progress, no searching for themes fitting his genius, no dallying (like Irving) with themes that give an opportunity for style. He sweeps together whatever memories of his youth, legends of the countryside, products of his reading, or social ideas then oppressing him happen to be handy, warms them up in a preliminary chapter, and dashes in on his story. If he has too much information at hand, as in "Lionel Lincoln," he dumps it by paragraphs regardless of the plot. If his story runs short, as in "The Deerslayer," he fills in with discussion; if long, as in "Afloat and Ashore," he carries on through another volume. If the real material of his own memories is not sufficient, as in "The Pioneers," he stretches it upon his usual plot formula. If he prepares for an event, as he clearly prepares for the marriage of Cora and Uncas when he so elaborately discloses her mixed blood, and then sees a better solution, in comes the new solution while the earlier preparation stays too. It is not surprising that when he changed the heroine's name in "The Pathfinder" halfway through, he forgot to alter the earlier references in the proof of his first edition. Loyalty, friendship, love, hate, and revenge interest him as inciting causes, but other motives, or indeed any motives but the unsubtlest, trouble him not at all. Anyone can be in peril at sea or in the forest for no good reason, and in the midst of that peril can stop to discuss philosophy, ethics, religion, politics, or woodcraft. He was an amateur even in the thing he could do best, and would stop a good story anywhere to scold his contemporaries or express his opinion upon matters that had little or nothing to do with the plot. Through a long series of tracts for the times, which did not sell and were not wanted, he was as obstinate in lowering his literary reputation as most men are in making one.

It is the amateur in Cooper that has so seriously threatened a position in literature that is still high, and should be higher than this generation will admit. Working at a novel with the patient industry of a man of business, setting down every fact of costume with precision,* dictating notes while he is ill for the fight between Chingachgook and Magua, rewriting in proof with a gentleman's care for corrections, and an amateur scholar's concern for nicety in language, he never seems to have concerned himself with conciseness, balance, condensation. He is the careless American, strong in energy, weak in craftsmanship except when by chance he falls upon his "gift," a Jack-of-all-trades a little ashamed to be just a writer. Of the two attributes of style, movement and order, Cooper had movement, but order he lacks. That is the chief reason he has suffered in time.

Yet Cooper's style, though amateurish, is by no means

* Dr. Francis in the "Memorial of James Fenimore Cooper."

the careless instrument that many have thoughtlessly called it. He never wrote with distinction because, in spite of his fussiness over pure English, he was not really interested in words, yet in spite of a commonplace vocabulary his diction can carry the mounting excitement of a chase, or depict a forest or a seascape with a justice and a vigor that are better than niceties of language. Conrad can beat him by the sentence, but when it comes to movement by paragraphs—great frigates rising into clouds of sail, or the quick changes of sea battle—Cooper is more lucid and more broadly pictorial. In dialogue, the style mounts to stiff unreality in direct proportion to the gentility of the speaker, especially if feminine. Yet in general Cooper's style, like Scott's, is adequate. It is in his mixture of themes, when, like a careless lecturer, he will not keep irrelevant ideas out of his discourse, that his amateur conception of the art of writing is most fatally displayed.

5.

It is impossible not to conclude after reading Cooper's novels that in so far as he wished to write at all, which was not much, he would by choice have been a historian and critic of society. It is difficult to escape the conclusion that he wrote pure romance to give the public what he knew it wanted and himself what he most enjoyed, but social criticism to fulfill a clear call of duty and intellectual desire. For this service, his equipment, admirable for romance, was not sufficient, and his circumstances unfortunate. He was an amateur in criticism as in art. This peppery squire was too heavy-handed. When he invented a society of supercilious monkeys in the South Seas, he spoiled a good idea by exaggeration, and made "The Monikons" the least readable of his books. He exaggerated as Dickens exaggerated, but not humorously. Humor was not in Cooper's armory. He deplored its lack in American

literature,* praising Irving for his unique possession, and
at the time he wrote, he was right. And next he was too
personal. Mr. Cooper's difficulties with Cooperstown tres-
passers, and Mr. Cooper's feelings as an outraged gentleman, are always intruding under very thin disguises. The
truth was that after his active youth Cooper was too withdrawn from normal currents of life to satirize his times
with point and pungency. From beginning to end his career was abnormal—abnormal, that is, not for an American, but for a social historian. He lived in the backwoods,
at sea, retired on a farm, abroad, and finally immured in
a family circle from which he emerged only to print his
books. Of all the works that he would have called serious
efforts only his dignified history of the United States Navy
survives, and that has been so overshadowed by his romances as to remain unknown to the general reader. His
shouting at the tides of democracy and commercialism,
his pleas for American Utopias inhabited by Coopers,
Natty Bumppos, and a few family slaves, and run on
Quaker principles with a Church of England respect for
class distinction, seem a little absurd now. As for his books
on antirent agitations, antijury trials, and anti many
other things, they are neither wise nor witty. Of the whole
series only "The Crater" deserves resurrection. His instinct was sound when he confessed to George Washington
Greene his partiality for Leatherstocking, saying that he
had intended to carry on his adventures into the Revolution. It was more authentic than his "call" to save his
country by means of irritable books.

6.

YET Cooper's reputation has not suffered because of these
digressions (which he felt to be major operations) into
amateur economics and sociology. He never had a repu-

* See "The Travelling Bachelor."

tation from them great enough to suffer. They were not read widely when written, they will never be read again except by students of the developing American civilization, who will omit them at their peril. If his once great fame has diminished it is for a very different reason. He was fatally an amateur in his literary borrowings.

Cooper's mother (like many Quaker women) was a great reader of romances. One of the few indications we possess of her son's early taste in literature is that he read "Don Belianis of Greece," and proposed to write a story like it. "Belianis" is one of the continuations of that exercise in rarefied chivalry, "Amadis of Gaul," and came into English in 1598, to be companioned with Sir Philip Sidney's "Arcadia." The heroic romance of the seventeenth century, where knights and ladies live in an exalted world of fine speech and fair deeds, is the final blooming of "Belianis" and its like.

When Cooper the squire became, somewhat surprisingly, Cooper the popular author, he drew heavily—at first preponderantly—upon his early reading. The chivalry of such as Belianis, the romantic melancholy of Byronic heroes, the mystery of Scott's Unknowns, the elegant aristocracy of Shakespeare's ladies (Shakespeare was his chief reading in maturity), all floated in his head. The nodes of interest in his plots are usually Laras, as in "The Red Rover," or Black Knights or Ivanhoes, as in "The Spy," which was published the year after "Ivanhoe"; and these, like their British prototypes, hark back in their conceptions of duty and honor to the earlier heroic romance. But the romantic shadows of Byron and Scott have in themselves little power of survival and Cooper's copies of a copy are still feebler. Harvey Birch has moral qualities that give him some distinction, but the Red Rover, Paul Jones, Washington, the ancient patriot in "Lionel Lincoln," and all the rest of Cooper's merely literary figures are incapable of interesting a sophisticated generation. They rust and crumble in the fabric of his narrative like bolts in a wall. They are the products of reading, not experience, and better suited to the movies than to literature.

So with the majority of his soi-disant humorous characters, always excepting woodsmen like Kirby, or sailors like Boltrope. They are studied from Shakespeare or eighteenth century fiction and their humor is as mechanical as their method of creation. So with his ladies. The sombre figure of Ishmael's wife in "The Prairie," an epic conception, Judith in "The Deerslayer," and a few other women of the lower classes, Indians, or slaves, are vigorous.* But his ladies are accoutred with such delicacy, such oppressive refinement, and so many attributes of modesty and reticence as to pass out of the realm of romance into sheer comedy. They cannot run, they cannot speak out, they have no ankles (not to speak of legs), they can only faint, cherish, and be loved. "Lovely innocent" is the term by which they are commonly addressed.

A study of "Precaution" is enough to prove that these too are literary conventions, borrowed from the sentimental novel of Cooper's youth and glamoured o'er by romance. If they outsigh and outshrink their originals, it is because their author's taste in scene and plot involved them in gales and forest fires, and hurried them from the boudoir to the scalping knife. Yet the fervor with which he describes his ideal female is more than literary. Cooper believed that women should be as literature had painted them, and he realized his ideal in his own family circle. His letters, and especially the memoir of his daughter (she who destroyed his papers at a word), give an impression of females who carried this theory of feminine gentility to an extreme eminently satisfactory to the novelist.

* Cora of "The Last of the Mohicans" gains character from her mixed blood in proportion as she loses gentility.

7.

But we can no longer join Cooper's Indians with Cooper's women in a common dissent. They are not amateur in any sense. Although these Indians were romanticized as his women were sentimentalized, the first were based upon a type generalized from life, the second upon bad books badly read. The Indian, as Cooper must have first known him in the days of the settlement, when only broken and degenerate stragglers were left in the great woods of New York, is probably represented with exactitude by the old sagamore of "The Pioneers," a little stupid, a little drunken, and noble only in his death. Gregory Paine * states that Cooper's historical knowledge of the Delawares, and even his name Chingachgook, are derived from the account of the Indians inhabiting Pennsylvania and the neighboring States, written in 1819 by the old Moravian missionary, John Heckewelder. It is here that Cooper got his background of Indian conflict and the exaltation of the Delawares above other nations. Mr. Paine is troubled by Cooper's adherence to this unhistorical preference for Delawares over the "Mingoes," the famous Six Nations, but it is obvious that as a novelist celebrating the epic warfare of two Delawares and their adopted white brother against ancient enemies, such a conception was dramatically necessary. Nor is it improbable that Judge Cooper, who told his son Indian stories, and perhaps old Shipman, should have given to the youth in the wilderness an idea of Delaware courage and Delaware virtue that Heckewelder merely confirmed.† In any case, Cooper's Indians were by no means all studied from Cooperstown

* "The Indians of the Leatherstocking Tales," *Studies in Philology*, January, 1926.

† It is traditional at Bethlehem, from which Heckewelder was sent as a missionary to the Indians of the North, that Cooper and Heckewelder were often together; and it is of course very probable that, like so many others, the missionary should have stopped at Cooperstown on his way.

vagrants and the pages of Heckewelder. Before his later books he had seen the unspoiled savages on their journeys East and accompanied at least one delegation to Washington.

Whatever may have been his personal experience, it is now certain that he did not falsify the primitive red man, not even in the increasing romanticizing of Chingachgook through the succeeding books of the series. The weight of modern study of the ethics, the religion, the poetry, and the character of the American Indian, indicates that Chingachgook or Uncas would have been at home among the Sioux or the Navajo as sympathetic and scientific observers have recorded them. Even the speech of Cooper's braves is not more poetic than numerous versions of actual Indian speeches and legends. Cooper adopted a common device of romancers—he made good Indians and bad Indians, and divided Indian faults and virtues very evenly between them. And yet he did better than Scott with his Highlanders, for by a skilful play of light and shade he kept racial traits in both, while emphasizing what he desired. Chingachgook, who murders the friendly French sentry in "The Last of the Mohicans," is never anything but savage, even though poetic, loyal, brave, aristocratic. Magua, in the same book, is only Chingachgook with an evil disposition and an unfortunate tribal connection. Together they fairly represent the Indian chief as the anthropologists see him, as his own arts testify him to have been, as no one else has been able to put him into literature. Romanticized of course he was, but it is fortunate that Cooper sprang from the Quakers, always friendly to the Indian, that he read Heckewelder, that he wrote sympathetically of the Indian, who even to Simms was the enemy, and to most Americans a figure half devil, half brute. Nor should it be forgotten that in the eyes of most of the characters who accompany Leatherstocking—

Hurry, the casual officers of the tales, the squatters of "The Prairie"—these heroic figures are only dirty savages, to be killed, or used, as the case may be. It is a tribute to Cooper's art that we, the readers, see his Delawares as he conceived them; and it is more than probable that on the romantic plane we see truly.

Cooper's America, as I have said, was moving too fast for him. Gentlemen were growing scarce; the tradesman, the capitalist, and the manufacturer were beginning to dominate; the cunning, disputatious Yankee was subjecting the land. He turned to the Indian with the sure instinct of one who seeks a symbol, and found it in these unfortunate relics, noble but not in a useful fashion, courageous but sure to be defeated, wise but not in trade, cruel but not mean. The Indian "gifts," like Cooper's political idealisms, were not wanted: he took pleasure in exalting them as Scott took pleasure in chivalry. Yet of the two, it is probable that Cooper's Indians have more truth of human nature as well as truth of origin than Scott's knights, and are likely to outlive them in literature. Between Uncas, idealized as he at least unquestionably is, and Ivanhoe, the choice is quickly made. And if Cooper's romantic reading led him to romanticize Old Indian John into a heroic chief, yet more than literary convention went into Chingachgook's making, and he lives while the white knights fade.

And again, the fierce independence, the intense patriotism, the disdainful courage, the complete self-reliance, that Cooper held as his own creed, were unquestionably Indian virtues. In romanticizing them he was romanticizing himself. Add the piety of Natty and his faith in simplicity to the aristocratic traits of the good Indian, and one gets Cooper's own ideal of fundamental man.

Cooper was less fortunate when he adventured in actual history. He can display the background of the American

scene with excellent art but when he links his characters
with historical happenings there is the break in continuity
that one gets sometimes between caption and picture in
the movies. Compared with Scott, he is an amateur in
this blending. Neither the identity of his Unknowns nor
the results of his long pursuits on the sea or through the
forest had much significance for history, and hence when he
introduced known events, as he constantly endeavored to
do, they remained undigested chunks apart from the story.

The memory, amply developed, of his own youth is the
source of Cooper's enduring reputation. The sea, the
forest, Indians, scouts, sailormen, negroes, moved him to
narrative that was not imitative and romance that was
not merely literary. And when Cooper's social ideas, elsewhere tiresome, inspire the speech of Natty, the self-
respect of Chingachgook, the religion of Tom Coffin, and
are reflected in the true republicanism of the forest and
the decorous authority of the sea, then romance itself gets
a weight and validity that gives it purchase upon time.
His best books, with the possible exception of "The Last
of the Mohicans," will have to be blue-penciled to rid
them of critical digression and stale romantic convention
before they can regain the popularity they deserve, but
in spite of the impurities the gold is there.

8.

THAT so much of Cooper can be blue-penciled rather
easily, and with little loss, is just another proof that he
was an amateur of genius in the art of writing. Amateurs,
however, sometimes make the most original craftsmen because of their recklessness.

Cooper wrote by formula. In all his good novels there is
a chase—and the chase is the plot. In all his novels, good
or bad, where the scheme would in any way allow it, there
are two character types, the romantic Unknown and the

humble (though often romantic) Naïf. The Unknowns, as I have indicated, are literary, the stock in trade of the romantic movement. The Naïfs are sometimes literary also. The idiot boy of "Lionel Lincoln," the surgeon of "The Spy," the scientist of "The Prairie," and even David, the psalm-singer of "The Last of the Mohicans," smell of the source book. Nevertheless, while the Unknown is this practical man's rather mechanical gesture for summoning romance, the Naïf, thanks to the influences that I have described before, sometimes sprang from Cooper's inner life itself, and eventually ran away with his stories. In "The Spy" he raised the naïveté of Harvey Birch into a melodramatic heroism that made him famous. Harvey was both Naïf and Unknown. In "The Pioneers" the parts were differentiated. Young Effingham had all the literary trappings, Natty Bumppo, the Naïf, must depend upon the simple nobility of a faithful heart for glamour, yet even so as the story develops he takes the lead. In "The Pilot," it is Boltrope and Long Tom, Naïfs both, who stir the author's talents to complete success, but the Byronic Unknown is still given the spotlight. In "The Last of the Mohicans" the process is complete. Leatherstocking has become a romantic hero without losing his naïve simplicity, and, in place of refurbished aristocrats, emerge with savage brilliance Cooper's great Unknowns, the Mohican chiefs. Paul Jones no longer thrills, the Red Rover is faintly absurd, Harvey Birch seems a figure of rhetoric and false psychology, but the Indians lead their kind and Natty is one of the great figures of English fiction. It is his monument in bronze in Cooperstown that fitly celebrates his creator's work and reputation.

Thus the formula that a none too original artist borrowed from Scott released the best that was in him—but remained a formula still. Cooper could transcend, he could not change, it.

So also with his left bower of technique, the chase, which was his plan of action and led his Unknowns and Naïfs sometimes on a forest-tracking, sometimes to hide and seek, as in "The Pathfinder" and "The Deerslayer," "The Spy" and "The Pilot," sometimes on a straightaway half across the world and back, as in "The Red Rover" and "Miles Wallingford." In itself this is one of the simplest and most effective ways of story-telling, but it requires two things for its success, a realizing sense of accompanying detail, which Cooper raised to genius, and single-mindedness, which he did not always possess. It is not so much the chase that fascinates Cooper and his readers—this is but the tension upon interest—it is what happens in the chase, the search for the print of a moccasin, the pirate ship seen for an instant in a flash at night, Deerslayer's silent laughter in his mask of bearskin, the sudden swing of canvas as the frigate breasts the shoal, the rush of boarders over the rail in "Miles Wallingford," the breathless suspense in Deerslayer's hidden canoe. Invention based upon a highly technical experience, enriched by careful research, was Cooper's forte, and it is interesting to compare his flow of complex incidents, each and all part of the chase, with the careful fabrications of Hergesheimer, which depict but do not move the story. It is the moving picture versus the "still."

In the details of movement Cooper has never been surpassed and seldom equaled. His "gift" would be a fortune for movie directors, who, like him, are unliterary men, interested chiefly in effect. The escape of the sloop in the fog of "The Pilot," the pursuit of Magua in "The Last of the Mohicans," the prairie fire in "The Prairie," the forgotten chase by French privateers in "Afloat and Ashore," are superb examples of narrative art.

But Cooper was professional only at his best. As I have said before, he would not stick to his story, he would digress. At a moment of desperate dangers the group of "The Pathfinders" can talk philosophy in their scarce hidden canoe. The author, unlike his Chingachgook, will stop while the trail is warm to tell British and Americans, snobs and the sophisticated, of their respective sins. Thus a Cooper novel is seldom a perfect work of art, but rather a set-up of familiar characters, part real and convincing, part literary and conventional, a mystery, a peril, a chase, sermons by the author, more chase, and a happy ending. Thus was the naïve, yet authentic, talent of the foremost American romances exhibited, like a great picture badly hung and badly lit. Yet when this art embodies his own ideals of simplicity, courage, spiritual integrity, in characters however rare and in passages however brief, we cannot withhold the adjective "great" from the few books in which they predominate.

"The Last of the Mohicans" and "The Prairie" are remarkable books by any standard of judgment. The one for the forest, the other for the plains (for it was not the real prairie of which he was writing), have that lift and scope of the imagination which is a sure sign of literary creation beyond the common. They added two new realms to fairyland, the primeval forest and the Wild West. In these two books also, and particularly in the first, where Cooper's aroused fancy escapes from dogmatism, the character of Deerslayer reaches its finest development, and Chingachgook, Uncas, and the Pawnee, Hard Heart, supply those aristocratic virtues for which there was no room in the Quaker scout. Some faded remnants of fashionable romance and literary convention persist in the women and the officers of "The Mohicans," and the not very humorous scientist of "The Prairie"—works of the head, not the heart. Yet perhaps nowhere in English is a happier combination of romantic ideals attained in settings of convincing reality and carried upon more exciting plots.

JAMES FENIMORE COOPER

If "The Prairie" has never had the recognition of the earlier story, this is because it is the more studied of the two. Cooper never knew the plains at first hand, and yet Ishmael and his sons are surely not literary invention, nor are the old man and his wife unworthy to rank with Magua as a fitting symbol of the malign strength of the wilderness. Indeed, they are the best representations in American literature of that reversion to barbarism which was so typical of the real frontier. The professional realists are just beginning to give us their like, but border history is full of their prototypes. "The Prairie" is the most skilful of Cooper's books, even though it lacks the rich imaginative memory of "The Mohicans."

The sea stories must go in a lower rank. Even "The Pilot" is adulterated with quasi-humor, complicated by a sentimental plot, and weakened by ladies whose only legitimate excuse for existence is that their presence necessitates so many brilliant sea manœuvres. Cooper probably knew the sea better than the forest—he had been a professional on the ocean—and for that very reason it gave him an opportunity for too much virtuosity. His scenes, like that of the British fleet emerging through the fog in "The Two Admirals," are superlative; but in spite of clear runs of incident that outdo in sheer excitement anything else written of the sea, he plays too much with plot, character, and description, ballasts his best narrative with the most egregious Unknowns, and seeks glamour by devices less fresh than the events of the forest.

It is impossible to lift into the category of "The Mohicans" and "The Pilot" his other stories that still deserve reading. "The Spy," which gave him his first reputation, was much overrated. It was successful because its romanticism was in the mode, and because of its novel theme of American patriotism. All the lesser desires of romanticism were satisfied by the gloomy self-sacrifice of Harvey Birch, the rapid alternations of failure and success, the abundant villains, and the shadowy figure of a great hero behind. The formula of the later novels is here. The Cowboys and the Skinners are bad Indians, the hearty Virginians represent Deerslayer to the rescue, the novel is one long pursuit; but the elaborate paraphernalia of social relations among the gentry and the heavy comedians of the lower parts weigh upon the story. As for "The Pioneers," it is one of the best pictures we possess of early frontier life; no wonder its appearance was, as Bryant says, startling in its realism, for it was faithfully studied from Cooper's own youth. In outline it, too, is the familiar formula, a wronged Unknown, a Naïf to the rescue, a pursuit. But the pursuit is too long delayed, the plot is too obscure, and most of the story must depend upon its frontier scenes for interest. Here Cooper had his first sight of the material he could best use, the material of his youth, but he had not yet learned to blend it with romance, which had to pass from the conventional ladies and gentlemen of the plot to Natty and the Indians before good description became a narrative art.

9.

THERE remains to say a word as to Cooper's relation to the great surge and flow of Western literature, of which English literature is the tide on far-stretching shores, and American literature in this early nineteenth century a wave only.

The subject has been made difficult by well-meaning critics whose nationalism has been stronger than their judgment, and equally so by their opponents who in a rage at petty distinctions have disclaimed the effect of nationalism altogether. For the latter, American literature is a part of English literature, with no sufficing distinction except that it was written west of the Atlantic.

The case of Cooper is illuminating for such a discussion.

JAMES FENIMORE COOPER

It is clear that philosophically considered he is a part of the romantic movement that throughout Europe was bent upon expanding the personality and intensifying the egoism of man. Wonder, mystery, opportunity, progress, escape, excitement, were qualities of the philosophy of Rousseau, the humanism of Goethe, the egoism of Byron, and the escape into the past of Scott. To the means by which man's spirit could be expanded, and his imagination set free, Cooper contributed the endless forest, and taught the novelist how to go competently upon the ocean. In this aspect, he was, like so many Americans, an inventor, who applied old principles to new circumstance, who was crude and imitative in his romantic ideas but strong in his grasp upon new things.

And yet it was precisely when he was most European, and specifically most British, in manner that he was least effective, most the amateur dabbling in literature. His Unknowns, his delicate ladies, his historical inserts, his polite conversations, are in the British romantic manner, and they are, with scarcely an exception, inferior to their originals. It is only when he is inspired by the sea, by frontier simplicity, by the Quakerism of the woods, or warmed by his curious republicanism, which is so characteristically American as to deserve a more specific name, that he wrote as of himself. And it was only in scenes and subjects, usually American, which served to discharge these native emotions that Cooper was roused to his full possibilities in art. A child of Europe, like all of us, he is best when he is most American in his theme, and is best appreciated by those who understand his American traits, which is a conclusion so natural and so generally applicable to all the really excellent American writers as to occasion no surprise and necessitate, one might think, no defense. The philosophy of Rousseau, which filtered down to Cooper through Jeffersonian democracy, the impulses of general romanticism that it would have been difficult for him to escape, interpenetrated his native edifice of romance. Yet it would have been better if he had never read European literature after his youth, particularly if he had never read Byron and Scott. Independent as he was, and committed to a lifelong crusade for the intellectual independence of his country, he was not keen enough to see that his own romances contained as much evidence of the dangers of imitation as of the value of fresh terms for the human spirit.

I make no extravagant claims for Cooper. He was not original except in the invention of incident, the use of new scenes, and a very few characters; he lacked utterly the patient determination of Irving to "do it beautifully"; he was no philosopher and was as uncomprehending of the necessary evolution of his country as of the political necessities of Europe; his sense of form was active only for one mode of representation, the pursuit. Yet his truculent honesty, which made him a persistent critic of developing America, is itself an index of the American mind. He is one of the really important interpreters of America, even when you must read him backward to get at the truth, and this not unimportant fact may be added to his achievements in pure art—the art of the forest, of the sea, of the plains, in terms of romance. Cooper, I think, was a great man, inhibited, handicapped, diverted in action, but free with his pen, whose work for these very reasons shows traces always of a heroic mould, and can be judged only in large measures, generously appreciating what the writer could have done and sometimes did. When the whole man comes through, he may fear comparison with neither Hawthorne, Hugo, nor Scott.

The interesting study of Cooper in D. H. Lawrence's "Studies in Classic American Literature" (Chapter V) concludes its brilliant whole and half truths with an apotheosis of Deerslayer, the vital American: "True myth concerns itself centrally with the onward adventure of the integral soul. And this, for America, is Deerslayer. A man who turns his back on white society. A man who keeps his moral integrity hard and intact. An isolate, almost selfless, stoic, enduring man, who lives by death, by killing, but also is pure white. This is the very intrinsicmost American. He is at the core of all the other flux and fluff. And when *this* man breaks from his static isolation, and makes a new move, then look out, something will be happening. . . . All the other stuff, the love, the democracy, the floundering into lust, is a sort of by-play."

It is not a byplay, nor is the struggle, as Lawrence romantically thinks, a conflict between a disintegrating white civilization (for Lawrence carries on the eighteenth century belief in the decadence of man and all animals on the American continent) and some dark dæmonic spirit of the land that Cooper symbolizes in his red men and vainly endeavors to bind in friendship to the white. The struggle is internal: it is in Cooper himself, who is as much of a man and a type as Natty his creation. It is the American with Europe on his back and in his veins endeavoring to grasp and hold and understand the opportunities of a new liberty in a fresh continent. Deerslayer is a symbol of escape from the problem by renunciation and native simplicity. But what gives Deerslayer his pathos, and Cooper his significance as a creative artist, is the pause— at the borders of the wilderness, on mid-ocean, for a moment in time—of the onward rush of the world muddle of waste, greed, vulgarity, pretension, while the story is told. Natty Bumppo fades into the wilderness. He will never come back. His kind of moral integrity must be compounded with different elements in order to meet a new civilization. Cooper dies quarreling with half his country, a belated aristocrat preaching a democracy that is neither equalitarianism nor mediocrity. His conflict was never resolved and never will be. Like his forest hero, he remains a figure of aspiration, of regret, of the might-have-been, a romance of an American ideal.

Ralph Waldo Emerson

WE have made a dim and dusty figure of the greatest intellect, pure if not applied, in American history. Emerson, whose mind lived with an intensity of a general's on campaign, has become a figure for schoolrooms and the entablatures of public libraries. The realists have chosen him as an archetype in their rather ignorant war against Puritanism. In literary history he has been subject to philosophical analysis and, reduced to terms of Neo-Platonism and Transcendentalism, has become an abstraction and often an inconsistency.

I shall discard terms that have become mere labels and try to recall, by a just method, some of the light and vigor of what to me is the most interesting mind in the formative nineteenth century, studying Emerson as in his frequent introspections he studied himself—a New Englander in the stream of time, and an intuitive mind reflecting upon the triple impact of Puritan moralism, experimental science, and the industrialism that was about to determine an epoch in all Western culture. Also as an American poet and man of letters trying to express what he had wholly divined and partly rationalized.

It is as great an error to interpret Emerson solely in terms of European thought as by the single light of his American significance. He was, of course, a world figure, in whose consciousness an unusual arc of world thought in both time and space was always present, but also very

143

specifically American. There is a fallacy now widely current in opposition to the flatulence of patriotic criticism, that when Poe has been coupled with German romanticism, and Emerson with Plato, Goethe, and Fichte, the important word has been said. Culture, however, is continuous in its influences, and the mental baggage a thinker takes aboard shows whence he comes, but not always where he is going. The life of his thinking must derive from his own idiosyncrasy or the impulse of his environment. Without the romantic movement, as Professor Norman Foerster * says, American literature would be inexplicable, but it is not explicable by means of it, or the other waves from Europe that run through our sea of the ocean of culture. Nor is Emerson more than located by the Platonism upon which he fed and the Orientalism from which he drew what he could and no more.

Hence if I write of Emerson with emphasis upon New England and America, and with more insistence upon his training and his personality than upon his documentary sources, it is not to write as an American, but rather as a critic aware that if a man lives in time he lives also in space; aware also that as it is the expression that gives the face its individuality regardless of the inherited bony structure behind, so it is the Concord and the America in which Emerson lived that determined not the core, but certainly the visible periphery and differentiation, of his thought. What was true of Cooper, was true in a larger sense of him.

And this distinction is particularly useful because Emerson was not a philosopher but a man of letters who thought philosophically, and still more a prophetic preacher obsessed by a sense of duty to his audience. Emerson the philosopher has been analyzed as a salt is taken apart into its constituent elements. I write rather

* See his "Nature in American Literature" and his "American Criticism."

of Emerson the essayist, poet, lecturer, dedicated preacher of New England, and prophet to the new scientific world.

2.

THIS approach has a further value, not always considered in literary history, of being interesting, for certainly New England in the first half of the nineteenth century was one of the most interesting communities in the Western world. It did not seem so to worldly visitors, who found gayety conspicuously absent. It has not seemed so to later historians, who have sought the drama of American history in war, and its romance in pioneering. But the twentieth century must think differently. For in New England, in the presence of the new industrialism, still dominated by the will to salvation, acutely self-conscious in politics, and curious in science, the American first began to express his own problems of the spirit.

I say first advisedly. The strong intellectuals who governed morals and thinking in the Puritan period were concerned with will in its relation to salvation, which was a universal problem and New England merely its test tube. The Great Enlightenment of the eighteenth century, in which Edwards was a leader, was as international as romanticism. The Unitarian secession at the turn of the century, and other relaxations from Calvinism, were inevitable results of secular prosperity and intellectual interests turned away from the problems of God to the interesting manœuvres of man. And although the progressive commonwealth of Pennsylvania in Franklin's time could provide a background for science, and the whole seaboard thought about economics and politics in general as well as in local aspects, concern for the relation to conduct and hope of the man living under strictly American conditions and an agent responsible for his own evolution, had not shaken free from conventional doctrines.

It has never shaken free and at the same time mounted to audacious, vigorous speculation except in New England and in this brief period. The soil and the time and the men were ripe. New England in the second quarter of the century was at a moment not duplicated before or after, a pausing time between first development and the quicker tempo of the Civil War and subsequent industrial prosperity.* Wealth enough had accumulated to give leisure for thought and experience; new wealth was for the moment not readily acquired at home. The West was draining young and active bodies; the town, newly industrialized, was draining the country. Shipping was beginning to decline, agriculture was definitely going backward, machine industry was still in the experimental stage. The population of New England through these years of the twenties to the forties increased but slowly. In some States there were actual declines. It was stock-taking time for an old country at the edge of a new continent.

It was a moment also when the balance was nicely held between a country (not a forest) environment and the new city, which was no longer an outpost of Europe or an overgrown village, but a unit of a new megalopolitan culture, where men were insensibly transformed. Boston, New York, Philadelphia, Charleston, were civilizations, especially Boston. And Emerson, thanks to the circumstances of the moment, could live outside in Concord and be a Bostonian. Both cultures were his—and neither a shadow of the other. "Good-bye, proud world! I'm going home," he wrote when at nineteen he escaped to the "wilds" of Roxbury. But the gesture had other meanings. He was city-broken and city-trained, but a rural philosopher.

The quality in the air of this middle age of New England that made it unique was a sense of moral duty which

* A possible exception may be noted for the turn of the 1900's.

became creative as soon as it escaped from the "you ought" to the "I." Emerson was living in the tradition of dedicated men and women who had made conceptions of the right will dominant if not common in the community. Speculation upon conduct was as natural to them as breathing. The will had been set free by the breakdown of Calvinism, made free by the absorption of new and liberal ideas from science and philosophy and new and liberal ideas as to the rights of the individual, but never for one instant was it freed from the necessity to think for the spiritual benefit of man. Two centuries had made that sense of necessity as native to the New England intellectual as shrewdness and ingenuity to the Yankee trader and manufacturer.

There is a letter written by Madame Emerson to her son William at Harvard that is indicative—"You did right to give me so early proof of your affection as to write me the first week of your college life. Everything respecting you is doubtless interesting to me, but your domestic arrangements the least of anything, as these make no part of the man or the character further than he learns humility from his dependence on such trifles as *convenient accommodations* for his happiness. You, I trust, will rise superior to these little things, for, though small indeed, they consume much time that might be appropriated to better purpose and for nobler pursuits. What most excites my solicitude is your moral improvement and your progress in virtue. . . . Should Paul plant and Apollos water, it is God above who can give the increase." *

This letter might be coupled with many others in the period of American austerity, from parents who felt that prayer was more important than a carpet, but its intellectual background cannot readily be duplicated. The dedicated intellectual in New England breathed a moral

* "Society and Solitude," Centenary Edition, noted, p. 355.

air in which responsibility was a live and creative thing.

And Emerson was so much a creature of this tradition that with all his challenging he never seriously questioned the fact of his moral responsibility. His fine free mind was played upon by the rays of a moral influence so native to his light that like the violet rays of the sun they were felt without conscious sight. He was one of those lucky men who are borne on the crest of the wave of time, already of the future, but swung on by the past. By a happy blend of environmental necessity and personal choice he stood between two worlds, the moral-ethical interest in ideas and conduct of his traditions, and the scientific interest in habit and practice of the modern world. He carried the will to salvation of theology into the individualism of personal responsibility, and so became the first great mediator between God and the machine. More of this later.

This dedication to spiritual welfare (I will not for the moment try to define the term) is obviously the first objective in a critique of Emerson. It is, as the behaviorists say, his conditioned reflex, and it is also, in a sense that behaviorists do not admit, the will of the man himself. Being what he was, in Boston, in Cambridge, and in Concord, he could not do otherwise. In a strong and growing country, such a habit of mind as the New England Puritan's does not die with its logical premises, it sublimates, transfers its object, becomes as among the English Puritans of the Revolution a discipline, or among the descendants of the American Puritans, a will to succeed. Take away the felt necessity of placating an angry God, and the tension presses elsewhere—upon ends and aims indifferently material or moral according to the nature of the man and his experiences. Emerson, who was a churchman, and a priest by inheritance of a strong church that had made a government, did not leave it by resigning his pastorate because its doctrines were still too little individualistic for his temperament. He remained in the church militant, dedicated to the saving of men's minds and through their minds their souls. As the most representative man of a thinking, aspiring New England, his will is the shadow of the American energy that subdued the West, organized the greatest capitalistic state in the world, exploited the resources of a continent, and controlled nature beyond every experience. Or his will and hope are the substance, set more and more remotely from our actual accomplishment, and our energy in business is the shadow, now by extensions grossly perverted! Emerson, the Civil War, and Henry Ford were all hatched from the same nest.

It is the conscious and inevitable dedication that set this fine figure of a man, with his deep blue eyes, slightly stooped head, and persuasive voice, apart from the American men of letters of his time who were not born in and of New England. Unlike Cooper and Irving, he was a thinker by conscious training, a difference that accounts for the world away of his masterful prose from Cooper's slouchiness and Irving's borrowed polish. This writer was inevitable, Cooper by accident, Irving by ambition and imitation. From Poe his intellectual heritage makes a fundamental difference, although in other respects the men are more alike. Poe was born poet and made himself a critic by the crooked road of journalism, but Emerson, as his "Journals" show, took to thinking not as a means of livelihood, or even as a necessity for self-expression, but as the first duty of existence. He wrote as a mind responsible for truth, which accounts for his success as a prophet but strictly limits the kind of pleasure to be got from him. He is a Sunday man, where Cooper, Irving, and Poe are good for weekdays also. Truth may be identical with beauty, but which the seeker chooses for emphasis makes an important difference in his work. Emerson sought beauty because of its relations to the truth to which he was dedicated. This, and his temperament, and Concord, set him apart from Cooper, Irving, and Poe as Wordsworth was set apart from Byron, though both were English romanticists.

Nevertheless, Emerson was as American as Plato was Greek, more deeply American, I think, than any of his contemporaries in literature, for Poe was an accident in our culture, Irving's Federalism a phase, Cooper's romantic republicanism is a dream, while Emerson, peculiar product of a peculiar sectionalism, made American idealism conscious, and self-conscious, and stamped it with a mark that may be indelible. Like New England itself, he has educated America by problems that, however general, were first raised in Massachusetts.

3.

REDUCED to general terms his ideas are not as original (one supposes) as Plato's. But warm from their New England nest they have the durable form that comes from a vital relation to immediate circumstance. The relativity of truth explains this seeming contradiction. The immediate, when truly observed, has a validity denied to more abstract considerations. And so it is with Emerson, who sometimes transcends philosophy when he is least logical, because he pointed always home—a home that, as it happened, was the cradle of a generous share of the Western future. He proposed to shape a people—no less—toward a destiny that he believed to be possible, and began, being shrewdly Yankee, with his own folks. He failed, naturally, but may yet succeed in so far as success is given to such efforts. For Emerson is not yet done. He does not belong with the philosophers whose criticism, like Carlyle's, has gone into the abstract of useful generalization, but with the prophets whose time is not yet out.

His gospel is worth understanding, then, for more reasons than one. It is a true gospel—a religion, not a philosophy, although its philosophic bases and ornaments have misled the Emersonians into trying to systematize it throughout. Vain endeavor, for what logic ever embraced the intuitions of the creative mind! The essence of this gospel is reasoned faith, its strength not consistency but insight. And it is as clearly a gospel for America as Paul's was for the Thessalonians, and with the same extensions of adaptability to a wider world. Furthermore, it is a gospel in time as well as in space, and far more richly documented by thought upon the circumstances of a new industrial, scientific, democratic, age just beginning than students of sources have realized or seekers for inspiration cared to know.

Emerson's doctrine is simple, his applications are not difficult except when in his later years a preacher's enthusiasm whirls him over difficulties with a mystic optimism; it is his rhetoric as of a Delphic oracle that seemed difficult to his contemporaries, although chiefly, it would appear, when he was read, not heard. So is the New Testament difficult in its prophetic passages, and Isaiah or Jeremiah even more so. The seeker for the One Truth, for Harmony, for a Revelation, must by rhetorical necessity flash and reflash his thought through the world's obscurations, experimentally adjusting his inner light to shine upon diverse circumstance. It is this which makes the Orphic utterance, the prophetic staccato of the oracle. The thought runs not forward in a line, but back and forth from the centre to the periphery—from idea to subject. Emerson must be read like a translation of a classic text, with constant reference to the original idea. There is no incoherence and no real inconsequence in him, but (as in the Bible or his early admiration, Bacon's "Essays") a progression in which he moves ahead by diagonals instead of a curve. Compare a paragraph from Macaulay with the Emersonian mosaic of apothegms, which he lifted usually from his "Journals" and joined to each other by a basic thought; as for example in "Experience"—

"How easily, if fate would suffer it, we might keep forever these beautiful limits, and adjust ourselves, once for all, to the perfect calculation of the kingdom of known cause and effect. . . . But ah! presently comes a day, or is it only a half-hour, with its angel—whispering—which discomfits the conclusions of nations and of years! . . . Life is a series of surprises, and would not be worth taking or keeping, if it were not. God delights to isolate us every day, and hide from us the past and the future. We would look about us, but with grand politeness he draws down before us an impenetrable screen of purest sky, and another behind us of purest sky. 'You will not remember,' he seems to say, 'and you will not expect.' All good conversation, manners, and action come from a spontaneity which forgets usages and makes the moment great. Nature hates calculators; her methods are saltatory and impulsive. . . . I would gladly be moral, and keep due metes and bounds, which I dearly love, and allow the most to the will of man, but I have set my heart on honesty in this chapter, and I can see nothing at last, in success or failure, than more or less of vital force supplied from the Eternal. The results of life are uncalculated and uncalculable. The years teach much which the days never know."

The gospel of Emerson is as consistent as his applications are sometimes inconsistent.*

Nature in its broadest sense is the serene and inviolable expression of the Creator. Spiritual and immaterial in its essence (as physicists later were to discover), it is a phenomenon that is the present expositor of the divine mind.

---

* It is interesting to note his rationalizations, first of pacifism and then, under the stress of conflict, of war, as recorded in his "Journals."

Man as a function of nature is a creature of the same divine will. He is the entrance to thought and virtue, its faculty for consciousness. Hence his duty and opportunity is to control as much of nature as he can (including naturally himself), and his method of control is to put himself in harmony not merely with this or that, but with as much of the all as he can grasp.

This nature is to be loved, but not believed in (since it is probably immaterial), except in relation to ideas. For ideas are immortal, necessary, increated natures. "No man fears age or misfortune or death in their serene company, for he is transported outside the district of change." And since man himself through nature has access to the mind of the Creator (for the world proceeds from the same spirit as the body of man), is indeed himself the Creator in the finite, it is ideas that he will seek in nature, and specifically the moral law, for nature is highly useful to us only in its moral relationships.

Whatever befalls is part of the lesson, ugly, beautiful, good, bad, for there is only a whole—each creature is only a modification of the others, all is a unity. The discovery of truth lies in a harmony between man and his total environment. Art is but a representation of the truth to be found in nature, a plotting of certain curves; logic, the plotting of other curves; science, the relating of some causes with some effects. A great man—a genius—embraces more in his scope, a weak man or a gross is narrow in his grasp. We take what we can, and also what we will.

"All science has one aim, namely, to find a theory of nature."

"Every rational creature has all nature for his dowry and estate. It is his, if he will."

I have taken the preceding paragraphs chiefly from Emerson's first essay on nature, which contains in its fresh thinking, either directly or by implication, all the best in

Emerson. In his idea of nature lie, half unfolded, "The Over-Soul," "Self-Reliance," "Compensations," and the creative religion of the "Divinity School Address." Grant the unity of man and nature and God, grant moral responsibility, grant the possibility of control by harmony, and everything else follows. Even so, without a luminous faith and constant application to known and vital circumstance, this fundament of Emerson would be a cold idea, such an abstraction as is Platonism for the scholar in philosophy. But held as a glistening touchstone against the world's thought and his own experience, made to seem possible by his own environment of serene woods, of dedicated men and women, and given the sinew of opposition by the Yankee realism of a race that was already bent upon turning nature into cash, it became a diagnosis and a prophecy, a faith and a religion.

To call his religion Transcendentalism is to disregard Emerson's plain dissatisfaction with the term. Transcendentalism for him was only a definition of his method. The professional Transcendentalists of his day he regarded as useful fanatics who, like the research scientists of ours, might discover the unexpected because their method was right. To define his faith as the religion of optimism is equally inadequate. Emerson's idea was capable of a turn either way. Recognizing the inexorability of a nature that sacrificed the individual to the race, and accepting whatever lesson it taught, he was able to trust it only because he found a slight balance on the side of good and reason.* When he had an overdose of Alcott's bright hope that by taking thought any New Englander might soar above his mills and pine trees and merely exist in the æther of pure idea like a swallow in a vacuum, he could believe in man degenerating beyond the possibility of harmony with nature. And in "Experience," where he tests his philosophy

* See "The Young American."

by his own least cheerful observations, he is almost a pessimist. To say that Emerson's religion is a negation of misery, sin, degeneracy, and pain, is nonsense. It is a synthesis of them, with the emphasis placed, where he felt it, upon other elements of life. He knew the irreconcilable when he saw it, but, good preacher that he was, threw his voice toward the outlet from the dilemma. If he was an optimist it was because his New England wished optimism and could do more with it than pessimism. He believed it to be the "higher reason." Christian Science, philosophically considered, is an imperfect generalization from Emerson, and would certainly have been repudiated by the Yankee and the rationalist in him, though the mystic would have suffered it gladly, as he suffered the New England reformers. The weak, idealistic optimism of good Americans who expect wars' ending and the disappearance of vice by pious wishing is the decadence of Emersonism—wish without idea or will.

Emerson's religion is better defined as the faith of a moralist who believed that the divine will was implicit and perceptible in the universe. With such a belief the inheritance of Puritan will was bound to set a weight of responsibility upon the individual to feel and see and know. It was an individualist's religion. Thus Emerson is more rigorous than Calvin, who said do so and so and you may be saved, whereas this New England gospel declares, seek, try, find, know, and if you fail it is due not to original sin or to a lack of grace, but to your own disabilities. The Quakers were content with inner light, but Emerson, sprung from a harsher discipline, and a stronger will, rationalizes this inner light and lifts it out of mysticism into a doctrine for intelligent men. The Quaker sought peace, but Emerson, action—a "practical idealism."

Both the Quakers and Emerson narrowed religion to the individual, but the Quakers sacrificed the intellect to

contentment and a good conscience, while Emerson broad-
ened his religion to pervade man's contacts from wild
nature to the last efforts of a sophisticated society, from
the south wind to the political state. Passion alone he gave
little thought to, because, except in ideas, he never felt it.

You must take Emerson as an authority upon microcosm and macrocosm, upon the whole man and the cosmos,
or not at all. His interests involve capitalism and the rhodora, evolution and friendship, the direction of thought
and the exhilaration of walking in the woods. As a religion
his gospel is limited only by its logic, which provides for
no personal warmth in the Deity, and by the temperament
and training of the founder, who disregarded some of the
evident facts of humanity, which his enthusiasm left lying
like blocks unfitted for the arch. Thus it is too much to
say that Emerson is either all right or all wrong. Yet one
can safely assert that his belief in the possible perfectibility of man through self-development, into a harmony
with the evolving idea of the world, is either folly or, in
principle, universally applicable and relatively true.

4.

MY BUSINESS is not with doctrine, but with what Emerson
himself might have called the pragmatic value of his religion for life and literature.

The moral responsibility of Emerson has but lightly descended upon our shoulders. We are moralistic here in
America, but not thoughtful. Nature in a boy-scout world
is a recreation and a discipline, scarcely a responsibility
and a religion. But in one respect Emerson's conception
of self-reliant man has profoundly influenced our thinking.
His philosophy is evidently shot through, determined as
to its immediate ends, and defined as regards its social
purpose, by a passionate obsession with democracy. His
philosophy is the spiritual ultimate of the town meeting,

as the government of Connecticut was its political ultimate. Emerson himself was a democrat only by relativity.
He was aristocratic in intellect and the descendant of conscious intellectual aristocrats. His tastes were aristocratic
—eminently so in books, and in wine, for which he had a
gentleman's taste. He longed for hearty contacts with un-
discriminated man but held back, protecting himself "by
solitude, or by courtesy," to conceal "his incapacity for
useful association." * I doubt whether he was troubled by
what used so to distress his Aunt Mary, the waste of time
that might have been spent in contemplating God. He ate
apple pie for breakfast—as is described in an unpublished
anecdote—with an air that left his rather horrified hosts
of a less crusty region impressed and shaken in their idea
of propriety.

But as a man thinking he was committed to the theory
that good resides in the potentiality of men, if not every
man, and his whole philosophy may be construed as a
defense of the thesis that, given the opportunity, we can
grow strong if not great, achieve harmony with nature if
we are not born harmonious. The world for Emerson was
and remained a Concord, where of one hundred men and
women, seventy were rising in the world, economically,
intellectually, or spiritually, five had symptoms of greatness, twenty at most were clods, and five imbecile, degenerate, or rawly Irish. From no other society could a theory
of the infinite potentiality of man on his own responsibility and by his own endeavors have so easily arisen, and
even so it took the will to success of Puritanism to give it
such splendid confidence. No, only a New England, with
a boundless West over the Alleghenies and a Europe across
the seas loaded with importable riches of the intellect,
could have formed an Emerson.

They say that this idealistic cement of democratic

* "Nominalist and Realist."

thinking has crumbled from Emerson's program; that democracy, having proven not to be like Concord, not to be an increasing harmony with nature, but rather out of tune with every finer note, is proof that he belongs with Alcott and Owen and Fourier, and the other dreamers of a hopeful day—sentimentalists who set too high an estimate upon fellow man. In a class there is hope—in democracy none.

But this is a judgment as absurd as it is premature, whether passed upon Emerson's idealism, or upon the heartier democracy of his disciple, Walt Whitman. The relativity of truth was familiar to Emerson before it was deduced from the science of Einstein. He wrote of a possible New England, as George Fox wrote of a possible world of Friends. His eloquence made it seem probable, but in any case it remains an ideal, which is all that can be asked of a political philosophy. It is not difficult to assemble from the essays and lectures a prophetic picture of the United States as it is today,* a capitalistic plutocracy, intent upon comfort, not blind to spiritual and intellectual uplift, but vague in all aims except the material welfare of the average man. Nature, he felt, proceeded by such exaggerations, and it is clear that the argument works as well against progress as for it. But unless there are physiological handicaps that Emerson did not suspect, or unless there is truth in the Spenglerian thesis that cultures move by cycles in which the will to be better which Emerson counted upon is slowly drained from the race, there can be no denial that the potential development of the individual is a practical ideal that may again overturn our social orders and remake society. And Emerson's belief that by controlling nature man can represent more of God in himself, as a religion and as a philosophy is more tenable, more fruitful, and more probable than the ab-

* See, for example, "Nature" in "Essays, Second Series."

stractions of the rights of man and the romanticism of the noble primitive with which democracy began. What is obvious is that Emersonism in its social phases sprang from American circumstances, and has profoundly influenced our ideas of social and political development. We are still democrats by faith if not by practice, and when we think now of democracy it is in terms not of Jefferson but of Emerson, of potentiality, not of right.

5.

EVEN more cogent to problems of the only time that is vital for us, our own, is another aspect of Emerson's prophecy, his religion of science.

And here it is essential to alter completely the conventional idea of Emerson.* He was a moralist certainly, who considered art, politics, sex relations, nature, social intercourse (the English, he said, joked too much), and science no less, as means for the conduct of life. Who shall deny him the right to do so, however it colored his definitions and limited the truth of his observation! At present the reverse is in favor, where, by a curious perversion of logic, all conclusions are suspicious if they can be used for moral ends. We believe in nature as a mechanism that governs our supplies of heat, light, food, and power, but distrust any further significance. Emerson trusted the significance but believed only in the idea behind the phenomena. It is nip and tuck which is right, but the odds are on Emerson. Pragmatically speaking, each faith gets what it seeks.

But granted the Puritan moralism, Emerson was its Dionysos. He is the vital spirit of intellectual joy breaking out in a New England become numb and dead except to industrial development and dry moralizing. Boston,

* A detailed study of Emerson's knowledge of science has been made since this chapter was written, by Harry Hayden Clark, and published in *The Philological Quarterly*, July, 1931.

says Henry Adams, was by 1800 intellectually dead. The effort of Unitarianism was negative, not positive. It said what not to believe; there was relief but no fire in it. Emerson, so cold and shy in his personal relations, was in faith, hope, and creative thinking a white fire burning through convention and all hindering obscurantism. He spoke to the young—as he may again. He sought tinder for his spark; he made tinder; his essential warmth is revealed in his eloquence, where alone he could make literature, but still more in the intellectual emotion of which that eloquence, so often happy in its rhythms, so often phrasing itself in apothegms that have passed into world circulation, was the garment.

And if nature in its abstract aspects was the subject of his most ardent contemplation, in the concrete his mind was most quickly lit by experimental science. He belongs to the romantic age of modern science. The basis of mathematical theory lies behind him in the seventeenth and eighteenth centuries. The shift to large-scale experiment with an improved technique came in his youth. The first startling innovations of applied science were under his eye. The great discoveries of Lamarck, Tyndall, Pasteur, electricity, thermodynamics, biology, are contemporaneous with his own intellectual development. Evolution was a familiar with him before Darwin stated its terms in exact observation; he guessed at the new physics—guessed, for example, that science would demonstrate the immateriality of matter; was cognizant of sociology; traced in his writings the curve that mounted toward the control of natural phenomenon. Crystals, water power, plant structure, psychology, were germane to his thinking. There would be little to surprise him in the twentieth century, unless it be our faith in material comfort as a safeguard of civilization. He read the Greek and Oriental philosophers and Shakespeare and the seventeenth century poets in order to enter into the heart of what the best men had felt about their world, but his fascinated obsession with science (in striking contrast to all other American men of letters except Thoreau, and in his amateur, romantic fashion, Poe) is proof that he felt the presence of new evidence and guessed that a time for a new synthesis was inevitable. In England it was the men of science as much as the men of letters that he wished to meet. Of his two terms, man and nature, he saw that nature certainly through a wide arc, and man in his physical aspects, were to have a new analysis that would give a philosopher, poet, and prophet an opportunity denied since Aristotle. He was premature, but probably right. *

Science to Emerson was not an end in itself, but a new tool for thinking. That is why he is so tremendously excited by scientific ideas. He saw, as if by miracle, the lost pieces in the world's picture puzzle being picked up and dusted one by one. The puzzle was all he cared about. He was no seeker of parts. It was the whole or nothing for him. Science that stopped with dissection was useful only for dissection. No knowledge was possible by facts alone. "Therefore the soul holds itself off from a too trivial and microscopic study of the universal tablet." "Empirical science is apt to cloud the sight." "The best read naturalist . . . will see . . . that much . . . of his relation to the world . . . is not to be learned by any addition or subtraction . . . of known quantities . . . but by untaught sallies of the spirit." As Horatio said in "Hamlet," to consider too curiously is to befog all conclusions. Yes, know the plants and birds as Thoreau did (the modern naturalist would say better, Thoreau as a scientist was a

* The obvious parallel person is Goethe. The two men should be discussed in comparison and in contrast. Emerson's lack of a creative imagination in the concrete was no handicap to his philosophic perceptions, which reach further ahead than Goethe's.

bit of an Emersonian), study the elements, classify the animals, disintegrate atoms, but do not forget that all this has no significance except as it enables man to relate himself to nature and thus increase his happiness and elevate his conduct.

And furthermore (heresy and damnation for the modern researcher) investigation must be a controlled research, not controlled in the scientist's sense, who speaks of a controlled experiment, but controlled in its issues. "In inquiries respecting the laws of the world and the frame of things, the highest reason is always the truest." "Nature is useful only in its moral relationships" (he means useful for the soul—he would have willingly used an electric refrigerator and been enthusiastic over an airplane, but for practical use, not for wisdom). The most industrious scientist will never be a great man if he keeps his reasoning down to the level of facts—if he says, here is a brachycephalous skull, I care not what it means—if he spends his one life on a fact without turning that fact again to life.

Here is the source and spring of Emerson's weakness as a contemporary thinker, and here, by a strange paradox, is his strong value for the present. His genius saw the complete implications of scientific research in its very germ and bud. What he did not see, what temperamentally he could not see, what his preoccupation with moral values prevented him from seeing, was that scientific analysis had to be carried through to the end before final conclusions were drawn. I mean carried through to the last detail even if, according to his own prescription, it was concerned only with the higher reasons that teach the meaning and conduct of life. He went gladly into the laboratory, but as a preacher seeking a text, not as a scientist determined to get to the end of fact, not even as a philosopher resolved to base his conclusions upon every evidence. He accepted "whatever befalls as part of the lesson," but he was much more concerned with the lesson than the befalling. He grasped evolution, but applied it to moral values before anyone knew how, or if, it really worked. Today he would grasp the theory of mutation as a prime cause of animal change, or electronic structure as a proof of non-materiality, without waiting for further evidence. Emerson's doctrine throughout, whether in its reference to democracy or to the unity of nature, suffers from premature generalization. He guessed too soon. Three quarters of our valid additions to specific and indubitable knowledge of the nature of matter, animate and inanimate, would still be unknown if the scientist had controlled his investigations according to Emerson's own practice.

Like most poets, preachers, and metaphysicians, he burst into conclusions at a spark of evidence. The new science had discovered fundamental laws of nature: ergo, man, being a moral creature, would use these laws for his own self-development. There are three assumptions here —that they are laws of nature, that man is a moral creature, and that self-development means what Emerson wanted it to mean. We now have reason to doubt the laws as such, are less sure than Emerson that man is potentially moral, and have learned much more about the nature of self-development in the human animal than he so much as guessed.

But in philosophy it is the wrong who usually are right. The audacious spirit springs after elusive truth and catches at least a tail feather while duller minds are still beating the underbrush. It becomes clearer and clearer that in principle Emerson was poetically, prophetically, and even scientifically right. Research in facts approaches its term so far as the nature of life is involved, and can go little further in conduct without the aid of philosophic thinking. Physics has demonstrated the non-existence of matter in any definable sense. Biology may be on the eve of proving that the development of living forms—which being matter are themselves non-existent in the material sense—is subject to controls not determinable by cause and effect. Spengler has dared to assemble from all history what he regards as proof that cause and effect are not the determinants of the life of cultures, which mature and decline for reasons inherent in the force that makes them. The time for controlled investigation, in which "the universal tablet" shall be studied for the significance of facts not in themselves significant, if not overdue is soon to be expected. We have an unbalanced civilization in which we can control nature for our comfort, but not ourselves, nor even direct our thinking toward any explanation of progress that would satisfy a second-rate philosopher. Even the inarticulate scientist of our day has begun to speculate upon the meaning of his discoveries, and he sounds like a childish Emerson.

The man was clearly right. We must find what science means—if anything—for man as a moral animal, as a conscious mind endeavoring to represent a harmony. Hygiene, diet, prosperity, behavior, adaptability, tool-using, are all secondary to the desired end. And even if there is no harmony, but only incoherence outside the efforts of the reason, even if Emerson's man thinking in harmony with the creative will is an artifice, the problem is not altered. The will to create such a man is precisely as valid an entity as the description of a cave dweller. Not knowledge, but knowledge controlled for conduct as we control it now for dynamos, is the desideratum. Becoming, enjoying, being, not knowing, are the only ultimate justifications of experimental research.

Prophets are not good at details. Emerson was precipitate, as fortunate men are likely to be. For him the rhythms of his pine woods and the discoveries of his scientists toned by gradations not always logical into a unity.

He had the aristocratic faculty of disregarding the petty, the gross, and the insignificant, whether in men or in art. His intuitions worked in a happy environment dangerously electric for a hopeful nature. Like earlier prophets he seized upon signs and portents at the moment of their rising. If he did not deduce war from comets, he drew a new God from the first hint of a nebular hypothesis. He could not wait for proof. But we all come back to prophecy sooner or later. We learn that the rainbow is made of water drops; we learn that drops of water split the white light ray; we learn that light is a vibration that can only be metaphysically considered; and so we come back to the rainbow and the meaning of beauty for man. Well, that is Emerson.

6.

BUT how shall we rank this poet-prophet, this scientist-preacher, in literature? He believed that substance and form were identical, one determining the other, and that if he should speak true he would speak beautifully. Can the pulse of his thought be taken by the form he gave to it?

In the few university classrooms where American literature was discussed twenty years ago, a favorite subject for argument was whether Emerson should be regarded as a man of letters or a philosopher. Professor Beers, of Yale, an acute and sympathetic critic who had known Emerson, held, as I remember, that he was too philosophical for literature and that his essential worth was in ideas, not in belles lettres.

The argument, I now believe, was idle, for the terms were wrong. Emerson was a poet by bent, a philosopher by training, but in the synthesis of all his faculties and most of all his will, a preacher—and preaching, good preaching, is literature. His philosophy is a preacher's philosophy, his science a preacher's science. As a man of letters he was conditioned by the preacher's need precisely as Mark Twain was conditioned by the lecture platform, or Sheridan by the stage. His merits are the qualities of controlled and eloquent persuasion; his faults the faults of a pulpiteer.

Oratory in college and afterwards was Emerson's particular study. The technique of delivery and diction was as native to his environment as woodcraft to the pioneer. He was born of a long succession of public speakers, accustomed to command by the voice. *To express*—whether by poetry or prose, pen or speech, pulpit or platform, essay or sermon—was not only his ambition but his confident expectation from his earliest years. His astonishing Aunt Mary wrote to him and talked to him, to draw out the answering mind. His Journal, in which for a lifetime he set down, not incidents so much as every idea, problem, observation, all moulded into expression and ready for use, was a preacher's storehouse—the richest of barrels—from which he drew whenever he spoke or wrote. It was in 1824 that he wrote in this Journal—

"I inherit from my sire a formality of manner and speech, but I derive from him, or his patriotic parent, a passionate love for the strains of eloquence. I burn after the 'aliquid immensum infinitumque' which Cicero desired."

It is a corollary, not a coincidence, that Emerson was born in the age of the lyceum lecture. A people that had taken their intellectual satisfactions in the dialectics of theology, now transferred the same kind of interest to mental and moral improvement. As the expressive Yankee phrase put it, they wanted to know. It was a symptom of the transition from the will to be saved to the will to succeed.

But this corollary was important for Emerson. He was a man of slender means who had to get additional income. When he left the church, he had no choice but to sell his

166

expressiveness, either to the eye or to the ear. Teaching was the first resource of every New England intellectual, but for a man with a preacher's training and ideas lecturing was an easier and more profitable way, and the lyceum lecture system made possible a career. It was a compromise that has wrecked many an American writer since, who finds that he can wholesale his thoughts, making large profits out of a quick turnover, instead of speculating in new models. But Emerson was a professional. The lecture confirmed his habit of preaching, but the necessity for carrying, as the preacher and lecturer must, a single idea into complex experience, was exactly adapted to a prophetic doctrine simple in itself but cosmic in its applications. All that he had of poetry, all that he had of orderly logic, which was not much, all his great powers of eloquence, were fused by a sense of audience into a prose that must be compared with the great divines of seventeenth century England, with Bossuet and Pascal, with Augustine and Paul, in order to orient its literary bearings. He made a platform his pulpit, and humanized into literature what was too heterodox for the church.

Forensic literature asks for an immense preparation in thought, but an informality in actual expression, as of talk where the idea flows and flashes. Its unit is not the paragraph as in essay-writing, or the stanza as in poetry, but the sentence. Its coherence is not so much the logic of developing thought as a process of saturation. What is said must open the mind and then sink in, and it must open and sink more than once. An effective sermon or an effective lecture is like a stream trickling over sandy ground, flowing by pools and runs; here it races, there it reaches its objective in a perfect mirror of thought, then it turns back to follow the dip of the thirsty land. And the style of forensic literature is a style of eloquence—eloquence in the two senses, first of perfect expression (like the forensic of Pope) and second, of emotion rhythmically phrased, and lifting into beauty.

Emerson's prose was an echo of his own free-moving intuitions but it was ordered by the subtle needs of an audience listening to the spoken word:

"In this refulgent summer, it has been a luxury to draw the breath of life. The grass grows, the buds burst, the meadow is spotted with fire and gold in the tint of the flowers. The air is full of birds, and sweet with the breath of the pine, the balm-of-Gilead, and the new hay. Night brings no gloom to the heart with its welcome shade. Through the transparent darkness the stars pour their almost spiritual rays. Man under them seems a young child, and his huge globe a toy. The cool night bathes the world as with a river, and prepares his eyes again for the crimson dawn. The mystery of nature was never displayed more happily. . . .

"But when the mind opens and reveals the laws which traverse the universe and make things what they are, then shrinks the great world at once into a mere illustration and fable of this mind. What am I? and what is? asks the human spirit with a curiosity new-kindled but never to be quenched. Behold these outrunning laws, which our imperfect apprehension can see tend this way and that, but not come full circle. Behold these infinite relations, so like, so unlike; many, yet one. I would study, I would know, I would admire forever. These works of thought have been the entertainments of the human spirit in all ages." *

This is eloquence of one kind, but more notable are the passages of apothegm in which Emerson has entered world literature:

"A sect or party is an elegant incognito devised to save a man from the vexation of thinking."

* "Divinity College Address," 1838. Or see the opening paragraph in "Nature" of "Essays, Second Series."

"Whoso would be a man must be a nonconformist. He who would gather immortal palms must not be hindered by the name of goodness, but explore if it be goodness. Nothing is at last sacred but the integrity of your own mind."

"Beauty is the harmony which nature offers to a great and harmonious soul."

"So much of nature as he is ignorant of, so much of his own mind he does not possess."

"An institution is the lengthened shadow of one man."

These are chiseled phrases, but between their niceties Emerson preferred to fly upon winged words. He was trained to soar, and this is his weakness. He cannot patiently write except for an audience. His essays, as I have said before, are rows of brilliant apothegms united by runs of eloquence, and transitions that do not so much lead on as prepare a setting. An Emersonian essay is made of sparks, glitters, and set pieces; these, with the central idea, is what one remembers. The preacher presents not an argument, but a series of amplifications of his text. The fiery wheel turns, but there is no more movement ahead than in a pinwheel; a gush of shining words flows out from the centre. It is the very method of the greatest of poetic prose, the English of the psalmists and the prophets in the King James version. In style, as in purpose and accomplishment, Emerson may be a minor poet, but he is a major prophet in the tradition of the oracles.

It is not necessary to cite Emerson's lack of ear, and his insensibility to music, to explain his failure to be the poet of his dreams. He had not the patience for poetry, and his rationale for poets—that art is the path of the creator to his work, and in following it the poet is warmed and carried away by his thought *—shows too plainly that labor grew irksome to him once his prophetic soul was aroused.

* "The Poet."

His insistence upon expression as both the result and the test of truth is as modern as Croce, but he was widely inconsistent in practice. For his preacher's purpose, delay was fatal. He would rush the boundaries of expression like a man talking, and for such eloquence the irregular rhythm of prose was the better medium. His poems, with few exceptions, are like hurdle races; only at intervals does he rise in easy flight to poetry, in between he is bound to an earthy beat. He would not work on a regular rhythm because a regular rhythm was not what he needed. How tame his rather tiresome four-stress metres are beside the surging eloquence of his best prose! How feeble and limited his scope in verse by comparison with the lilts and golden moments of his lectures! It is significant that his favorite instrument was the inconsequential, irregular Æolian harp, sounding to the caprices of the wind. The genius, he thought, should let God flow through him; immediate inspiration, it appears, makes better prose than verse!

Indeed, the merits of Emerson's poetry are prose merits. He has written great lines of poetry as has every prose writer, but they are lines, such as

> And striving to be man, the worm
> Mounts through all the spires of form,

or the famous lines of "Brahma" or "Forbearance" or "Forerunners," or the end of "Voluntaries," in which the idea reaches final expression in a passage that happens to be verse. They differ in no real sense from the poetry of his prose. It is all in "Merlin":

> Great is the art,
> Great be the manners, of the bard
> He shall not his brain encumber
> With the coil of rhythm and number;
> But, leaving rule and pale forethought,

He shall aye climb
For his rhyme.
"Pass in, pass in," the angels say,
"In to the upper doors,
Nor count compartments of the floors,
But mount to paradise
By the stairway of surprise."

Emerson, in short, preferred the elevator to the old-fashioned stairs. He had no time to be a minor poet of perfection, the author of a hundred poems as good as "Days." His inclination, though strongly poetical, was bent away from a technical perfection by an urgency to use not the best words in their best order, though this he often attained, but the best order for his persuasive thoughts. It was not poetry he wanted, but to use poetry. One of his few bad judgments in literature was to put Tennyson of "The Idylls" above Shelley. He was a preacher.

7.

EMERSON's writings, with the exception of a few poems, were all produced in middle age. His first book was published when he was thirty-three, and if this rightly famous "Nature" contains the heart of his thinking, it was a result of long pondering, amply recorded in his earlier Journal. The later essays and poems are followed in the notes to the Centenary Edition by trains of parallel passages, earlier phrasings, and repetitions in different figures. There was time therefore to rationalize by his theory of the representative nature of art everything that he cared to preserve in print.

Good painting, good poetry, good architecture, like the good acts of good men, he believed to be the capture of wider arcs of nature than ordinary men could see. They represented a true perception of the harmony between man and the creative spirit exhibited in the universe. This truth, divined and organized, became beauty. Talent forced its way toward the harmony, the lucid perceptive mind of genius let the harmony flow through. This is the Emersonian æsthetics, and Emerson's own attempted practice. Expression was his goal, not the beauty of form for itself that Poe felt so keenly. He knew that beauty also, but would ask, what was the truth it represented? For himself he preferred to know what he was expressing. The artist, he said in "Culture," should have no wife, no family; he should be a devotee to his art. But Emerson had a mistress, duty, and in a more concrete sense, a congregation, of readers and listeners that wanted to know, that had to be exhorted, striven with, taught. His æsthetics was an æsthetics of controlled self-expression precisely like his rationale for science. Art was something to be used—for the highest uses certainly, but still to be gauged by its ultimate usefulness.

Such ideas, consciously held, put limits upon his appreciation as well as the scope of his work. He distrusted all novelists, believing that in their so facile attempts to make man they had stacked the cards for their own purposes. The reader got amusement, but not truth. Hence his somewhat patronizing attitude toward Hawthorne. He believed in him, but not in Hester. She was not truly representative; there was more artistry than nature in her.* Hence again his disdain of "chatterers," like Jane Austen. Worldly, unimportant people, humorously expressing foibles of no "survival value," as the biologists say, seemed to him unworthy of attention. With his eyes always on the top of Olympus he could not be amused by the pleasant inns on its slope. Emerson was often happy, but seldom amused. Humor was not his gift. Prophets seldom possess it.

His æsthetics hampered him, but he could have used no

* His comment on Hawthorne is well known. I deduce his opinion of Hester.

other. The man was bent by circumstance toward art as duty, but he bent readily. Unlike Goethe, who of all moderns most resembles him, he had little creative power within the human image. Goethe could make a man who, henceforth, walked and talked for himself, while Emerson could only point out the relations between the Creator and his work. This was due neither to training nor to environment, although his Massachusetts did not favor imaginative invention. He was shrewd enough in his judgment of characters more earthy than himself, but to him they were only interesting representations of the divine, imperfectly expressed. He could not, like his infinitely (and perhaps enviously) admired Shakespeare, make them. His instinct for greatness was sure. The great character builders—Sophocles (but not Euripides), Homer, Shakespeare, Montaigne (in a different sense)—got his lasting homage. They made creatures that were not only men but significant. But he himself could imagine only the way of personality, not personality itself. He could create a new heaven and a new earth (in principle) but not the new man (except in principle) to inhabit them.

And I suppose that there is a direct relation between this deficiency in creativeness, which forever prevented him from telling a story (I doubt if he ever wanted to do so), and his inability to perfect his lyrics. There again he was a narrower man than Goethe. For the poem or the play, like the man or woman, is a whole, a thing in itself, and answers a question in terms that we accept without analysis. Prince Hamlet is better reasoned than "Self-Reliance," and the "Ode on a Grecian Urn" nearer finality than "The Over-Soul." Critic yields to maker, but a great critic—and perhaps this is the most lucid description of Emerson—only to the greatest. His imagination is steel and diamond beside the shoddy romanticism of his lesser contemporaries.

8.

BUT there was one theme in which that contemplative mind, so passionately wed to duty, was as free as a child and always fortunate. Nature, and especially New England nature, wild yet proximate, untamed but humanized, was his escape, his solace, and his happy inspiration. He is most eloquent when he describes fields or the forest, most poetic when a flower is his subject, least the preacher, most the creative spirit, when nearest the woods.

"In the woods, too, a man casts off his years, as the snake his slough, and at what period so ever of life is always a child. In the woods is perpetual youth. Within these plantations of God, a decorum and sanctity reign, a perennial festival is dressed, and the guest sees not how he should tire of them in a thousand years. In the woods we return to reason and faith. There I feel that nothing can befall me in life,—no disgrace, no calamity (leaving me my eyes), which nature cannot repair. Standing on the bare ground,—my head bathed by the blithe air and uplifted into infinite space,—all mean egotism vanishes. . . . I am the lover of uncontained and immortal beauty." *

He rationalized this haunting passion, which is so much a part of the man's temperament that he would not be Emerson without it. His first book was "Nature," the word is constantly on his lips, his metaphysics turn upon nature as a major premise. But before Emerson thought, his love of nature was—a love happily bestowed upon a rural New England that, more than any other region with which I am familiar, combines the wild with the pastoral. Europe has been too slow in the making for such results. Her wildernesses, even in Wordsworth's day, were merely land unclaimed. But Emerson stepped from his garden

* "Nature," pp. 9-10.

into the porch of the great forest that was still reminiscent of the primeval.

His was not an interest in details, like Thoreau's. It was seldom the vesture of nature he saw, except under guidance, and at nineteen he was still capable of making the English blackbird sing in his woods.* It was a spirit, which to him, and many like him, is a melody unheard, a presence, a rhythm of life, a harmony more powerful for serenity and spiritual confidence than any artifice of men. The sincerity of Emerson when he writes of nature is complete. Of men and cities, of society, both gay and intellectual, of great men and events, of love and friendship, Emerson got enough and came home. He made no strong attempt to see again the pictures of his hero, Michelangelo. One view of the three men in Europe who most drew him thither—Landor, Carlyle, and Wordsworth—was sufficient; for if he went again to Carlyle it was because convenience offered. The critic-philosopher took what he needed and went home. But of nature he never had enough. You could find him in his pines. There is something fundamental here, and explanatory. It may well be that for his purpose, which was to pierce the veil and discover harmony in the universe, wild nature was more documented than cities and civilizations. The key was there. As he said in "Nature," "In the wilderness, I find something more dear and connate than in streets or villages."

In every wood lot in New England the wilderness still followed its own laws. A temperament like Emerson's could not escape a religious emanation stronger, deeper, and more subtle than churches provided. There was no data, no interpretation, little description of this American nature. Wordsworth even, at first, seemed alien to this seeker who wanted to know the secret of his own woods.

---

* "Good-Bye." Of our two common blackbirds, one does not sing at all, and the other but creakingly, and never in the "groves."

They were virgin in the intellectual sense, though a lum-
berman would have called them second growth. Their impact upon the sensitive mind was direct—no dryads, no
shepherds even, no "dewy lawns," no "haunted shades,"
screened them with words. Nature was his love, and out
of nature manifesting in a fresh continent he made his
philosophy. Here is something deeper than the "influences of romanticism" that bore him on his way.

9.

NEVERTHELESS, in his literary study of nature, as in his
poetry and his philosophic essays, Emerson, as a man of
letters, was conditioned by his preacher's complex and
confined by his preacher's technique. He was oracular here
and elsewhere, because it was the oracle he sought. The
surréalisme of the moderns, which finds the only reality in
mental impressions, he would have very well understood,*
passed over indeed as too familiar; but reality for him
was only to be found in the *significant* impressions. It was
the higher not the lower reason that he chose as truth.
We who are accustomed to the non-selective methods of
later periods, who have been taught that the worm's digestion may teach more than contemplation of the nature
of God, find this oracular view of the universe trying. It
may be our error, not Emerson's, though we have the advantage of knowing that there was more to the worm than
the not too particular scrutiny he recommended would
ever have found out. But we keep our prejudices. The art
of the nineteenth century was sickened by ideas, and the
whole movement of realism may be regarded as an attempt to get data of actual experience that would burst
the patterns of conventional thinking. Emerson, as
preacher and as oracle, drives by hammer blows into a
modern mind that detests preaching, precisely what that

* See R. Michaud's interesting "L'esthètique d'Emerson."

mind in the lag of romantic idealism and in the era of things is reluctant to receive. Hence these essays, which have penetrated second-hand and adulterated throughout American education and literature, are themselves neglected. Emerson remains as a classic and will rank as a prophet, but lives only by passages of great eloquence and transcendent insight, floating up from the temporal and casual that already weighs upon his preaching. His seat is not with Shakespeare, or Sophocles, but with Marcus Aurelius, Isaiah, and his dearly loved Montaigne.

That he was a very great man I do not doubt. There is a command in his name, a challenge in his life, and a consistent quality in his mind, that will not let the individual sink back into a history of a reputation. His deficiencies are themselves arguments, for they would go unnoticed in a lesser man. Imperfect relationships with the active world, emotions that burnt white like cold light, indestructible and undestroying, will that was not obstinate so much as obsessed with the duty of uplift, tensity and the complete absence of that humor which is so often keener than thought, quaint confidence that "we needs must love the highest when we see it"—all these are qualifications of genius, inwrought in the texture of the man, and equivalent to the opposite faults of self-indulgence, egotism, and passion uncontrolled of great men of a different genre.

Saint, however, is not his term. Saints may be oracular, but they are also apocalyptic. They do not think, or at least do not expect to grow by thinking. It is true that Emerson's special greatness lay outside the realm of struggle, in an energy formed for contemplation and issuing in pure idea.* He exactly conforms to those happy beings described by Jonathan Edwards, who are born with a will to live in the certainty of grace. There are many such

* See, for example, his attitude toward reformers in the essay of that name.

in history, but few with the energy and the luminous ease of Emerson. This is greatness both born and achieved, yet it is not saintliness, which withdraws from the world, whereas Emerson focused his whole being upon conduct in a progressive society. He is absolutely Western—the first and sanest of the many in our time who try to reconcile perfection of soul with control of nature.

There is always a certain naïveté in this attempt, the naïveté of practical idealism that Europeans find so often in America. It was naïve to imagine an ideal New England and build upon that a world philosophy. But there was Yankee shrewdness too. The strenuous races are the least cynical. American ethics, American religions, the wooden nutmeg, and the chase for the dollar, all began in New England. Emerson was a happy mutation resulting in a man whose difficulties were only shadows of himself, and whose deficiencies were merely the absence of energies centred elsewhere.

I have already given my opinion of the quality of his work. *Ought* and *is* are its prevailing words. It is great teaching and great criticism, but it is questionable whether literature in which man always appears as an abstract of potentialities can endure except as a summary of wisdom perfectly expressed. In English belles lettres Emerson must take his chance with Pope, not with Milton or Shakespeare.

The extent of his influence—and not merely in America —has been obscured by the absorption of his ideas into common thinking, and their inevitable degradation. He is the prime speaker for the liberated Puritanism of the nineteenth century, which to *will* of the Calvinists, and *love* of the Methodists, added the idealism of minds seeking to find new paths from man to Deity. Carlyle beside him is a mighty voice roaring confusedly, Ruskin, a narrow rhapsodist, Arnold, a bound and melancholy spirit.

RALPH WALDO EMERSON

He belongs not with them but with his opposites who were his analogues in their own field of progressive materialism: Mill, Spencer, Huxley. Carlyle and Ruskin are almost meaningless today, Arnold a historical regret, but upon these others we are still building. Our thinking is a criticism of theirs, baseless without it. Only the prophets who prophesied in terms of science belong on the typical curve of the nineteenth century, and of the thinkers on science only Emerson was a prophet.

And indeed his chief claim to greatness may be that he was in his own best sense a representative man, not only of the nineteenth century in its moral aspect but of his own race. It is not often that a cumulative energy like the New England will so perfectly transmutes into moral philosophy and discharges into the storage battery of literature. The will to duty which rationalized an ardor for conduct that had survived its theology, became in Emerson an idealistic philosophy at the very moment when, in its materialistic phase, it was subduing a continent. Like the spiritual river flowing through Musketaquid that

> Unbounded goes
> Through flood and sea and firmament;
> Through light, through life . . .

Emerson was sweeter and finer than New England, and in perfect opposition to one half of its dualism, yet the waters of his imagination were not vaporous but knew a spring and a course.

If it be objected that this last is not influence, the answer is that representation is a prerequisite for influence. If there is a valid backward relationship, there is sure to be a forward one also. Of this, Racine and Voltaire, Shakespeare and Milton, Dante and Cervantes, are evidence. We take out of the past only what is alive and useful for us, but what is alive now must have been alive in

179

its own present. The immortals in literature were closer than others to the essence of their own times. The best writing for the future is the best writing of the present. Thus the simples of Emerson's thinking, which were never without reference to his own America, have had an almost biological history. We of the fourth generation from him inherit Emerson in our education. Ethically and spiritually he has passed into the future of American life.

Appeal to the moral idealism of the American democracy and you are sure of a response. It is a language they have been made to understand. Cravings for spiritual perfectibility (thanks to this pervasive Emersonism) they know to be theirs. Woodrow Wilson, inheritor like Emerson of the Calvinistic will to uplift, spoke the Emersonian ethics. He believed in the moral will of the crowd, and at his words the American people were more profoundly stirred than for a generation, stirred—and at last wearied, like the modern reader with Emerson—by the tensity of moral concern. Wilson also confused potentiality with possibility, and since he was politically minded, with much more serious results. He asked his democracy to act, and for an act he required a majority, whereas the wiser Emerson urged self-development. There was no great reformer in Emerson's day, and therefore we cannot judge what might have been his criticism of Wilson's mighty effort by his remarks upon "seekers" and fanatics. That he would have preferred him to Daniel Webster there is little doubt: that he would have described Wilson as a genius crippled by too little knowledge of nature is probable; that he would have recognized his own ideas of a moral state at work in both leader and populace is sure.

10.

THERE is a special consideration for Americans in reading Emerson that should make them patient with his intensities and his preachments. All, without exception, of the great American writers have been radically in opposition to the materialistic trend of our civilization. Cooper, Hawthorne, Melville, Mark Twain, Whitman, were active rebels, Poe and Irving passive ones. They have been to a man protestants against a culture increasingly engrossed in material comfort. That is why there are only two humorists among them, both of whom wrote satire. But Emerson is the incarnation and rationalization of this civil war of the American spirit, although not its realist. He best represented the moral ideas and the conception of man that caused the revolt, and at the same time possessed that passion for an ideal democracy and the large tolerance of human error which the others, except the unphilosophic Whitman and Twain, so decidedly lacked. Whatever he may be in world literature, he is the prophet of a nobler way for Americans—and an American way, in its intense individualism, at that.

Emerson's America, where moral enthusiasm seemed able to accomplish anything, and did precipitate a war, where shrewdness and courage guaranteed economic success, is almost dead, as dead as the privileged Europe he knew, where the ideas were forged that a new continent tried to work into immediate furnishings for Utopia. His pausing point at the juncture between conduct and science is long overrun. His life of a rural town, conscious of the city, yet not of it, has become a rarity for Henry Ford to collect. In an urban civilization, industrialized to the point where individualism must be standardized to survive without exceptional effort, his large hopes for a democracy of nonconformists seems absurd. We control them as we control nature for fear that we will not keep up with industrial progress. Nature, indeed, has been controlled with a vengeance, and her chemistry and physics are slaves that do not need great men for masters. Executive skill and technical ability are demanded, and the call to idealism is heard but not heeded. We are too busy elsewhere. It is a radio sermon, accepted as familiar and obvious, but not vitally important. We tune out when the telephone rings. There will be no Emersonian democracy in this culture cycle, and nature struggling for life is not likely to provide harmony for her vivisectors.

Yet beware of Emerson's own fallacy, which George Fox shared, that potentiality and possibility are the same. These were minority men. When the Quakers became a majority they sank into quietism. When Emerson's idealism mixed with the Methodist fervor and became a national ethics it gave us twenty commandments before we had learned to observe the first. Emerson's religion is useful to individualists only, and there will never be a race or a culture of individualists. He is a voice speaking to man, not men. He is not dogma or a document but fire that lights only where it can. The tinder is preparing in the great swing back from the mechanistic philosophy that has been the unconscious religion of the West, toward a metaphysics that will supply some new basis for faith. Postscientific man will make more of Emerson (or some renewal of his prophecy) than we do. It may be that his eloquent English prose will carry him through to that day.

He went as far as he could, further indeed than his facts warranted, and it was some realization of his overweening that is expressed in "Terminus."

> It is time to be old,
> To take in sail:—
> The god of bounds,
> Who sets to seas a shore,
> Came to me in his fatal rounds
> And said: "No more!
> No farther shoot
> Thy broad ambitious branches, and thy root.
> Fancy departs: no more invent;

Contract thy firmament
To compass of a tent."

He had lived through the Civil War and saw that Faust the entrepreneur would have his day. He may have guessed that his New England was dead. Yet he wrote in his Journal, "Within I do not find wrinkles and a used heart, but misspent youth." He might well have recalled the words of his "Experience," "Up again, old heart, . . . the true romance which the world exists to realize will be the transformation of genius into practical power." The returns were not yet all in, and what was "practical" perhaps only the romanticist and the optimist had guessed. Even the leaders of the industrial age begin to realize that man does not live by bread alone and that to hunger, fear, vanity, and greed, must be added as a prime motive for humanity that desire for spiritual content through self-mastery which some call happiness, others religion, and which Emerson defined as the harmony of man with the creative force of the universe.

We shall take up Emerson again, but as a prophet, not as a preacher, as individualists, not as a congregation. And who shall say that when he wrote in this same poem of renunciation, "Leave the many and hold the few," he did not mean men as well as gifts, hopes as well as purposes in life?

As the bird trims her to the gale,
I trim myself to the storm of time.

Well, that is the fate of all philosophers and prophets and their dogmas and idealisms. Fortunate the man whose craft has been built in his dooryard, and is rigged to sail up the wind a little way toward the future.

CHAPTER FIVE

Henry David Thoreau

I've searched my faculties around,
To learn why life to me was lent;
I will attend the faintest sound,
And then declare to man what God hath meant.

———

That my weak hand may equal my firm faith,
And my life practice more than my tongue saith.

A SMALLISH man but long-legged, firm-set, with high cheek bones like an Indian's, a powerful nose, and gray-blue eyes—"terrible eyes," as Emerson said—that looked you through and through, his face bearded in later life, but in mid-career islanded in soft brown whiskers, dressed always for rough walking, an old music book under one arm for pressing flowers, an umbrella often as not in the other hand—even in the Maine woods he carried an umbrella. Here was Thoreau, as by luck you might have seen him in the brush or swamps, or crossing the Concord road by a fox path. And this is the man whose essay on "Civil Disobedience" came, in 1907, into the hands of a Hindu in Africa who was already meditating passive resistance as a defense of his people. Mahatma Gandhi, whose name is now known wherever news goes, found his ideas confirmed and apparently clarified by a statement of principle that embodied firmness without violence and a devotion to truth, and the word "Satyagraha" was coined to express the civil disobedience that has become the weapon of the Hindu nationalists.* Little wonder that, even in a town of peripatetic philosophers, Thoreau was a marked and a markable man.

With reason, for here was one of the world's rare originals whose eccentricity comes from being too sane. The farms of Concord, he said, were his by right of free enjoyment: he had the best of them, the air, the soil, the flowers, the views; he got their best crops. In like fashion, Thoreau got the best of Concord itself, was its eye and central mind when the others, even sometimes Emerson, were limbs merely that went sprawling about business of no ultimate concern. He was the man most alive in Concord—few men in the world of his day anywhere were more alive than he.

To live so heartily and honestly in one patch of land and its culture was very emphatically to live in history. And indeed Thoreau's roots struck into soil that cannot be described by any modern geographical name. *His* Concord was older than New England, which owned only the thin crust of modern culture of both soil and mind, and his intellectual sources were as deep and as broad.

Indeed this man's rarity is to be explained only in large terms, and by a duality commoner in the seventeenth century than in the nineteenth. He was a Renaissance man with the adventurous passion for sheer living of the

---

* See "Gandhi of India: His Own Story," edited by C. F. Andrews, pp. 193-96; and a letter from Gandhi's collaborator in the editing of *Indian Opinion*, Henry Polak, in *The New York Evening Post*, May 11, 1931. Without the full text of Gandhi's autobiography, which has not been translated, it is impossible to tell how much beyond support and confirmation he owes to Thoreau, but apparently "Civil Disobedience," which he read and reproduced in *Indian Opinion* and circulated in pamphlet form just before the essay competition on the ethics of passive resistance that resulted in the term "Satyagraha," powerfully influenced his new policy. "The principle, called Satyagraha," says Gandhi (*op. cit.*, p. 95), "came into being before that name was invented. Indeed, when it was born, I myself could not say what it was." It was at this time that he read Thoreau.

Renaissance and both the will and the ability to create a life for himself that should be "inviting and glorious"; not a scramble for pennies like the gold rush of '49, but such full-blooded days as Sidney and Raleigh, Hotspur and Bassanio and Mercutio, sought. He could seem "blessed" in clear November, he inhabited his body "with inexpressible satisfaction," he could "feel the juices of the meadows," he loved his "fate to the very core and rind." "Heal yourselves, doctors; by God, I live!"

I think that he quotes more often from the Elizabethans and their immediate successors than from elsewhere in English. Raleigh, who had "a breathing place between his sentences" was, I think, his best-loved author in youth, a man whose outward history was in complete antithesis to his own, yet who made his tower prison a Concord when he wrote his "History of the World."

Indeed Concord to Thoreau was a New World rich in discoveries, and his life work, which Emerson described as pounding beans instead of empires, and which certainly contained no conquests of Armadas and Guianas, was a journal, a journal of experience and reflection recording a passion for this "brave world" which is so far from being ridiculous because frogs, sunsets, swamps, and ideas are its events and its heroes, that only the ebbing vitality of the American imagination has kept us from realizing what a man we had in Thoreau.

His gusto for living, like so many of his tastes, is akin to the seventeenth century, just as the raciest American English so often has its closest affiliations there. But the nature of his will finds its source three generations later when Protestant ethics reached its creative height and the spiritual foundations of New England were laid. For Thoreau was "one of that class," as he said of John Brown, "of whom we hear a great deal, but, for the most part, see nothing at all—the Puritans"—the real Puritans, he

186

might have added, who live intensely by and for principle, the heady blend of which Miltons were made, intense personalities controlled for moral ends. Rejoicing to be alive, a "protestant à l'outrance," as Emerson said, taking his philosophy from the Oriental scriptures as a tonic against materialism, yet conditioned by New England, here is a man who deserves a better description than rubbishy talk about a hermit and nature-lover.* With all his limitations there is no literature that might not be glad to claim Thoreau.

So much for generalities, and for encouragement to readers who know their "sweetness and light" and their "French Revolution," but have never read "Civil Disobedience," nor realized that the one ringing challenge to the industrial revolution has come from a Thoreau who is still little known in American universities, nor thought of except as a wild man with a perverse passion for the woods. It is one of the ironies of American education that of the six most remarkable books of our single century of national existence—"Walden," "Moby Dick," Emerson's "Essays," Poe's "Poems," "Leaves of Grass," and "The Scarlet Letter,"—only Emerson's "Essays" and Hawthorne's novel of adultery are thought to be proper for teaching in schools!

2.

THINK of Emerson and you think of New England, for the bounds and scope of his effort were set by the ideals of a Massachusetts intellectual; but Thoreau was much more his own man. The immemorial Concord of the Musketaquid was his pasture, but to the peculiar civilization of New England and of Concord, he owed only the felt responsibility for uplifting his neighbors that no first-

---

* He refers in "A Week on the Concord and Merrimack Rivers" to the "mealy-mouthed enthusiasm of the lover of nature," preferring the surliness of a woodchopper.

rate mind east of the Hudson could escape. It sat uneasily in Thoreau, who in youth feared that he was grown too unhealthily moral, and was careful to apologize, even in his tirades against slavery, for his concern with a matter of less essential importance than the business of his lonely walks. He took his moralism with a difference. The Harvard education and Concord environment were irritants. Instead of a call to preach, they aroused in Thoreau a passion to contradict and overthrow. That which made Emerson prophesy, made him rude. He challenged false opinion, like George Fox in the "steeple houses," and if he never looked for trouble (except when slavery was the theme) he never avoided it. He shared the sententiousness of Emerson, because that was the fashion of Concord, and the way of argument for a solitary man. Conduct was his concern even more than Emerson's, and if the conduct he urged was not New England's, it was proposed as an answer to questions that church, state, and business in New England insistently raised. In the seventeenth century Emerson might have written metaphysical poetry in Herbert's rectory, and Thoreau an "Anatomy of Nature" where there would have been more sweetness and fewer explosions than in "Walden." But the resemblance between the two men ends with their love of nature and their responsibility for uplift. It was Emerson's business to prophesy for New England, Thoreau's, to create a life and then report upon his experiment. (Emerson, as Thoreau very wisely implies in "Walden," took little thought of what *hindered* Divinity in man.) That both drew upon a common reservoir of moral philosophy and used a language mutually intelligible, that both made books of collected epigrams made into paragraphs, has given them a delusive likeness. Thoreau was not Emerson's man, although Emerson perhaps thought so.

And yet all that I have said of the oppressive background of New England moralism must be applied also to Thoreau. I shall not repeat it. This Puritan, who was remorseful on one occasion because too much indulgence in huckleberries had clouded his intellect, was Puritan also in his will to "declare to man what God hath meant." Every intellectual Yankee of his century believed in the duty to teach!

And Thoreau was almost aggressively Yankee. If he refused to fool himself or others with wooden nutmegs, yet he could make them if he wanted to. He learned to shape the best pencil in New England, and then stopped. He went peddling with his father as far as New York until he could support himself by less irrelevant labor. He was a typical handy man, self-reliant anywhere, from making a fire to mending the roof, such as New England sent out by thousands all over the West. Like the New Englanders in the Revolutionary Army, who shocked the French and Hessian officers because they were innkeepers, tradesmen, or artisans in off hours, he despised no useful labor, but was logical enough to despise all labor that did not lead to a genuine welfare. Precisely those New England qualities of shrewdness, self-reliance, and independence of spirit which made New England mistress of the trading sea, and mother of the successful pioneer, sent him to Walden on a cash basis. Like Emerson, Thoreau is one of the Mendelian variants of the New England breed. His Journal is the spiritual analogue of a notion shop, and if he did not make his fortune it was only because he was more ambitious than his fellow countrymen, and dealt in ideas instead of dry goods. And Thoreau was more eager to perfect his goods than to sell them. He had no time to get rich.

3.

HE WAS a Yankee, too, in his relations with the Transcendentalists. What he needed of their philosophy he took freely, what was not practical for his idea of living he let drive past. He certainly did not believe that Alcott was an old fool with some angelic attributes, as modern critics like to assume. But he was not even interested in Alcott's dreams of super New Englanders self-supported by theories of agriculture while they thought. Let the individual solve his own economics first, he said, before setting up a Utopia for philosophers.

And yet Transcendentalism was so self-evident to Thoreau that he was even willing to be called by its name,* the only label, I think, except "saunterer," that he ever accepted. Transcendentalism came to him from his Concord associates, Emerson especially, as easily as breathing. That the mind can perceive directly spiritual truths was self-evident to a youth who found wild nature at his back door confirming the truths of the Bhagavad-Gita; that the universe was a unity he profoundly believed, that the black swamp water and the rhodora above it were manifestations of a single force he knew, and he accepted without argument the corollary that evil and good were phenomena of a life stream that was as homogeneous as Concord water. He wrote in "Walden," pp. 489-490:

"We can never have enough of Nature. We must be refreshed by the sight of inexhaustible vigor. . . . I love to see that Nature is so rife with life that myriads can be afforded to be sacrificed and suffered to prey upon one another; that tender organizations can be serenely squashed out of existence like pulp—tadpoles which herons gobble up, and tortoises and toads run over in the road; and that sometimes it has rained flesh and blood! With the liability to accident, we must see how little account is to be made of it. The impression made on a wise man is that of universal innocence. Poison is not poisonous after all, nor are any wounds fatal. Compassion is a

* See his "Journals," March 5, 1853.

very untenable ground. It must be expeditious. Its plead-
ings will not bear to be stereotyped." *

Or again, where the idea first appears, in "A Week on
the Concord and Merrimack Rivers"—"the secret innocence of these incessant tragedies [in nature] which
Heaven allows."

Nature for him was transcendental phenomena, and his
life labor was to collect her in her aspects of eternity, not
for classification, since he felt that mere knowledge of fact
led nowhere, but as evidence. Beyond this, since for him
nature was poetical, not metaphysical, his Transcendentalism did not go. Emerson complained that he never defined his nature, and the complaint is instructive as to
both men! Emerson's definition seemed more important
to him than his pine trees, but with Thoreau nature was
definition. I mean that he had the far more consistent
philosophy, since he believed that you could never reason
about nature (though you might speculate) until you
knew and felt everything in your own environment. He
never finished. A scientist would say that he never began,
for his study was always of the plant, stone, or lake water
in its relation to his own mind, seldom as to its structure
or physical essence. If Thoreau was a scientist at all,
which I doubt, he was a Transcendental scientist. "There
is more religion in science, than science in religion," he
said; and there was in his. In short his basic philosophy
was like that of most great protestants against the world's
follies—simplicity itself, practical not speculative, though
he speculated endlessly on phenomena and application.
For Thoreau, who could not live happily without four
hours a day of walking, who could look for fifteen minutes
at a tree or bird while the irreverent wondered, wild nature was the unglossed and uncorrupted text of whatever
truth the world contained before man began his editing.

* See also "Walden," p. 216.

There the truth behind appearances was most likely to be discernible.

A description of this truth he might very well have got from his Sanskrit scriptures, and indeed, as regards ultimate truth, Thoreau was and remained an Oriental, contemplating rather than defining, absorbing rather than explaining. It was in his beating of the bush for new phenomena and his sturdy protests against interferers that he was Western. And yet his serene confidence that his intuitions of the Good and the Beautiful and the True were faithful intuitions came, I think, from his association with Transcendental friends. Faith, like literature, comes strongest from a coterie. It is true that his tireless and sometimes tiresome moralizing came also from his education in Emerson's circle. It was a form of wit where the concrete is always shifting into the abstract, and is sometimes almost offensive, especially in his earlier work. At its best there is real wit:

"It is well to have some water in your neighborhood, to give buoyancy to and float the earth. One value even of the smallest well is that when you look into it you see that earth is not continent but insular. This is as important as that it keeps butter cool. When I looked across the pond from this peak toward the Sudbury meadows, which in time of flood I distinguished elevated perhaps by a mirage in their seething valley, like a coin in a basin, all the earth beyond the pond appeared like a thin crust insulated, and floated even by this small sheet of intervening water, and I was reminded that this on which I dwelt was but *dry land*." *

But *he* is dry sometimes, too, with his constant turning of substance into accident. No wonder he liked Quarles and the seventeenth century metaphysicals! Yet Thoreau owes only less to the Concord minds than to the Concord

* "Walden," pp. 137-38.

fields and woods. He would have been less sure if he had been born in the Brandywine valley, less articulate if he had wandered in Virginia.

Many a good reader has been put off Thoreau by these tricks, which are closely related to punning, of which he was reported to be too fond. Yet his first epigrams are made this way, which is further evidence that he tried to think and write in such a fashion, as did his seventeenth century predecessors. It was the conversational method of the Transcendentalists, if you can judge from their journals. Nothing was so interesting in itself as for its significance. One notes that when he slipped away from Emerson, his Journals begin to yield a larger and larger assay of pure observation, a fact of which his latest editor complains because they are dully repetitive. Credit then to the Transcendentalists. If they made him pedagogical, they also gave immense encouragement to a naturalist who at his best was never content merely to weigh and name what he saw.

But if I write in a somewhat sketchy fashion of Thoreau's Transcendentalism it is because I feel it is important (as with Emerson) only as a definition of what he believed, and far less important than what he did. It is like the Quaker's inner light, which Emerson wanted to rationalize. In itself it is a simple fact, but how to live by means of it is a subject for endless discussion.

4.

AND this leads on to the central problem in the life and works of Thoreau, which is a dualism in his nature. I have already touched on this dualism in one of its aspects by calling him a belated man of the Renaissance, Puritanized.

There are two Thoreaus, the Thoreau of want and the Thoreau of ought. What he consistently wanted, was to follow his own bent and belief and live in terms of closest intimacy with wild nature. *Not* because nature contained implications of the Deity and ultimate truth, although this he believed. *Not* because he was a Transcendentalist, although he observed transcendentally. But because to live in such intimacy was what he instinctively loved ("There is in my nature, methinks, a singular yearning toward all wildness") and, still more, because, in the Emersonian sense, he felt himself in tune with the universe when he was in the fields and the woods.

The very interesting chapter on "Higher Laws" in "Walden" may be readily translated into psychological language. Thoreau began, like most New England boys, with a gun and a fishing rod. He loved, as he says, the wild not less than the good, and his savage nature like his spiritual grew stronger in the woods. He had a taste for violence. But the wild thing captivated his imagination and stirred his mind. He sublimated his savagery into observation and comment. He sublimated his passions also into this single passion. As we find him in his Journal, he had apparently no amorous emotions which could not be satisfied by friendship, and indeed friendship with him seems to be synonymous with love, and is regarded as something to be won rather than enjoyed. He had dreamed of sexual intercourse as "incredibly beautiful, too fair to be remembered," * and had no patience with primness, though he was exasperated beyond measure by lewd talk. Yet love of woman for him was entirely sublimated into his passion for nature. I do not mean pantheism, or any ism, I mean a literal passion for wild experience. Hence the prime demand that society makes upon the individual meant nothing to him personally. He could love a sunset readily, but not a girl. His fright when one woman wanted to marry him is delicious.

* Letter to Harrison Blake, Sept. 1, p. 52.

HENRY DAVID THOREAU

The ferocity of sex pursuit bent away in him from sex to nature. He was clearly a lover in his walks, with a lover's jealousy for his solitude, and a lover's reticence as to his ends. I do not think this either morbid or pathological. The rather rarefied purity of his Concord circle made such a course easier than it would have been, say, in Italy, and it is more than probable that his rule of non-intercourse with mere society kept temptation away. But there is nothing surprising in his shift of love. It is a phase of the merging of the carnal into the divine familiar in other civilizations. There was nothing inhuman in Thoreau. With children he was delightful, and his fierce intolerance of polite conversation was unsocial perhaps, but certainly not true misanthropy.

He was, if you please, a "case" of the romantic movement, where nature becomes an obsession and loving observation a passion so satisfying as to engross the best energies. With Thoreau it was a permanent obsession. It is White of Selborne getting his love and his religion from the fruit of his sight. The "bliss of solitude" to such men is a passionate joy because the endless variety, movement, mystery, and beauty of nature satisfy every one of their emotions, absorbing their energies as fast as produced. Men in war and great adventure are so engrossed, and we take it with them as a matter of course. With Thoreau, it was doubly engrossing because his critical, philosophic mind hovered, like his favorite marsh hawk, above the sly coverts of his instincts, viewing each minute experience from on high as possible game for the soul—an ultimate secret slipping through the world's wild bush.

I emphasize this passion for the wild, because this is Thoreau's will and in a true sense himself. He is primarily a lover of life; and it is necessary to take his wilderness delights seriously, understanding that not Raleigh in the voyage to Cadiz, or Mohammed returning from the desert, was more urgently engaged in business of highest personal moment.

As nature's man, he challenges nobody. He wonders why a farmer drags a rock all day merely to ornament his gateway, and is sorry for poor rich men who weigh down their shoulders with responsibilities leading to no happiness. But he does not complain of Concord and the world because they do not seek out the sphagnum bogs or walk the foxways in moonlight. That is his joy, which he will communicate or will defend. But he is no missionary for nature, though its prophet. His successors in nature-walking as a means of recreation, John Burroughs in America, Hudson in England, have made more converts to wilderness recreation than ever Thoreau. He is an adept, a devotee, with every faculty engrossed in a study which is *his* religion, *his* happiness, and *his* hope of an ultimate justification of the life that to him "was lent." But it was Emerson, not Thoreau, who said "back to Nature." Thoreau is more like the Quakers who say that you must be a Quaker in order to become one.

Read, for example, Thoreau's admirable and too little known essay on Carlyle, one of the finest and coolest summaries of that honest blusterer. With the gentlest of needle pricks, Thoreau punctures the attributes of greatness that the philosophically romantic were attaching to the Scotch name. Carlyle is a reviewer of events and a great journalist, not a seer; he talks always of profundities without once being profound. Nature is a word to him. He lives in a bustle of activity, demanding talk and ever more talk as the breath of his life, and is preoccupied with passing events. All that he is, sincerity excepted, is antithetic to Thoreau. Even his Transcendentalism is skin-deep. And yet he is an honest man, a shrewd wielder of ax blows at sham and folly. Even if he is ignorant of the way, he is working out his own karma, living his own life, writing an English that only a robust heart could master. Thoreau thanks God for him.

I cite this rather remarkable essay, when I might have quoted more direct statements, because it indicates so clearly that Thoreau's own passion for nature was the passion of an individualist, his own faith and not a creed, a will for himself rather than a rule for others.

"We need pray for no higher heaven than the pure senses can furnish, a purely sensuous life," he said in "A Week," and meant his own way of experience; but so long as a man explored his own higher latitudes he was content with him, felt that he was one of those "for whom this world seemed expressly prepared, as if creation had at last succeeded."

> I love a soul not all of wood,
> Predestinated to be good,
> But true to the backbone
> Unto itself alone,
> And false to none;
> Born to its own affairs,
> Its own joys and own cares; . . .
> If not good, why then evil,
> If not good god, good devil. *

Thoreau, I repeat, was the prophet, not the preacher, of the woods.

5.

To THOREAU, the passionate lover of nature, I shall return for more intimate discussion. He is the positive Thoreau who unites seer and lover in happy union. Had he been as concerned with turning his life as a nature man into art as in governing and directing and defending that life itself, he would have very simply and easily taken his place in the literary hierarchy beside Izaak Walton, Hudson, Herrick, Marvell, Sidney.

But there are negative Thoreaus also: a protestant

* "A Week on the Concord and Merrimack Rivers," p. 94.

Thoreau, radical, rebel, economist, Puritan—an unwilling Thoreau who turned aside from his proper business with nature to protest against a society that bent a man toward its own misdirected aims; and again, a puzzled Thoreau, whose conscience would not let him escape a duty to the minds of his fellow men although he so readily shrugged off their companionship. Conscience also, he said, has its diseases.

The positive Thoreau is all rugged tenderness and shrewd and happy contemplation. He is not a mystic, and yet would have lived happily with his philosophy, fishing with Walton in "a wide halo of ease and leisure." But the negative Thoreau is either a seeker, eager to justify his idea of truth, or a fighter against a society that will not let him alone. It is this latter phase that I wish to discuss now, where the whimsical, the religious, Thoreau of the "Week" becomes spark and flint. Both the negative Thoreaus are Puritan. It was his innate Puritanism as much as the moralism of his environment that made him try to moralize nature. The two million words of his Journals are a tribute to duty. It was no essential part of his scheme of independent and individual living that he should set it all down and try to rationalize it for others. The positive Thoreau would have been content with poetry and essays, the Puritan Thoreau must prepare a vast storehouse of ammunition by which the world might eventually be driven toward truth. It was the Puritan Thoreau that turned, like an angry woodchuck, on an interfering world, gnashed at it with invective, scorned its idleness, and then prepared at Walden a thoughtful answer to the argument of industrialism that you must produce or be barbarous. I am concerned now with Emerson's "protestant *à l'outrance*." Still more with the individualist who, when Deacon Brown offered a pledge at the peace meeting, that they should treat all mankind as brothers henceforth, remarked, "I think I shall wait and see how they treat me first."

It was not nature but himself that he was defending. If his zest had been for textual criticism, or contemplating his navel, his cause would have been the same, his indignation equal, his argument as sound. Of the two Thoreaus, the one belongs to Concord, and with, as I hope to show, the true discoverers of America, but the other is an individualist citizen of the universe, who will not endure interference with his idea of living. He is a belated perfectionist set in sudden opposition to the new industrial slant of Western civilization, a Milton attacking not despots, but machines. This Thoreau belongs definitely and without reference to æsthetic values in the world movements of our time, and has a place in intellectual history that only the ignorant will belittle because his stance was merely Walden Pond and the village life of Concord.

6.

I shall not trace his protest against our civilization through his books and his Journals, but rather try to sum it up from his total conclusions. It is implicit in "A Week," which is a youthful book, lacking a theme and overstuffed with quotation, a record of a young man's thoughts when his reading intermingled with fresh experience. In that first sturdy chapter in "Walden," called "Economy," it comes out clear in a terse and powerful prose. "Civil Disobedience" and "Life Without Principle" are rebellion simon-pure.

For Thoreau's morality was that a soul should be

> Born to its own affairs,
> Its own joys and own cares.

His affairs I have described; they were "his Master's business, and his own joy." They seemed to him transcendentally important, and to them he devoted his leisure. He was able to support himself in a number of ways, by pencil-making, surveying, teaching, more doubtfully by lecturing, but no one of them could produce what Concord called a livelihood without impinging upon his priceless leisure. His happiness, which was to observe and meditate, was also his duty. If he could not think, he was, as he complains so often, asleep—no longer alive in the Elizabethan sense, no longer useful to himself, or even to Concord, for Massachusetts can get on well enough without his pencils, yet needs the wisdom he can draw from swamps and woods.

But in an America made by hard work on the land and now growing rich strenuously by steam and water, rails and looms, sauntering, as he called his profession, is peculiarly misunderstood, nature unprofitable except when dead, science idle unless in terms of measurement, religion suspect out of church. He is in a society unfit for the honest leisure that leads to mental enrichment, and that makes him mad. Madder still, because the pressure of subsistence upon opportunity is not heavy in New England. Food and shelter are readily had. It is easy to live, if hard to grow rich.

Thoreau's predecessors on American soil had found their leisure on the frontier. The wastrels and the idlers, the adventurers and the ne'er-do-wells, had taken to the woods, lived crudely in its plenty, drifted the streams, hunted in the forests, been so content, many of them, that it was a real question in the early 1800's whether the white man in the West would not accept the *mores* of the Indian. Thoreau envied the Indian, but not the pioneer white. He would have been able, I think, to accept savagery, but not barbarism. He had a mind to satisfy, and cultivated desires that asked more than a franchise in the wilderness. He needed books, companionship with his peers, leisure to study as well as to observe, to observe as well as to get food. His problem was a problem for civilization. Ten wild Americas could never solve it, and it is noteworthy that this lover of wilderness seldom speaks of the West, still untamed in his day, and made no strong attempts to see it until near the end of his life. He had nature in Concord; when he went to the Maine woods, it was to learn how the Indian lived.

His problem was normal, not abnormal; it was the dilemma that confronts millions of men and women in our phase of the industrial revolution. Culture and education have given them tastes and intellectual cravings that only leisure can satisfy, and our habit of life has crammed them with material wants for clothes, machines, cleanliness, amusement, and all the refinements of a highly mechanical environment. But leisure and luxury, or even leisure and comfort, they cannot have together. They must produce if they are to enjoy production, they must produce if the industrial machine is to keep functioning. Up and up goes the standard of living, lifted like the steel shafts of a skyscraper by all the engines of advertising. There is no end to wanting, because new necessities are created in endless succession. The best part of a life is spent "earning money in order to enjoy a questionable liberty during the least valuable part of it." * Bound to the wheel of the world, blind, and drunk with its speed, caught in the economics of production where want breeds want, we are citizens of a mad world where ends are lost in the means of living. Concord or New York—there is little difference between Thoreau's Farmer Brown expanding his acres until he dies crushed by them and the corporation lawyer working twelve hours a day in pursuit of a phantom competence that is never enough. There is only this difference, and Thoreau was aware of it: a mounting curve that industri-

* "Walden," p. 86.

alism was to push toward its logical conclusion. His dilemma is the true subsistence problem of the industrial
revolution, which gave us control of nature without control of ourselves. The mediæval donkey with his bundle of
hay has become a modern mechanical ass with automo-
biles, airplanes, the Riviera, Park Avenue, and bootleg
champagne hung before his straining eyes. We can never
catch up—and leisure lies beyond.*

The problem of course in its essence is ancient, and it is
because Thoreau found it so succinctly stated in Hindu
and Chinese philosophy that he is so Oriental in his quot-
ing. Gandhi saw in "Civil Disobedience" ideas from his
own India restated in new terms forced by new conditions
in the West. But Thoreau was no Oriental. Like Emerson,
he was a Westerner, a Yankee, who wanted to do, not to
be. Contemplating the navel is not his desideratum. He
wants leisure, yes, but leisure to be happy in his own individualistic fashion, and to make use of his happiness. He
went to Walden Pond "because I wished to live deliberately, to front only the essential facts of life, and see if I
could not learn what it had to teach, and not, when I
came to die, discover that I had not lived. I did not wish
to live what was not life, living is so dear; nor did I wish
to practice resignation, unless it was quite necessary. I
wanted to live deep and suck out all the marrow of life,
to live . . . sturdily and Spartan-like, . . . to drive life
into a corner, and reduce it to its lowest terms, and, if it
proved to be mean, why then to get the whole and genuine
meanness of it, and publish its meanness to the world; or
if it were sublime, to know it by experience. . . . Our life
is frittered away by detail. . . . I say, let your affairs be
as two or three, and not a hundred or a thousand; instead
of a million count half a dozen, and keep your accounts

* See his meditation on shad, "A Week," p. 44, where he prophetically views
the end of industrialism.

on your thumb nail. In the midst of this chopping sea of civilized life . . . a man has to live . . . by dead reckoning. . . . Simplify, simplify. . . . The nation . . . is cluttered with furniture and tripped up by its own traps, ruined by luxury and heedless expense, by want of calculation and a worthy aim. . . . It lives too fast. . . . We do not ride on the railroad; it rides upon us. . . . As for *work*, we haven't any of consequence. We have the Saint Vitus' dance, and cannot possibly keep our heads still. . . . Hardly a man takes a half hour's nap after dinner, but when he wakes he holds up his head and asks, 'What's the news?' . . . When we are unhurried and wise, we perceive that only great and worthy things have any permanent and absolute existence. . . . Children, who play life, discern its true law and relations more clearly than men, who fail to live it worthily, but who think that they are wiser by experience, that is, by failure. . . . Let us spend one day as deliberately as Nature, and not be thrown off the track by every nutshell and mosquito's wing that falls on the rails. . . . If you stand right fronting and face to face to a fact, you will see the sun glimmer on both its surfaces, as if it were a cimeter, and feel its sweet edge dividing you through the heart and marrow, and so you will happily conclude your mortal career." "If we respected only what is inevitable and has a right to be, music and poetry would resound along the streets." *

Thoreau went to Walden Pond to make a book from his Journals, to live under such circumstances as would permit him, the individualist, seer, and nature-lover, to be useful and happy in a high sense, but most of all to prove that in an acquisitive society based upon production and proceeding by competition, a man could do what he most wanted, even if there were no cash profits in it, and still subsist.

* "Walden," pp. 143-55.

Stevenson's idea that Thoreau was dodging life and its responsibilities is nonsense from a romanticist whose sacrifices were all capitalized. When Thoreau went to Walden, he walked toward the problem, not away from it. His answer was not an Oriental renunciation of all worldly things, whose logical conclusion is a seat in the dust and scraps of food from the faithful. His answer was renunciation of whatever does not primarily concern *you*—a sifting and threshing of desire until the chaff of imposed wants flies upward and the good grain of essential need remains. For Henry Thoreau, the woods, books, enough solitude, and the simplest food and clothing were prerequisites for successful leisure. "Walden" records the results of the experiment—and note that an equal emphasis in that well-digested book falls upon the fruits of happy contemplation and the means by which it was secured. The actual cash account of Thoreau's living is there, carefully set down. It is not your living, your wants—but he asked neither you nor anyone to come to Walden, and if he implores the generality to bind themselves like Ulysses to the mast of higher pleasure until the wasteful meridian of the dinner hour is past, that is his little joke upon hungry Transcendentalists who had to eat at a table. His is a type solution of which the principle is applicable in a thousand fashions. When he had enough of solitude (one factor only in his need) and another way of beating foolish labor around the bush offered itself, he left Walden and came to live with Emerson. Walden had served its purpose.

If the early converts to the British Labor party carried copies of "Walden" in their pockets, and knew long passages by heart, it was not because they hoped to set up housekeeping in the New Forest or upon Wordsworth's lakes. They saw that the idea of the book was not life in nature, but life for the sake of living, and how to live it. Living for them was a different problem from life in

Thoreau's semirustic world, but the principle was the same. Let us reform our ends and reconstruct our means so that each human shall be able to live in his own best way. It can be done—if not by going to Walden Pond, then by shortening hours of labor, distributing the products of machinery, and educating desire until we get and enjoy only the best.

Thoreau challenges the industrial order because he asks the fundamental questions: Where are you going, what do you really want? They were not questions in abstract philosophy merely. A German, named J. A. Etzler, published first in Pennsylvania, and then later in England, a book called "The Paradise Within Reach of all Men, Without Labor, by Powers of Nature and Machinery." Thoreau reviewed the second English edition of 1842 in *The Democratic Review* in 1843. It was a book that, with much romantic and sometimes absurd speculation, outlined the possible results for comfort and power of the use of machinery. The prophetic German prepared a control of nature by machinery and called upon mankind to create an immediate Utopia. There is not one of his descriptions of machine power quoted by Thoreau in his review that has not by now been fully realized. All the man lacked was specific knowledge of processes, all that is wrong in his scheme is the time element (ten years instead of a century), and his guess at the result for the human race. We are not so happy nor so comfortable as he thought.

Thoreau is neither incredulous of the Etzlerian dream nor dazzled by its possibilities. He strikes at the root of the fallacy. "The chief fault of this book is, that it aims to secure the greatest degree of gross comfort and pleasure merely. Nature is to be controlled, wealth is to be controlled, pleasure is to be distributed by a corporation, and not the slightest concern for the moral control of man and his wants." The horsepower of machinery is trusted for everything, and nothing said of the horsepower of love. Faith in that is the first reform; with that we could do without machinery. In physics, we can make the elements work for us, but to what use unless the moral force is also brought under control. "Nothing can be effected but by one man," the converse of which is that unless the man himself is clarified, machinery can add only to gross comfort and irking wants.

Thoreau's review is playful, but his life experiment in controlled living was as earnest as it was happy. His challenge to the industrial order came from a central principle of his nature, thoroughly rationalized. He was obstinate, but clear-eyed. There is really no other solution than his to the increasing ills of a state that we call sometimes progressive, but more often strenuous, nervous, febrile, aimless. The disease—which, like some selective malady, seizes upon our best, and fills sanitariums with nervous wrecks, homes with neurotics, cities with fine-drawn, irritable men, slaves of time whose hopes of leisure, and with leisure happiness, are always deferred—is susceptible to no other cure. Psychiatrists are patchers and repairers merely. They and the vocabulary of their science are inventions to describe the malady that Thoreau diagnosed. They cannot save the machine, and freely admit it. The only cure is moral, the only alleviation a robust discrimination in wants. Curious that our continent should provide the readiest escape into nature, where leisure is easiest, and also the most damning industrial competition. Curious, but inevitable. We have had the most nature to control, and diverted from the ends of common sense the most energy in order to control it for the sake of production. Babbitt was a symbol and a symptom of power turning into weakness. If Sinclair Lewis created him out of a thousand prototypes, Thoreau philosophized him in advance of his nativity. As nervous indigestion is the American disease, so Thoreau is surely the American philosopher. And he might have excepted his Journals when he wrote, in "Life Without Principle," that there is "little or nothing to be remembered written on the subject of . . . how to make getting a living not merely honest and honorable, but altogether inviting and glorious."

7.

IT WAS Thoreau the protestant, again, who wrote the essay on "Civil Disobedience." This time it was the state, not an economic system, that interfered with his individualism. When the state lets him alone, he will ignore the state, but if it forces him to participate in injustice then he is as wronged as when society refuses him leisure. I do not take too seriously his remarks upon slavery, which the Mexican question in 1849 had made an issue of violence. Slavery was repugnant to every fibre of a professional wanderer, and it was easy to be an Abolitionist in Concord. He was far sounder in his clear view that Massachusetts practices wage slavery than in his willingness to see the Southern problem cut by a single gesture. But his defense of his own integrity is unimpeachable. The state exists for individuals, not individuals for the state; patriotism is less than private morality; if the minority yields to the majority in essential matters it is soiled by the compromise. Only an honest man can be a good citizen. To force the support of injustice, even by so indirect a method as taxation, is an offense against moral liberty. Thoreau went to jail gladly on the issue, and indifferently came out. It seemed to him a petty experience—for the state! But with a community of Thoreaus to deal with the experience would not be petty.

"Civil Disobedience" and "Life Without Principle" are the most radical essays in American literature, precisely because they do not threaten property or counsel spoiling the fat for the benefit of the lean, but go to the root of the whole matter, where it is made clear that a life conducted for worthy ends and according to principles of elementary justice is the ultimate that must be preserved even if the state totters. Like Falstaff, they offend only the virtuous who have principles to lose. Admit this, make the individual responsible, and government becomes a machine, best liked when least observed. Politics and the routine of administration are *"infra-*human, a kind of vegetation,"* to be thought of as little as possible, *unless* they interfere; then there is only one answer to the state and that is to oppose it.

Such theories are dangerous, for they challenge the success of a state as such if it is not a success of men, and deny it the moral standards of expediency by which every state lives. When the Thoreaus and the Gandhis rebel there is no easy compromise. They cannot, like our own radicals, be satisfied by stopping their mouths with prosperity. But it is questionable whether Thoreau would have thought it worth his while actively to conspire and rebel. He did not want to reform society, he wanted to reform himself. Even the execution of John Brown could not rouse him that far. He would have given his life for his own principles, but would have been sparing of his energies in the doubtful endeavor to remake an institution for the benefit of other men. He was first of all an individualist. Let each man save himself and all will be saved. You cannot quash such a theory by saying that it leads to anarchy.

The most outspoken doctrines of resistance ever penned on this continent have been seldom mentioned in radical literature. They are too utterly un-European, too much the exact antithesis of either socialism or communism, which are the parasites of our industrialism; and that is

why, perhaps, that they have found their first broad application in the East. They require the kind of courage that
only individuals possess, and while we have had radical
parties enough, we have not had enough Thoreaus to overturn a state. And yet for Americans there is more dyna-
mite in his writing than in all Marxism. We might con-
ceivably, even yet, become radical his way.

8.

I DO not wish to write of Thoreau as if he were a Force,
although a latent force in his own mid-century of many
fanatics and a boundless optimism of opportunity he undoubtedly was, and an active force of slow-gathering mo-
mentum in ours. Both man and books are very human.
He was a failure in the world's eye, or rather in the eyes
of the little Concord world that knew him, and by no
means a success in his own. His lack of fame has not been
without reason and his success with a few devoted readers
has been a success almost by accident. A tip of the scale
and "Walden" would never have been published, or, if
published, would have come home to make another private
library, like the unsold copies of his "Week." The strength
of his program is that he actually lived and had faith in it.
There are limitations in his ideas fatal to general acceptance, even as there are shortcomings in his writings most
prejudicial to art. I believe him a great writer as well as
a great man, a critic of the first rank as well as a sincere
and candid individualist, but he never found the hound,
the bay horse, and the turtledove that he pursued through
life. These symbolized, said Emerson, his disappointments.

He was a happy man, happier even than Emerson, much
happier than his colleagues in American literature who escaped Puritanism altogether, than Poe and Mark Twain,
Irving and even Cooper. Only Walt Whitman, who drew
from Emerson's spiritual hope and was thus far a kindred

spirit, was happy with Thoreau's vigor. Thoreau was happy, but grave, a serious man in the French sense of the word, but not with the obsessive brooding of Hawthorne, or the prophetic seriousness of Emerson. Thoreau's deep gravity, deepest when he was alone, and often frosted with an autumnal wit in his writing, was due not so much, I think, to his contemplations of the universe, which were to him blissful, as to his own personal problems.

He courted solitude, for in solitude he could go about his business, but he worked for men. There is no other explanation of the two million words of his Journals. He proposed to learn what was the best life for himself so that others could profit by his experience. A Thoreau content to be a seer would be understandable, but this was not Henry. With infinite labor he made himself a teacher too. As I have said before, one had to teach, to uplift, in the proud, Puritan air of Concord. For what other reason did Thoreau publish books that brought less than nothing, when fame meant little to him though self-justification much? Why not survey in the forenoons and have the afternoons free to observe without further considerations whatsoever? He felt a duty, either to Massachusetts or himself—it makes little difference which—to mould his thought and express it. He had to make a gospel.

This granted, difficulties arose. Solitude was well enough for seeing, but in telling and teaching society had to be considered. That the gabble of social parties distressed him was of no importance, but his inability to meet mankind on a common footing in other respects was more annoying. "By my intimacy with Nature," he wrote in his Journal in 1852, "I find myself withdrawn from man." In pursuit of his hound and his dove and his bay horse he had sublimated all the human passions into love of the sunset, but how could a man who, beyond nature, cared only for a few intimates, prophesy for fathers and mothers, husbands and wives? Could he take a wife to Walden— breed children by a forest pond and feed them on beans and potatoes, educate them in a petty wilderness? Perhaps—but to lift individualism to its highest power while linked to a day and night partner, bound to her by passion as well as by economics, or as the father of children with wills not his own and temperaments inscrutably different! Yet that was the human problem!

He did not dodge it. It was not his own problem, and, good individualist that he was, he solved only his own equations. I cannot discover that he troubled his head about the corollaries of propagation; his paragraphs on love, marriage, and chastity might have been written in a community of Shakers. These were wants that he did not actively feel, yet as facts they surrounded his woods. He could not escape them. He could not get all the way back to mankind from his solitude with such impairments of sympathy. If his books seem cold, it is because their warmth is only for the austerely single heart.

Note that this does not affect the value of his principles. The harm was to the breadth of his doctrine, and still more to his own self-confidence. All of Thoreau's writings, with the exception of his essays in rebellion, are diffident. They proceed by bursts and reticences. His books are clearly put together from passages in his Journals most likely to reach an audience of an emotional quality different from his own. He writes as if he were addressing another sex. Something failed in his imagination when he turned to this audience, for an audience demands that ideas shall be newly created for it, and Thoreau did not know and did not trouble to know other men as he did himself. He could report, but not re-create his experience in terms of a general humanity that in practice he preferred to avoid. "I never read a novel," he wrote in the "Week," "they have so little real life and thought in them," and he ardently preferred the Hindu scriptures. So little real, he meant, of what to him was the reality of spiritual experience, so much of human relationship that to him was trivial or untrue.

There are other symptoms of this frigidity of temperament in the zone of general personal relationships, so different from Emerson's intense though rarefied flame of love. He was witty, but humor repelled him. Of Rabelais he said that it is "sport to him, but it is death to us. A mere humorist, indeed, is a most unhappy man; and his readers are most unhappy also." I can imagine no more disturbing visitor in Walden than Falstaff. The fat knight simply will not fit into Thoreau's universe. If Thoreau would not follow the crowd, it is also true that he was ignorant of the humors of the crowd. He was a good journalist, but would have made a wretched executive.

And yet it was his project to show that Concord was a microcosm of the world. The farmers he understood well enough, and the Transcendentalists, and the sauntering rogues and half-vagrant woodchoppers; but the tradesmen, the libertines, the mill-owners, and whatever echoed faintly in that prim community from the gayer world beyond, all he could say of them was *non simpatichi*. He learned the sweet rhythms of the universe from wild nature, and preferred his huckleberry hill to cafés and salons. That was his strength. But it was a drag upon his pen. If he would write for humanity, it had to be as prophet and philosopher. He could not speak as one man to another.

I think that if anyone wonders why out of an eager if short lifetime and a voluminous record of carefully noted experience and meditation, Thoreau made only two real books, this is one of the answers. He could not readily get back from nature to man. He had sold his heart to nature, as Faust sold his soul to the devil, and it was hard for him afterwards to turn back to the needs of the town. Except

HENRY DAVID THOREAU

when he is chafed in his sacred liberties, he speaks by paragraphs only, which seem almost reluctantly released from his meditations. He is most human, least esoteric, when he is in a rage.

9.

ANOTHER reason for his reluctance to publish is to be sought in his obscure relation to science. John Burroughs has justly said that Thoreau was not a good naturalist, and has caught him in several unpardonable errors, to which many more could be added. He does not seem even to have distinguished between the songs of the wood thrush and the hermit thrush, which is a reflection on his ear as well as upon his ornithology.* I believe that he was much more accurate in his botany, but doubt whether he would stand scrutiny there either. He observed closely but began to rationalize his frog as soon as he saw its spots. As a naturalist, he was a genius at collecting, but not a scientist at all.

But neither was he, like Emerson, a pure Transcendentalist in nature. He accepted Emerson's belief that facts alone were valueless, but he was never content to stop with Emerson's generalities. He went on collecting while he speculated. He set down and reiterated the same observations year after year.† Emerson observed with passion and his very passion carries him instantly up into metaphysics. But Thoreau is not satisfied. He sees the purple grasses waving and below them the tiny star of a new flower, which must be identified. He lies for hours in his boat watching the waving meadow grass of the river bottom. He notes how the woodchuck carries his tail, records the variant colors of Walden ice, sees all that eye

* See "The Maine Woods" *passim*. He refers constantly to the wood thrush where probably no wood thrush ever sang, and hermits are abundant. But the Concord dwellers were never strong on music. Emerson found it perplexing.

† See for example the books called "Autumn," "Spring," etc., collected by H. G. O. Blake from his "Journals."

213

can see. His measurements are surveyor's measurements, infinitely crude beside the exact and minute methods of science. And yet he will neither take his evidence into the laboratory (and would not if he had the best of laboratories today) nor give up collecting it. He is like a scholar bogged in a morass of texts.

Hence a confusion that went deep into his life and from whose perplexities he never escaped. Nature was for him an intense and continuous experience. But his faith, one might well say his self-respect, required that he should make something of it beyond the pure fabric of happy episodes that are so lovingly recorded in his Journals. He could not generalize, like Emerson, from second-hand information. He was too scientific for that. But neither could he stop to dissect a leaf when the secret of being was in all nature. In a world of which he was the only inhabitant he would have been a happy observer, content with his intuitions and constantly excited by discoveries that needed no words. But in a culture already electric with science, and in a New England vibrant with the desire to learn and teach, he was tensely indeterminate between research and philosophy. He knew too little to generalize; his intuitions were too deep to be sounded by a millimetre scale.

Thoreau never finished. In his forty-five years and his two millions of words, he had but begun his observations. Only his protests—against wasters of life, against infringers of liberty—came through whole and complete. "Instead of engineering for all America," said Emerson, "he was the captain of a huckleberry party. Pounding beans is good to the end of pounding empires . . . but if, at the end of years, it is still only beans!" That was Emerson, peevish in his grand manner because one of his representative men had not tried to make his America into Utopia. But with a shift of meaning, it was perfectly true. Thoreau was still pounding beans for the great synthesis when he died, pounding them harder than ever, as the innumerable notes of his Journals show. He never defined his nature. It was hard enough to make men see God in frogs, or bliss in solitude. All we have of Thoreau is a life that was itself a work of art, protests that are brilliant sparks of individualism still able to kindle, and the by-products of a hopeless task.

Hopeless, because he would trust neither science nor himself. But are not all great syntheses hopeless, all schemes of the universe valuable chiefly for what the poet or philosopher or research scientist finds on the way? The part is often more than the whole, the by-product more valuable than the contemplated fruition. And so was the work of Thoreau, whose passion communicates passion, whose protests are valid, whose living observations are more contagious and more truly informative than books of supposed fact. He mastered his life, if not his subject, and as a critic he reached results that no mere speculation could attain. If he had realized that at Walden Pond he had found all that he could bring back whole and complete, he might have troubled to organize his discoveries, and have made more books with beginnings and middles and ends, which would have long since had the recognition given to classics easily read and digested. But you cannot trim a sumach! Let him go, then, wandering like his woodchuck, striking back with a gleam of teeth when he is disturbed, never getting to a visible destination, but ineradicable, unforgettable when you have seen him on the border of his woods.

10.

IN DISCUSSING Thoreau as an artist and man of letters it is necessary to make distinctions he never made (since his life and thought, more than most men's, were unified) and think of him as poet, critic, idyllist, and philosopher.

Not perhaps in his style, though even here his nature narratives are distinguished by suavity, his criticism by terse strength, his philosophy by eloquence and often by sheer rhetoric. I do not think he learned to write except by epigrams and paragraphs until the epoch of "Walden." Then you begin to get his clear, strong English unimpeded, flowing like a spring brook with the dynamism of powerful water. He has not Hawthorne's mellow continuity, and yet by paragraphs it is a racier, more virile style than Hawthorne's, less mannered and more flexible. He is less eloquent than Emerson on his heights, but less wordy also; not so good a preacher but a better writer, with a finer ear for the strengths and subtleties of prose. He praised Carlyle for his escape from the pedantries and conventions of literary style, but deserves the praise much more himself, for he is strong and free without Carlyle's wasteful profusion. Thoreau neither flings about his words nor builds them in like bricks. Indeed, as in his thinking, this recluse is closer to the new age of plain and informal speaking than any of his contemporaries. We could learn to write from him, as never from Ruskin, Emerson, or Irving. He has the American accent, the staccato of short sentences, the sudden dips into the colloquial. Yet his English is always choice and pure. I should put him at the head and front of the fathers of a distinctively American prose, with those subtle differences of rhythm that spring from a different racial experience.

"I love to see the herd of men feeding heartily on coarse and succulent pleasures, as cattle on the husks and stalks of vegetables. Though there are many crooked and crabbed specimens of humanity among them, run all to thorn and rind, and crowded out of shape by adverse circumstances, like the third chestnut in the burr, so that you wonder to see some heads wear a whole hat, yet fear not that the race will fail or waver in them; like the crabs which grow

216

in the hedges, they furnish the stocks of sweet and thrifty fruits still. . . . How cheap must be the material of which so many men are made!" *

"For what is a man profited, if he shall gain the whole world, and lose his own soul? Or what shall a man give in exchange for his soul? Think of this, Yankees! . . . Think of repeating these things to a New England audience! thirdly, fourthly, fifteenthly, till there are three barrels of sermons! Who, without cant, can read them aloud? Who, without cant, can hear them, and not go out of the meetinghouse? They never *were* read, they never *were* heard. Let but one of these sentences be rightly read, from any pulpit in the land, and there would not be left one stone of that meetinghouse upon another." †

"The chief want, in every state that I have been into, was a high and earnest purpose in its inhabitants." ‡

"Some circumstantial evidence is very strong, as when you find a trout in the milk." §

Quotations scarcely do justice to the nature of his prose, which has the quality of nuggets in a vein, where the diversity is merit. And random selections often exaggerate the slough of literary imitation, seen particularly in the "Week," which he cast off later. Hazlitt, Lamb, and the contemporary virtuosos like N. P. Willis, and the English reviewers, are sometimes traceable, but he shook loose easily. I like him best when, in his mood of brusque opposition, which Emerson disliked, he swings his sentence like an edged and rhythmic bush hook on sweet fern and dead wood alike.

The more I read Thoreau, the more I feel that with all his faults of discontinuity, and occasional rhetoric, as of a

* "A Week on the Concord and Merrimack Rivers," p. 447.
† *Ibid.*, pp. 91-92.
‡ "Life Without Principle," p. 284.
§ "Journals," 1850.

solitary trying to write in the accent of a sophisticated society, he is one of the masters of English prose, purer, stronger, racier, closer to a genuine life rhythm, than any one of his contemporaries, in England or America. A perfectionist in philosophy, he can claim no perfection here—for in suavity and organization and the organ roll of phrase there are a hundred better than he. But his style is like a hill of sumachs and wild apples which has a natural subtlety of expression that partakes of the secret of nature itself, although man has been there, has cut if not planted, and perhaps made the harmony from his own imagination. The hill slope merges into woods, it is a moment only between the cornfield and the forest, and Thoreau is his best self only by paragraphs, but there a master.

Of his verse I say little, because even more than with Emerson, who rose occasionally to poetry, it is a function of his prose. Poetry, he said in the "Week," is an irruption, great prose of equal elevation commands more respect than great verse, it reaches "a more permanent and level height." It did with him. His best verse contains lines of point and power exactly equivalent to the epigrams that dot his prose. He had no rhythmic flow in poetry, but a recurrent rise and fall like the hum of his favorite telegraph wires. Poetry, he thought, was a subsidence, "drawn from under the feet of the poet," a vital function like breathing; the poet was more than the poem. In short, like Emerson, he would not constrain his nature to be beat up into a regular rhythm. There was too much raw material in his philosophy for sonnet forms. A journal, like his, is best kept in prose and indeed, as his translations from the Greek show, his ear was not set to literary cadences. It took nature to move him to poetry, but it was only by the poetry of prose that he could speak. Metre bound his tongue.

II.

STYLE aside, Thoreau must live by his descriptions and his criticism. When he sat down to expound philosophy as such, it was someone else's philosophy. His own he prefers to apply. When he is in the critical mood, when he compares his life and ideals with Concord's, when the ax touches his trees or the state puts fingers on his freedom, then the woodchuck turns and the man begins to write. No more absurd statement was ever made than that America has produced no critics. With Poe, Emerson, and Thoreau any half century might be content.

Why has Thoreau's criticism of literature and life been so little observed by historians of American literature? First, because he has been read by excerpts, or in his few books, which are excerpts from his Journals, and there the nature passages have always been given a preference. It is only in the twentieth century that we begin to realize the virility of the American mind in the first half of the nineteenth century, or comprehend that there is an increasing need for going back to Walden. And next, because Thoreau, like Alcott and Emerson and all the Transcendentalists—even such border men as Hawthorne and Melville—was a world-or-nothing man. He did not work in a category, was perhaps incapable of specialization, and certainly inimical to it, could not and would not write merely economic, or classical, or literary criticism. His idea of a pervading unity made it impossible for him to describe a wood mouse, criticize an essayist, or comment on a farmer's habit of mind without seeking relationships as far as Betelgeuse. Not that he was given to oratorical analogies like Emerson in his later years; no, this was what, in reality, his subjects were; every leaf had its aspect in eternity and that was the aspect which for him was real. It was the prespecialist age when philosophers were still just possible; and for a Transcendentalist to cultivate his garden was to write with the universe as theme.

For Thoreau, therefore, as for Emerson, the problem of truth was so extended that to put together his commentary by means of a logical plan was to submit to a discipline that seemed, and probably was, artificial. It was to make a novel out of life. Only the anger and the immediate need of "Civil Disobedience" and "Slavery in Massachusetts," or the intensely personal theme of "Economy" in "Walden," could provide such a restraint for his ranging intellect. Hence, like Emerson, who also took on the cosmos, he is at his best in epigrams, for epigrams are sharp glances into infinite truth; or in those paragraphs of his that move in one net-scoop of words. Is it the transitional character of our civilization, and the diversity and rapidity of its change that has given us so many good paragraphers among typical American writers, from Franklin and Jefferson, through Emerson and Thoreau and Mark Twain to the modern columnists? Thoreau, I should call a paragrapher of genius.

Hence also his books are always mislabeled. The "Week," which is a youth's philosophy, is listed under "Travel" with "The Maine Woods," which is a true travel book; and "Walden" goes with the "Excursions" under "Nature Literature." One might as truly call Shakespeare's English plays of kings, history, and Browning's "Ring and the Book" a detective story.

12.

I DO not intend for an instant to depreciate Thoreau as a master in the literature of nature. When it comes to mere information there are, it is true, many who can beat him at his own game,—which, however, Hudson, perhaps excepted, they learned from him. Burroughs is more consecutive in his descriptions, as well as more accurate.

Muir is often more picturesque. Even Audubon, with his quaint stilted style, can better suggest the vast diversity of an American wilderness.

But Thoreau lifts far above the latitudes in which these nature-lovers work. They are draughtsmen, he is the artist who sees the part in its relation to a whole. Nor are the achievements of "Winter Visitors" or "Wild Apples" or the river scenes in the "Week" or the literary geography of Walden, merely transcendentalized description. For Thoreau in his rôle of a relater and interpreter was attempting a feat beside which these other nature sketches were just literary games. He has a self-appointed task to adjust himself and his race with him to New England, with the full consciousness that, as a nature-lover, he is a pioneer on a new continent, which is known but not humanized as environment, whose airs, waters, flowers, birds, and stones are still alien to Europeans, who themselves are still squatters in its woods. See how carefully in all his descriptive writings he searches the records of the centuries of settlement, to find what Maine, or Cape Cod, or Concord was like in the seventeenth, in the eighteenth, century. How lovingly he lingers over the history of his river, letting his imagination drift down the history of its slow adjustment to the urgencies of civilized man.

This is the true explanation of his fervid and never-waning interest in the Indian. It was not Cooper's romantic attachment to a "nature man." Read "The Maine Woods" carefully and you will see that it was knowledge that Thoreau sought, that intimate knowledge of environment which every English poet has by inheritance, and even yet, few Americans. A most striking characteristic of American imaginative literature is its lack of roots in the soil. Even with Whitman, who belongs to the school of Thoreau, the relationship is indicated in broad terms, by strings of American things and names. Compare him in this respect with Masefield or with Tennyson. The Indian knew his forest as a cockney knows his street, and as no American knows even his wood lot. It was the reticence of the savage, not his romance, that piqued Thoreau into his Maine journeys. He wished to unseal the aboriginal lore of America.

I submit that this attempt to make the American at home in his land is of the highest importance æsthetically and psychologically—so vitally important, even in its utilitarian aspects, that much of our nervous unrest and feverish maladjustments to labor may be broadly attributed to a failure to heed the necessity that European man must adjust himself to a new climatic environment.

For Thoreau this problem was ever present, as can be denied only by those who have not read him. Indeed, I believe that he would be well content to live in the American consciousness as the interpreter of the American environment. There he has succeeded. Think of woods that no hand has planted, of pastures invaded by wilderness, and of the characteristic mingling of free forest and land subdued, that is still America, and you think of Thoreau. He is the medium. And thanks to the rush of industrialism in the East and the necessitous pioneering of the West that followed the Civil War, he is still the best as well as the first in the field. I know of no modern American who has felt his continent as Thoreau tried to feel it, unless it is Robert Frost.

This explains the extraordinary excitement of Thoreau at his best. When he tramps Monadnock, sounds Walden water, walks winter fields by moonlight, watches the ants battle, learns ancient history from the arrowiferous sands of Concord, it is a renewal of the romance of the explorers. No civilized man has seen what he sees. It is still a virgin land, even though battered, burnt, and cut by exploiters. New Yorkers, Chicagoans, San Franciscans, are at home in the city congeries they have made, but they and the rest of us are still alien to the land, still needing the spiritual maps of a Thoreau. Our woods, our farms, our suburban lots, the skies above us, are not yet our own.

And fortunately Thoreau's style, which could be austere, tense, uplifted, could warm and uncoil and glitter for his descriptions of nature. I choose these at random:

"The pickerel . . . is a solemn, stately, ruminant fish, lurking under the shadow of a pad at noon, with still, circumspect, voracious eye, motionless as a jewel set in water."

"Maples, full of glee and sap."

"It is candle-light. The fishes leap. The meadows sparkle with the coppery light of fireflies. The evening star, multiplied by undulating water, is like bright sparks of fire continually ascending."

13.

THE battle between the city and the country reaches one of its climaxes in Thoreau. The conflict between two ways of life, which is a deeper and longer conflict than any merely economic struggle, was sharply visible from Walden. He did not make the mistake of thinking that a man was a countryman because he lived in the country, nor commit the fallacy of praising labor with the plough in contrast to labor at the machine. He was free from this kind of sentimentalism, spared perhaps because the horrid results of factory life were less visible in New than in Old England. He was concerned rather with the deeper difference between accord with nature and its exploitation. The costliness of crowd living, the creation of artificial wants, the loss of aim in a hurried and fretful life, and an obsession with the means of living—these are what he meant by city life. He spoke of other disabilities—gayety, license, convention, the dissipation of time valuable for a naturalist and a philosopher. But these are the whims of a Puritan solitary. On the art of social living his views are about as valuable as his criticism of music and architecture! He knew Maine better than Boston, and because he was a right judge of sunsets cannot be allowed to deprecate a taste in wine. One may admire him and still tolerate Voltaire, Alcibiades, Pope, and Anatole France, even though none of them could have been happy overnight at Walden!

The democratic man, who, seizing his spiritual opportunities, should rise to all that Whitman and Thoreau offered, has of course never bestirred himself, nor been concerned with nature. He has taken, rather, to city life with rapture, and has filled the environs of every great city, and Walden itself, with blazing symbols of every abomination in Thoreau's calendar. The excrements of the city lie on the countryside. We have all risen like hungry fish to the lure of new desires. We want more a hundred times than in 1840, and advertising sets new wants before us in triplicate. We have sold our individualism to the radio, the newspaper, the weekly illustrated magazine, and the moving picture, and have accepted the ideology of a business world which believes that a man at hard labor is the noblest work of God. A Thoreauvian must think that there is more energy than health in American civilization, more noise than aim, more childish intent to pile block on block than philosophic consideration for the happiness of man. Yet like children we have learned something in our play. We have gone through that necessary stage where the means for living without digressive effort are readily provided. Machinery, not the Transcendentalists, made this possible. The plain man has acquired civilized luxuries, if not civilized tastes. He has learned how to be comfortable, if not how to be happy. He has leisure if he wants it, and lacks only the knowledge and the will to control his own

future according to ends that may be regarded as best.
Men by no means plain are no better off. We are ripe for
a dose of Thoreau.

But it takes—at least in the industrialized West—an
aristocrat to read him. In spite of his rough boots, worn
coat, and brusque manners he was every ounce an aristocrat himself. He had his idea of what a man owed to himself. He had his code. It is clear that wealth and material
power and, what is more unfortunate, dynamic ideas are
in the hands today of men whose keenness does not com-
pensate for their lack of insight and of self-knowledge.
One kind of aristocracy died with the old South in the
Civil War, and if it had survived might have taught us
something of value in social intercourse almost lost today.
Another aristocracy waned with the New England individualists, and this was the more valuable because its discriminate renunciation and its positive grip upon fine
thinking are not only in sharper opposition to the tendencies of mass living, but far more transferable to the conditions of that life. We can provide Waldens anywhere
today if we can breed the men to want them. We must
breed Thoreaus somewhere, or see this machine society
stuffed and stifled by its own superheated desires. One
cannot walk down Broadway without praising God that
sane men once did live here. Thoreau is their prophet.

He is not dead yet. He is more alive than Emerson, because he is more timely, because the oversoul at best can
stir us on to metaphysics, whereas a possible way of happy
living is a need at every man's door. There is still a minority determined to live their own best lives, at Walden
or elsewhere, which is what one has to do in order to become a Thoreauvian.

CHAPTER SIX

Hawthorne and Melville

NATHANIEL HAWTHORNE was a mystery, even to himself, and, like Melville, he has remained a man of mystery in American literature, whose heart successive biographers have tried to bare, each one with a different explanation. Emerson beside him seems transparent, Thoreau definable. And this mystery is not only in the man, it extends to the profound impression made upon the whole English-reading world by books that, in some of their aspects, are stiff, crude, and conventional, in others garnished with a romanticism already outmoded and even in his own time unworthy of a great imagination.

He was naïvely proud of his "depths," even to the point of denying their mystery. "A cloudy veil stretches over the abyss of my nature," he wrote in a letter to Sophia Peabody in 1842, but adds that any mortal "capable of full sympathy and therefore worthy to come into my depths" is welcome to penetrate his heart. "I abhor [mystery]," he says elsewhere, "and have often felt that words may be a thick and darksome veil of mystery between the soul and the truth which it seeks." Words are "poor rags and tatters of Babel." * "Secrecy and darkness," he did not love. Yet with a reticence, a reserve, and a passion for solitude seldom equaled, he practiced them all his life.

* "Journals," 1840.

HAWTHORNE AND MELVILLE

There is no great philosophic secret in the abyss of Hawthorne's nature. There is not even a mystery. He was not a mystic. He belongs with the artists who ask "How?" rather than with the philosophers who learn "Why?" His reticence comes from finding no solution to the problems that constantly beset him. His reserve and love of solitude were the defenses of an imagination formed by peculiar circumstances and playing upon circumstances still more peculiar. What profundity he has is by intuition, not by logic, and his success is the success of an imaginative dreamer (not a thinker) with a genius for looking backward at the very moment when the rest of his generation were absorbed in what was ahead.

2.

I SHALL not attempt to retell the familiar story of Hawthorne's life, for it needs no retelling, but only a redistribution of emphasis. Mr. Lloyd Morris * sees in him an inhibited adventurer, irked by the wild blood of his sea-captain ancestors. Mr. Arvin † would have him to be a man ruined by habits of solitude; but a taste for solitude is a symptom, not a cause. If his biography is to be rewritten, it is the Bowdoin years, rather than the Salem withdrawal in a family that kept by choice not only out of the world but away from each other, which might be given more amplitude. In his college days he led a gentleman's life, with wine and cards and good talk in it, a life whose impress shows clearly still in the face of the much later portrait in the Philadelphia Museum of Fine Arts, the face of a man of the world, who belongs, except for the deep-burning eyes, to the company of Irving and Cooper, rather than of the "ugly [so he called him] . . . uncouth and rustic" Thoreau. Hawthorne is neither a

* "The Rebellious Puritan," by Lloyd Morris.
† "Hawthorne," by Newton Arvin.

227

Melville estopped from adventuring, nor an Alcott devoted to asceticism. He seems—and was—a rich nature, caught and held (not unwillingly) by circumstance, and so become a spectator, not an actor, in the great drama of life.

Indeed, what I chiefly draw as significant from a new scanning of Hawthorne's life story is his distaste for what we call action. This was not merely an inhibition. When he wanted money, he went into what amounted to business to get it. He was a good custom's officer, and a good consul. He was persistent and not unhandy in disposing of his literary work. But in business, in action in the world, whether economical, political, or social, his interest was perfunctory. The energy of his American period never excited him. He was like a reluctant schoolboy with his book open but his eyes elsewhere.

It is hard, of course, for us who have yielded to the industrial revolution and cherish its fruits to understand the shrinking back of a Bowdoin gentleman, Salem recluse, Concord moralist, from the machine age just beginning. For us the lovely New England village, created by men who believed that order was heaven's first law, is a museum piece. We hope, some day, to achieve by machines an equivalent excellence, but what we see is only a relic happily preserved, not the thing itself. The Hawthorne I am trying to interpret saw the New England town in its first real decadence, a civilization breaking up. He saw all about him (and constantly records) the new machine industry, which on country streams and in mountain valleys was penetrating New England like a fungus growth, sapping the last vitality from farm life, but bringing a new and rapid prosperity. The machine to him was what the machine is to that contemporary romanticist, Eugene O'Neill. Indeed, he sets down in his notebooks a plot of a steam engine that catches and finally crushes a man to death which might have suggested "Dynamo." But with Hawthorne it is disinterest that defines his attitude, not dislike. The mechanical age did not catch his attention except as it suggested figures for his symbolism. He drew moral imaginings from the new age as Thoreau got music from the wires of the telegraph. His face was far from this our war, and for good reasons. The first ingredient of Hawthorne's so-called mystery was that he did not want to act, did not want to live in any sense that his age, either its practical majority or its transcendental minority, called acting and living. This, of course, irked him, made him unhappy, sapped his self-confidence, gave him Freudian dreams of his classmates who went on to success while he lagged behind. It accentuated a desire for solitude, which his love of brooding had already made characteristic. It made life difficult, as all maladjustments make life difficult. This is the true Hawthorne, uncomfortable in his solitude, but not frustrated. You cannot be frustrated by failing in what you never really want to do. This is the true Hawthorne, who joined the communistic experiment at Brook Farm neither to reform the world nor to escape it, but only in the hope of making a living in the least uncongenial circumstances.* This was the Hawthorne who, like the woodchuck, never came out of his hole except to eat.

3.

REALITY for Hawthorne was moral reality, and it was the lack of a moral element in which he could believe that made his own times unreal to Hawthorne, and action in them, beyond the necessities of existence, futile. Still quainter to us than the old village, still further from practicable living as we know it, was the life governed by moral duty or devoted to a search for God that had been the ultimate reality of the Puritans. Against Puritanism

* See his letters to his future wife.

as a theology and a system of ethics he was in lifelong opposition. He had thrown over its Calvinism and he gave his best imagination to depicting the terrible results of its austerities. Yet, though he freed himself from its precepts, he never escaped from the brooding upon sin and the moral life that was the cause of Puritanism and its legacy.

It is impossible to comprehend Hawthorne without the Puritan background. Puritanism, for him, was a fortress from which he had escaped and was glad to be gone, and yet looked back to as a city fortified and strong in its certainties while he was a wanderer, clear-eyed, but uncertain and weak. The Puritan age and its sure morality was an obsession in his life. It was still the norm from which deviations could be measured. If success for his contemporaries was measured by action, and his failure to be interested in action depressed him, his real concern was with ideals diametrically different. They were the ideals, though not the fact, of Puritanism. Spiritual failures, moral failures, were for him, as for the Puritans, the great theme, and his great characters can all of them be described in no other terms. Calvinism had broken down, but the world for Hawthorne remained nevertheless a moral world, in which the new energies of industrialism were exactly equivalent to the commercialism of earlier ages, which was never, even in Venice or Constantinople, a norm for good living. Business has always until today been regarded as a necessary evil of civilization, and the whole of modern literature up to the early summer of the industrial revolution may be cited directly or indirectly as evidence for this statement. It was so regarded by Hawthorne, and by business he meant everything that interfered with his concern for the soul escaped with its scars from the Puritan citadel and wandering, uncertain where to go.

Nor had the age of trade and production in Hawthorne's day revealed itself as a revolution whereby mankind was to use the machine to make something better or worse, but certainly different. Hawthorne, looking back to the strong city that the Puritans had built about God, saw in later generations only series of mysterious and romantic tragedies where prisoners, escaped from it, died of their wounds, and freedom brought moral disintegration. This was the real world for him, and beside its problems "progress" seemed irrelevant. The "new" men in his stories, by which I mean the types that have close analogies in the leaders of our civilization today, are all subordinate characters, either insignificant or unworthy. The bankers are sly, the tradesmen petty, the industrialists morally stupid and uninteresting. Indeed, the New England world of State Street and the mills seemed as dull to Hawthorne as the country to Pope. Emerson was on fire with prophetic glances at the science of the future, but Hawthorne was untouched by the new births of modernism about him, except for the natural depression of a man who cannot think with his neighbors. The decay of the old world excited him where the grossness of the new merely inspired distaste. He saw in the breakdown of Puritanism moral issues that had some aspects of eternity, but in the upbuilding of a new economic state, none that seemed to him significant.

Transcendentalism, of course, that refinement of spiritual unrest which filled New England and the New England West with a cloud of "seekers," "come-outers," and enthusiasts, could not fail to attract him, but only because of the companionship with fine minds it promised him, not for any hope in its doctrine. Through his own and his wife's friends he entered that circle of the rebellious who were opposed, like him, to the materialism of the new industrial age; Emerson interested him, Margaret Fuller fascinated him, Thoreau got his admiration—but Transcendentalism as such touched him not at all. It could not

arouse him, for enthusiasm and optimism were both foreign to his nature, and the fact of moral disorder and
decay stirred his imagination where the possibility of
moral regeneration by pulling on mental boot straps left
him cold. Ways of reform did not interest his skeptic nature, ideas for a future society could not hold his attention
long, because he had the novelist's, not the philosopher's,
eye, and human failures and their causes were more interesting to him than prophecies of success, one might truly
say than success itself. Margaret Fuller's transcendental
heifer that kicked over the milk pail at Brook Farm was
his symbol for the rebellion of these intellectualists. He
did not expect to escape from the "chaos" of time by the
transcendental route. He was not, I think, really interested in escape, except in moods of financial discourage-
ment.

Rather, his sensitive mind, released, as was Emerson's,
from the straitjacket of Calvinism, turned back like the
convict to his jail, to brood and speculate upon the ulti-
mates in human nature of that sin which the Calvinists
had thought to chain forever. Not hope, not faith, not a
new revelation, and not, therefore, the transcendental, but
rather the actual moral world seemed to him the business
of the moment—the unfinished business, if you please, of
a dying Puritanism. And in the moral world it is the failures, complete or qualified, that a novelist finds most interesting, and a novelist like Hawthorne, brooding upon
the breakdown of a great system, would inevitably choose
for his themes. To escape transcendentally, like Emerson,
by arguing the insubstantiability of life, and the superi-
ority of the good spirit over mortal flesh, was, for an artist,
simply to destroy the problem itself. Hester's hopes (in
"The Scarlet Letter") of a new sex relationship would, in
such a conception of life, become more important than her
own story—and this was to turn art into philosophy.

Donatello's symbolism would become more significant than his tragedy. If Hawthorne had not been skeptical of Transcendentalism, he would have turned away in any case the instant he began to write. For his mind was set on truth, not hope, and truth for every man resides only where he most feels reality.

And hence, in the feverish activity of the forties and the fifties, and in the felt presence of that unrivaled optimism which was already stirring Whitman to pæans of democracy, Hawthorne chose for his characters the weak or the wounded from the great battlefields of Puritanism, or the dreamers and the self-deluded who wandered vainly in search of a new security. Is it necessary to specify, to name the personnel of "The Blithedale Romance," "The Marble Faun," "Septimius," "The Scarlet Letter," the short stories? They are all moral failures, whether victims, like Donatello, Hester, Ethan Brand, Hilda, or would-be conquerors, like Hollingsworth, Zenobia, Septimius, who are too often self-deceived. They belong one and all to a world of moral speculation in its last orbit, already eclipsed by industrialism, and to be darkened forever in New England by the Civil War and the decades succeeding. A world in Hawthorne's day still dramatic because its failures were on the grand scale of moral perfection, but significant only in art, since the attention of society had shifted from being to doing, and the spiritual conflicts that had shaken the past were already degenerating into taboos, reform complexes, faddisms, and gross superstitions.

Think of Hawthorne, then, as a man conditioned by Puritanism, though quite free from its theology and skeptical of its ethical code. Think of him as an observer set at the very moment when the sense of sin and the will to moral perfection alike give place to a justification by material success. Think of him as a skeptic among his fellow idealists who sees that the present is rushing on and away from the place of conflict where the secret of human destiny seemed about to be revealed, and turns backward brooding on the wreckage of the past, finding more to engage him in broken wills and frustrated hopes than in prosperity, and more wisdom in failure than in rosy Emersonian hope. Grant this, as one must, and it becomes easier to explain his broodings, his seclusion, his increasing maladjustment to life; and also his rather astounding success as an artist, a success caught at the very edge of failure. Here is to be found the reason why this gifted observer with "something of the hawk-eye" about him, turned instinctively to the methods of romance.

4.

FOR this success his skepticism was largely responsible, more so, I think, than his susceptibility to the romantic movement, which after all only gave him his opportunity. With Melville and Twain, he is one of the three great skeptics in American literature. Melville's skepticism became in the heat of his ill-regulated imagination a rebellious positivism that melted the conventions of his upbringing. He wrote one great book in which natural man, surrounded by the similitudes of all his instincts, cruised madly to revenge himself upon the malignity of the universe. Afterward in the attempt to rationalize a hidden world of the emotions that the new science had not yet begun even to consider, he set down his discoveries in symbolic narrative, defying a public that wanted stories, not prophecies. I cannot do justice to him in this chapter since he is a perplexing figure of major importance, not yet in perspective for a summary criticism, although I hope to be able to show here the relation of his successful books to Hawthorne and to literature. But Hawthorne was a true, a congenital, skeptic, who kept his heart in security no matter how wildly it throbbed, and never let his obsessive interest in the moral problems of humanity deceive him into certainty.

He was a skeptic of Puritanism, inevitably. He knew its annals, bore them in his own heredity. He had broken from its creed with his generation, even though he never escaped from the problems it had tried to solve by *force majeure*. The New England world was one pattern for him, dim in the distant past, sharp in the background, raveling into tatters at his feet, but woven through with the same themes of sin and grace and will. He did not believe in the Calvinistic dogma, and therefore could see it objectively from its source in the secret springs of error to its widespread and powerful effects.

He was a skeptic, as I have said, of the new "alleviation," the optimism of the Hollingsworths and the Septimiuses, who by reform or by a magical ethics would bring about a new and happy world. Emerson to him was a man with a sunbeam on his face, yet a man deluded, who, denying the power of evil, denied something vital in character itself. He stood with him, watching the breakdown of a moral order that had been as complete ethically as the system of Aquinas, but he looked at men to see how they were affected, not forward rejoicing in the possibilities of a different future.

He was skeptical of the new economic world where science was to right all ills, but skeptical with the mild interest of a man who looks upon what does not concern him. Only his humanitarianism was touched by the symptoms of the new era,* he did not follow through, did not face this new world like Emerson, who transcended the conflict, like Thoreau, who offered a determined and obstinate refusal as unlike Hawthorne's indifference as the sun from moonlight. He was too skeptical of the values of

* See his horror at English industrial poverty.

industrialism to be dazed or angered by its confusions. The human problems resulting, about which one could not be skeptical, were all that really aroused his fascinated concern.

Skeptical of all cures, indifferent to what was itself an increasing indifference to the moral problems, he kept his head and his heart, and while others prepared for the Civil War and the physical development of the seventies, and Christian Science, and the triumph of mechanism, he went his own way and, like the captain of a derelict ship, made observations of the sun, the stars, the currents, eternal verities independent of time and taste.

To speak in plainer English, it was the thing itself—character, human nature, the soul—that interested Hawthorne, not tendencies, reconstructions, theories, and hopes. And when the dull soullessness of the immediate present of commercialism repelled him, and his transcendental friends' obstinate pursuit of their dreams left him cold, he turned backward in his brooding to the New England past (so close to his childhood) and found there one of the great treasure houses of human experience, a civilization characteristic and unique, built upon moral ideas that he understood to the core of his being, powerful with a dogmatism worth wrestling with, and illustrating in a thousand fashions those frailties of human certitude which skeptics love to brood upon; furthermore, a civilization rich for the artist in dramatic conflicts between the good will and sin. For there in early New England, at the dramatic moment when the old order degenerating died in the midst of the new, and vivid fire shoots of the ethical imagination were released from the theology of necessitarianism, was a store of material, of stories that told themselves, and meant more than their plots. And this material *now*, though not at the time of its making, was romantic in the truest sense, could be viewed through mists that suggested more than they revealed, could be expanded into a type experience of humanity. And in this civilization, or in the shadows it cast over the present, he did his best work.

5.

HAWTHORNE's natural bent was toward realism. The "Note-Books" are almost naïve in their painful attempts to provide a clothing of verisimilitude for the moral ideas that were the staple of his thought. "A person to catch fireflies, and try to kindle his household fire with them. It could be symbolic of something." "The smell of peat . . ." These items of observation, laboriously recorded, and often transferred with little change to his stories, or made into stories, are meant to hold the pen to its object. The object is exact realism in a world where reality could be only a shadow of moral truth. They do not seem romantic, even when they record the bloody footsteps, poisoned drinks, old unhappy incidents, that served afterward for tales which we (and he) called romances. Seldom has a recluse looked upon the current of life with a more sternly focused eye. Indeed when Hawthorne left home and routine at all, it was seemingly to fill another notebook with pictures of how the world looked. It was the realism of his early sketches, "A Rill from the Town Pump," and "The Celestial Railroad," that gave him his first success. "The Marble Faun" is still a guidebook to Rome. Children learn of the Puritans from "Twice-Told Tales" and "The Scarlet Letter." He was capable of realism, although he used it only to give names and local habitations to his moral imaginings.

But realism alone would not serve his skeptical purposes. It is true that skepticism is antiromantic, and indeed, while Hawthorne's methods are borrowed from the romantic fashions of the day, I cannot see anything essentially romantic in his mind. Nor are the great passages in his best books romantic, if the term has any meaning beyond imaginative excellence. The first and last, those superb chapters of "The Scarlet Letter," are no more and no less romantic than the great chapters of "Tess of the D'Urbervilles." They have a setting exotic in time and removed from the familiar, they are generalized into universal qualities, but this does not make them romantic. To call "The Scarlet Letter" a romance, is as useful as to call it a story of the Puritans. Neither description defines it.

The obvious romanticisms in Hawthorne, those mysteries laid down in "The Marble Faun" like obstacles in a road race, pictures that take on life, witch brews, magnetisms, resurrections, potions, portents, mystic resemblances, are often (let us be frank) the shoddy in his work. The death seat and death stare of Judge Pyncheon is something to frighten children with (and is so used), the kidnapping of Hilda is cheap Gothic machinery, little Pearl with her witch soul is psychologically untrue and a blemish in a great book. Some of the short stories are too elementary in their melodrama even for the movies.

The romantic movement did not give us our Hawthorne, even though he spelled out German stories with a dictionary and read, like every other American in his period, widely in romantic literature. But romanticism, and especially the late Gothic, pseudo-German romanticism that attracted Poe so strongly, gave Hawthorne his tongue. It was already decadent in Europe, but (as has happened before and will again) reached these shores to be taken up by minds fresh and vigorous and with a new subject matter full of vitality. Repelled by the present, in which (as he says so eloquently in his "introductory" on the customhouse before "The Scarlet Letter") he could find nothing that stirred him, those veils of illusion, this retreat from immediacy, these resorts to the mysterious and the picturesque which were the romantic formula, were welcome and especially to a man who chose to write of the past, and was fascinated by a dying morality and its diseases.

And thus his native skepticism found in the language of this romanticism a happy medium. It was a happy choice; not the great victory of a genius who resolves the spiritual problems of his age (a Goethe or a Shakespeare), but the victory of an artist who achieves expression by discovering a medium adapted to his talent and calling forth his powers. Let me go into more detail, for this description of Hawthorne is crucial for his position as an artist.

While he had shed Calvinism and distrusted the new spirituality, Hawthorne had kept much more than Emerson, and almost as much as Longfellow, the conventions of New England moralism, especially in matters of sex. He still assumes a profound connection between sexual irregularity and irretrievable sin. A woman who is not innocent is not damned, but she is blackened. A curse is on her, which she must struggle against, may profit by, but from which she can never escape into happiness. Even the nude in art shocked Hawthorne, as one sees in "The Marble Faun." It is never certain in that book whether the sin with which Miriam worked such havoc upon the inhuman purity of Hilda was sexual immorality or violence leading to murder. There is no hope for Hester Prynne except in a new society where her impulses might sublimate differently. Hilda, of these three women, is the most significant, for she, in her hysterical agonies over the sin about her, is Hawthorne's own tortured belief that purity in itself should be able to give character to the soul, like sin and remorse. Hilda is the conscience of New England struggling against disillusionment.

The characters of these women, and their problems, are a credit to Hawthorne's creative genius, as may be said also of Donatello, his image of childhood wronged; but their fates are not inevitable. These are determined by a convention that Hawthorne retained from the Puritanism whose theology he had discarded. Hester and Miriam and Donatello must not escape their sins, Hilda must be saved and forget. Admirably consistent in his psychological analyses, when this great observer turns moralist he reverts to convention. Sin and remorse he knows, salvation or damnation he takes ready-made from the remains of his creed, where skepticism had not yet penetrated. The story must always in Hawthorne be balanced between the realities of the individual and the requirements of a theoretical morality. The artist, skeptic and creative, writes the narrative, the Puritan adds the dénouement. Realism becomes dogmatic with such a contradiction at its heart. It imposes a philosophy, as George Eliot did in her moral novels, or it breaks down in the impossible task of recording and explaining human nature in the same document. But romance, with its symbolisms, its peeps and withdrawals, its retreats into allegory and flights to mystery, can preserve the balance between indecision and insight and yet keep the story vital, the characters true.

For Hawthorne, then, with his really profound insight into moral situations and his skeptic inability to solve them philosophically, or solve them at all (except by conventional punishments), romance was an obvious escape from intolerable difficulties in expression. The veil of unreality, the reticence of the indirect, the indefiniteness of fancy, which hold the interest yet never commit the writer to a final solution—these were tricks of the romanticist's trade ready at hand. What he would have done in periods less romantic I cannot tell, but I hazard the guess that in 1730 or in 1930 Hawthorne would have been tongue-tied and kept silent. That he had to choose romance, being what he was, writing when he did, seems obvious. He says so, and repeats it. His ideas are mere moral abstractions of the most obvious sort, dressed in cold observation, until by the devices of romantic machinery he is able to build them up into a story where what he knows of character becomes impressive in its insight, and what skepticism forbids or convention insists upon is toned down or wreathed in veils of romantic mystification.

One does not romanticize in familiar speech and perhaps that was the reason for Hawthorne's well-known taciturnity, which might have extended to pen and paper also if he had not picked up the fashionable story-telling methods of the day and found that when, thinking as a New Englander, he wrote like Tieck or Hoffmann, he could say enough and not too much. I do not mean that he was inhibited in the modern sense. I mean rather that he was cautious with a Yankee cautiousness, afraid to commit himself in daylight, where all could see his uncertainties in matters in which everyone else seemed confident, and (like the professional conjuror) glad of a make-up, with some mumbo-jumbo to fill up the gaps between his admirable perceptions of humanity under stress.

The mumbo-jumbo (which one must admit does not seem to have been distasteful to him) is painfully visible in most of his stories: climaxes of sensational horror, unnecessary mystifications. The end of "The Marble Faun," the end of "The House of Seven Gables," the end of "The White Old Maid," may be due to time-serving concessions to romantic fashions, which, like the clothes of Concord and the domestic manners of the Americans, were already outmoded abroad. But I should charge this, and every dependence upon the machinery of romanticism, not only to the use and wont of the American magazines for which he first wrote, but also to Hawthorne's need of whatever favored reticence and avoided conclusion. His imagination could clothe itself only in symbolic representation and that he found in romance. If he found there also folderol and bunkum and kept them, give him credit for rejecting sentimentality. I do not see by what other path his peculiar genius could have found expression.

6.

EMERSON said that Hawthorne was greater than his books. This remark, which has often been turned against that shrewd critic, was a proof of his shrewdness. He did not say that Hawthorne was a greater thinker than his books would indicate. Indeed, I believe that it was precisely the lack of profound thought and the evidences of spiritual conflict and mental confusion in Hawthorne's books that repelled the sage of Concord, who liked to see the intellect conquering uncertainty by great lifts of spiritual confidence. Alcott, who rose never to come down again at all, was more sympathetic to Emerson than Hawthorne's brooding skepticism, which could neither extinguish doubt nor give up trying. Hawthorne—if I interpret rightly—seemed to Emerson, as they talked and walked together, a far greater man than his childish mystifications, his naïve sins clad in rich, strange garments, his gurgling throats, and theatric scenes of romantic fancy. In the bright air where lived the oversoul, this trifling with stage sets seemed unworthy. Philosophically considered, Emerson might have said, Hawthorne never got beyond the fact of sin, and wonder at its interweaving with the stuff of virtue; nor had he any solution except remorse, or death.

Emerson did not like fiction.* Character and personality meant little to him unless they had transcendental aspects. Reality, he said, dissolved in his hands. A small man (philosophically considered) like Dickens, who

* When he called Poe the "Jingle man" he clearly spoke in derogation of Poe's whole literary effort.

worked in a minor art that was useful, amusing, revealing, but of the kind that would vanish at the first toot of the trumpet of doom, a man who never tried to be a philosopher, he could understand fairly well, and like his books, as Æschylus might have read with patronizing approval some human, humorous tale from the Orient. But Hawthorne was not a small man, and he did not deal in the appearance of things. He cared for significance, yet stuck fast, so Emerson must have thought, in circumstance. It was only in that least regarded chapter of "The Scarlet Letter," where Hester adumbrates her new world for the sexes, that Emerson, I suspect, would have seen the Hawthorne he admired beginning to come through. The rest was a staged statement of a moral problem without a philosophic answer. It was like the ballet he once attended, and found valuable as experience, but not to be taken seriously by a man who could not stop with men and women in his search for God.

I say that Emerson was shrewd, because it is clear that Hawthorne himself was not content with his rôle of observer and felt that, in this respect, he was a frustrated man. He desired (like all the Concord men) to see through the mystery, and the best he could do was to record the failure of men and women to solve their problems, in stories which he felt (quite rightly) that his Puritan ancestors would have regarded as trivial. And to make his unsolved problems interesting, to express them at all as problems without committing himself to an answer, he had to charge and overcharge them with romance.

Indeed, as I have said, all of Hawthorne's best books are stories of failures. Couples, like the daguerreotypist and Phœbe in "The House of the Seven Gables," or Kenyon and Hilda, escape, but to a rather tame and uncertain future. The great figures—Hester, Dimmesdale, Zenobia, Miriam, Ethan Brand—all fail. And the books themselves are relative failures. In none of them, except perhaps in "The Scarlet Letter," does Hawthorne blend in one luminous whole both the significance and the reality of the life he depicts, as Dostoevsky, Hardy, even Fielding, all have done. He is always driven back (flies back would be a more accurate figure) to his romantic symbolism, which is left to be read in two or three possible ways, or made cloudy, like Melville's, who himself was also a frustrated philosopher. He romances sadly, not like Scott in joy, or like Cooper with a single interest in the romance itself. He turns and twists in his lonely Salem room from a life outside that repels him to a brooding that always hesitates this side of conviction. And his books hesitate and turn also, and take refuge in mere observation crudely moralized. They, like him, retreat from life at the moment of grasping. And if greatness lies in a quality of spirit, then Hawthorne was greater than his books, because they represent his compromises with an active world that otherwise got from him no real concessions. If he had not been happily married to a safe woman (who edited the eccentricities out of his journals) he would probably have kept silent after his first failure to put his inner being into acceptable words and, like the rest of his family, taken to his room for life. She put just enough heart and self-confidence into him to go on, as his letters to her show.

Emerson wrote much, and sometimes wisely, of art, but he had too little patience with its preliminaries. He could not understand that in records of failures which were in themselves failures to record completely, there could be virtues that his own serene elucidations could never pretend to. If he was right in feeling that Hawthorne was one of the great men of his hierarchy, then he was also right in believing that the greatness of a Dante or a Shakespeare had failed to consummate in his friend's work. But, as usual, his eyes were on the stars and he missed more earthly achievements. Hawthorne's obstinate tarryings with circumstance gave him a concentration that more expansive romantics never attain. If he did not philosophize sin, he gave us the most powerful portraits in English of the moral sinner. If he never reached a *Weltanschauung*, he did put into imperishable prose the ripe and overripe fruits of the deeply significant civilization of New England, itself the end of a cycle.

And in one respect at least Hawthorne did reach the scope of what we call world literature because it is typically expressive of humanity always and everywhere. His plight was typical. That passionate brooding on the whys and wherefores of human conduct which reaches no conclusion but relieves itself by a sudden outpouring of confession and description, is characteristic of all the moments in history when the skeptical mind, just escaped from dogmatic certainties, has refused to bury itself in the unreflecting life of action. Sometimes the result has been satire, sometimes romance, but the motive is always the same—to make a fresh reading of the problem that is man.

7.

THIS irreverent generation has mocked at Hawthorne's struggling souls who torture themselves over peccadillos like adultery and are morally wrecked by obsessions that (so it is assumed) any good psychoanalyst could remove. Studies in nerves seem to us more important than studies in morals, and certainly we are right in supposing that common sense and a working knowledge of science would have prevented half the casualties of literature. Hawthorne might retort by saying that without a moral sense you have of course no moral tragedies, and an observer of both epochs might add that the value of his literary psychology lies not in the deeds analyzed but in the picture of a struggle between right and wrong where the state of mind of the characters in conflict is immensely significant without regard to the rightness of what they think right or the wrongness of what they think wrong. If the plan of action seems great, not petty, that itself is an argument for the importance of the literary picture.

And indeed there is a lack of consistence between the scorn that our younger critics shower upon Hawthorne's moral creations and their respect for his style. They admit a dignity in the expression that they will not allow to the thing expressed.

Hawthorne's style has a mellow beauty; it is sometimes dull, sometimes prim, but is never for an instant cheap, never, like our later American styles, deficient in tone and unity. It is a style with a patina that may or may not accord with current tastes, yet, as with Browne, Addison, Lamb, Thoreau, is undoubtedly a *style*. Such styles spring only from rich ground, long cultivated, and such a soil was Hawthorne's. It was his good fortune to become a moral romancer at the end of an age of reflection when those subtle and perplexing factors which lie back of behavior are and have long been the subject of earnest study and obsessive interest. His style is the fulfillment of a long culture, turning toward literature only at its close. That this culture was Puritan determined the quality of the soil from which his rhythm came, but its depth and richness was due to the almost hysterical intensity of this civilization, where both the rigors and the opportunities of a new country had packed time with significant incident. When Hawthorne in later life went to England he wrote of his "old home" in the language of one who is possessed of a culture more intense if narrower than the English, and as old. And his style, although owing much of course to the great English tradition, gets its dignity from a stable sense of the generations of moral thinkers behind him. He was a rebel to their works, but he speaks nevertheless for a New England that had long been making up its mind.

Carlyle, whom he read, had no power to influence him as he did Melville; he has none of the suave imitativeness of Irving. The grave and simple beauty of his style is an absolute expression of the high seriousness of New England moralism, even when the subject matter is skepticism or cloudy German romance. When it is homely it is homely with the shrewdness of New England, an old country, long peculiar, long articulate, more humorous than the Scotch, more concentrated than the English, more self-confident than the rest of America.

And much of Hawthorne's success as a stylist must come from the dignity of his themes. Holding back from the new life of America into which Whitman was to plunge with such exuberance, he kept his style, like himself, unsullied by the prosaic world of industrial revolution, and chose, for his reality, the workings of the moral will. You can scarcely praise his style and condemn his subjects. Even romantic themes that would have been absurd in lesser hands get dignity from his purpose, and flush his gravity, like Donatello's wine, into warmth and beauty. Indeed, I should choose his description of the Sunshine of Monte Beni as the best description of his own style:

"The wine demanded so deliberate a pause, in order to detect the hidden peculiarities and subtle exquisiteness of its flavor, that to drink it was more of a moral than a physical enjoyment. There was a deliciousness in it that eluded analysis, and—like whatever else is superlatively good—was perhaps better appreciated in the memory than by present consciousness."

But to return to the inconsistency of those who would question Hawthorne's subjects while praising his style, it is foolish to suppose that he has been preserved, like some virtuosity of decoration, by his style alone. His field, to use the jargon of psychology, was neuroses. It was essentially the warped or injured mind that interested him, yet, like great doctors, he was a specialist, concerned only with the great neuroses, where the world had been too much for a patient who suffered not from the ordinary maladies of greed or vanity, but from the great maladjustments where minds of more than ordinary moral calibre clash with the offspring of their own powers and disabilities. He dealt with sin in its metaphysical sense of a disturbing element, a force in conflict with good and yet a part of good itself. His patients suffer greatly because they are potentially great. Hester, the Gentle Boy, Miriam —blot out these tragic figures and the scenes in which they move lose their interest. They are the fibre of their world, without which it is morally dull (like ours) and, being otherwise limited, devoid of memorable humanity. Even the defeatists and the utterly broken, like Clifford and Hepzibah, are the cause and blood of the story.

Every powerful age gets its expressive writer, and though it was in a transition between two ways of thinking about living, one moral, one materialistic, that Hawthorne, fortunately for his skeptical and observant genius, was born, he is another instance of this fact. As Shakespeare, the Renaissance man, gave feudalism its final lift into the imagination, so Hawthorne, the skeptic with a moral obsession, raised New England Puritanism—not the theory, but the practice and still more the results in mind and spirit—into art. This lies behind his style.

8.

HERMAN MELVILLE's struggle for self-expression was fiercer than Hawthorne's because he was more of the world, less of New England. A rover, whose imagination had been disciplined neither by Puritanism nor by a formal education, he lashed, like his own whales, into bloody foam when the lance of doubt finally struck him through. Hawthorne, talking with him, thought his reasonings over "Providence and futurity" rather monotonous,* but that was Hawthorne's reaction to any abstract speculation. And Melville, in return, had little use for the majesty of dying Puritanism. These Puritans, obsessed with practical morality, seemed to him merely dull.

He was impatient both with inhibitions and restraint. Both men were puzzled observers of a world that did not seem to be explained by any formulas, but Melville's perplexity drove him to wrath, not brooding. Romance for him was not a medium and a means of escape, it was a positive that led to action, it was the human spirit expanding, rising above locality and the everyday into a transcript of the universe that rewrote the present. There was no Yankee caution in Melville.

"Moby Dick" purported to be a descriptive history of whaling—accurate, scientific, picturesque. It still is that, and must be cited in any book of reference, yet never did any book so transcend, while including, its purpose. Whales and whalers became texts for discourses on heaven and earth, and their adventures a new language of symbolism by means of which Melville captured and made concrete his own tumultuous skepticism.† He had neither Hawthorne's respect for the order from which he came, nor the historian's instinct. The limits within which Hawthorne worked, leaving the philosophy of the universe to hint and inference, Melville burst through in an orgy of words, where objective reality was sacrificed again and again to epic representation of the primal forces. It is a

* "Journals," 1856.

† It is true that Melville in a letter to Mrs. Hawthorne, still unpublished except in part, says that he did not see the allegory in "Moby Dick" until it was pointed out to him. Not allegory, perhaps, as the Hawthornes understood allegory, but that his imagination was not working, consciously and unconsciously, in symbols, is incredible.

difference between environments quite as much as a difference between men—a Salem bedroom and the seven seas, the moral liberalism of Concord and the memories of a man who had lived with savages, worked with brutes, and bent his untrained mind on ideas of life wherever and however he could find them.

Hawthorne's limitations were fortunate because they kept him brooding upon that New England theme which he was particularly qualified to raise into literature. Such glorious narrative of sheer action, symbolic yet concrete, as Melville wrote into "Moby Dick"—the most magnificent I think in modern English—Hawthorne was quite incapable of duplicating. Such breakings through into world philosophy as Melville constantly permitted were at odds not only with Hawthorne's reticence but with his own thinking. He had no such ideas to retail. He was no Emerson to possess them, no Carlyle to discharge them— good and bad, wise and ignorant—together. Melville, like a revivalist, stopped at nothing that would serve his end, and often seems, and sometimes is, a raver. Hawthorne to Melville, as is well known, seemed cold, unresponsive, reticent, and, perhaps, afraid. Two of the greatest books of ethical imagination in the last century, "The Scarlet Letter" and "Moby Dick," are intimate proofs of the dissimilarities of genius working in the same spiritual atmosphere but with different intellectual environments, different temperaments, different conceptions of means and ends.

And yet it is impossible to dissociate these two men. "Typee," as Lewis Mumford has ably shown,* is Melville's discovery of the error of the new industrial world. Here in a primitive atmosphere of unmorality he is curiously most like Hawthorne—gentle, reticent, idyllic, indirect, yet sure in his implicit condemnation of societies that are

* "Herman Melville," by Lewis Mumford.

forgetting how to live in the struggle for living. Hawthorne, had he followed his ancestors to sea, might have written "Typee," would have moralized it (as with "The Maypole of Merrymount"), but would surely have perceived the innate values of the Marquesans.

"Moby Dick" is a dramatization of the spiritual world that seemed so real to the Transcendentalists, who were Hawthorne's friends and Melville's tutors. It is a skeptic's dramatization, and its relation to Emerson and Carlyle is curiously like Hawthorne's own ironic bond. For in this book strange creatures break the calm sea of spiritual optimism and cruise madly over the waters.

"The whale . . . from side to side strangely vibrating his predestinating head, sent a broad band of overspreading semicircular foam before him as he rushed. Retribution, swift vengeance, eternal malice were in his whole aspect, and spite of all that mortal man could do, the solid white buttress of his forehead smote the ship's starboard bow, till men and timbers reeled. Some fell flat upon their faces. Like dislodged trunks, the heads of the harpooneers aloft shook in their bull-like necks. Through the breach, they heard the waters pour, as mountain torrents down a flume. . . . But as the last whelmings intermixingly poured themselves over the sunken head of the Indian at the mainmast . . . a sky-hawk that tauntingly had followed the main-track downward from its natural home among the stars, picking at the flag, and incommoding Tashtego there; this bird now chanced to intercept its broad fluttering wing between the hammer and the wood; . . . and so the bird of heaven, with archangelic shrieks, and his imperial beak thrust upward, and his whole captive form folded in the flag of Ahab, went down with his ship, which, like Satan, would not sink to hell till she had dragged a living part of heaven along with her, and helmeted herself with it.

"Now small fowls flew screaming over the yet yawning gulf; a sullen white surf beat against its steep sides; then all collapsed, and the great shroud of the sea rolled on as it rolled five thousand years ago." *

But this shrouding sea and its creature the whale is nature, Emerson's nature, not to be conciliated, controlled, as he believed, but deceptively beautiful, malignant, terrible at heart, scarcely to be conquered, never to be subdued. And Ahab, a mad man, pursues this nature, drawn on by his endless quest for mastery, sailing on a ship that is a symbol of human wills, with the courageous Stubb, the prescient and regretful Starbuck, the clairvoyant Malay, the two savages—Indian and African—resolute as nature herself from which they are only part emerged, all in a hopeless chase, engaged not because they must but because they will, until the ship is destroyed, carrying with it the little of heaven that man's feeble strength has been able to grasp, while the white whale still roams the seas.

This is Melville's answer to Transcendentalism and his wildly imaginative comment on the intellectual pride of the nineteenth century. Compare him with Browning or with Tennyson. He is much less coherent, but his rebellious skepticism is modern in its contradictions of hope, its dramatizations of will, and its projection of evil as nature, of which man, like the self-lashing tail of the lion in the bestiary, is part.

Compare Melville with Hawthorne, and see that both tell the same story with the difference that art and temperament provide. "The Scarlet Letter," "The Marble Faun," and "The Blithedale Romance" also answer Transcendentalism and scorn the materialist. But in these quieter books the response is distilled like an elixir into human character where, under the veil of romance, the

* From the end of "Moby Dick."

soul struggles with its own substance. For Hester has
yielded to nature because it was fair, and suppressing her
love suppresses part of herself. And Zenobia is the pride
that will overcome evil, and is self-destroyed by its own
pertinacity, and in that dark house of the Seven Gables,
in the deceptive innocence of Monte Beni, in Rome itself,
so lovely for the simple spirit as yet inexperienced, there
is a malignancy also, as in the white whale that swims on
eternally leaving wrecks behind it.

These two were skeptics at a turning point of civilization, when nature was so peacefully submitting herself to
man for profit and domination, when the old rigidities of
moral law could be loosened at last and seen in their absurdities, and will was free to follow its own desires, mad
for dominance, lax in pleasure, flushed in the materialists,
soaring in the spiritual into dangerous confidence, and
always disregardful of the truth that

> If the red slayer thinks he slays,
> Or if the slain thinks he is slain,
> They know not well the subtle ways
> I keep, and pass, and turn again. . . .
>
> They reckon ill who leave me out;
> When me they fly, I am the wings;
> I am the doubter and the doubt,
> And I the hymn the Brahmin sings.

It is as skeptics of man's escape from nature that Hawthorne and Melville are in deepest agreement.

"The Scarlet Letter," "Moby Dick," and Emerson's
"Nature" are three climaxes of the religious obsessions of
the American nineteenth century, different, but more than
temporally related. Captain Ahab is the madness of man
attempting to solve the greatest of moral issues by subduing utterly the unintelligent malignancy of nature. He
is self-destroyed. Hester and Dimmesdale in "The Scarlet

Letter" are two exalted spirits caught in the nets of the flesh, and unable to free themselves because the net and they are one; good cancels evil, evil fortifies good. Emerson rises above all such perplexities into an ideal unity, of which all truths are facets. He would call upon Tashtego to tear the flag of human idealism from the masthead of the sinking ship and with it walk the waters. A great period of spiritual conflict ends with these men. The anæsthetics of war, materialism, scientific advance, and the comforts of prosperity were to drug the next generation. Action was to provide happiness or its substitute, and the ship of state was to sail on, like a new *Pequod* with Moby Dick brought in tow at last to be rendered into oil to light a prosperous America!

9.

MELVILLE was a romantic by nature, not, like Hawthorne, by convenience, and therefore he tried to say it all, to burst through the restraints of theme and subject with a voice that would proclaim the Great Secret of the Universe. If he had read less of the windy and often self-muddled Scotchman who wrote so much of this Great Secret with such authoritative incoherence, it would have been better for his style. The weakness of the self-educated lies in too ready a yielding to a voice that seems to them erudite. With such an ambition in him and such handicaps, it is not surprising that after one great triumph he sailed into the doldrums of unsuccess. Beside "Moby Dick," the books of his American contemporaries, with very few exceptions, now seem insignificant; but it carries the seeds of disruption. His failure to convince his readers that it was more than a whaling story may have daunted him, and led him on into the defiant psychology of "Pierre," where the theme is morbid pathology and the method melodrama. But I cannot agree with those who say that Melville was suppressed by his American environment. If he went wild after "Moby Dick" and merely puzzled his readers, it was because he was both too late and too early to get the full effects of his genius. The days of the "seekers" were passing quickly, and Melville grew more metaphysical precisely at the moment when the age (not only in America) was aswing toward materialism. His art was too unrestrained for adjustment. In "Pierre" and other books this clairvoyant mariner was attempting to search out the psychology of motive a half century ahead of psychology, and by means of romantic, melodramatic narrative that only a Transcendentalist could have interpreted. Like the rhetoric of Emerson's later essays, his method obscured and still obscures the prophetic novelty of his theme.

In "Moby Dick" the balance between speculation and narrative is kept, just kept and no more. In the earlier "Mardi" and in "Pierre," it tips. The desire to tell of the inner nature of beauty or the warping of desire was stronger than the creative will: the story is a medium too thin in "Mardi," too thick and stiff in "Pierre," to dress the thought. These two books are profound, and, as wholes, almost unreadable.

10.

To RETURN to Hawthorne (for I intend no complete analysis of the baffling Melville in this chapter, but only a study of his characteristic qualities), the romancer of the Puritans attained some measure of serenity by a humbleness that Melville never shared. It was an instinctive rather than an intellectual humbleness, for Hawthorne, I am sure, like many another novelist, believed himself to be a philosopher, and was prouder of his "mysteries" than of his books. Although he never charged a human mind with more than it could bear in a human environment, as Melville did with Pierre, and successfully with Ahab, because in "Moby Dick" the environment transcended the human, yet he is always hinting at his own profundity.

Nevertheless, his skepticism was of the tenacious kind that keeps one humble, and it never let him go. It was that which held him back from the boundlessness of great literature, toward which Melville in "Moby Dick," with torn sails and erratic course, undoubtedly is voyaging. His Puritan will kept him hard for renunciation. Like Jonathan Edwards in his "Freedom of the Will," he stuck to a theme he could control, where his "gifts," as Natty Bumppo would have said, were sufficient. He was skeptical of all grand affirmations.

But though cool in his art, Hawthorne is far from unfeeling. There is more concentrated passion in the extreme reticence of Hester than in the uninhibited modern novel. Hawthorne himself is the daguerreotypist of "The House of the Seven Gables," skeptical as always, but pitying, vaguely humanitarian, appalled and fascinated by the ravages of greed, dogmatism, and suppression upon character; in love with innocence, but doubtful whether in so queer a universe it is not an abnormality, to be cherished and protected. He is the young poet of "The Blithedale Romance," a little outside of the tensities that shake the rich and subtle Zenobia and skeptical of their worth, yet drawn into the web of emotion because (again) the innocence of Priscilla inspires love and needs protection. Ethan Brand is a possible self that he could but would not be. Hester has the best of him. In her, his skepticism rises to great moral issues, challenges the existing order, plots the future; but he is not Hester. Hester had the resolution he lacked, the iron that ran out of his parental strain before he was born. He is Kenyon of "The Marble Faun," a man of sense and sensibility, understanding, though aloof from, the innocence of Hilda, puzzled by Miriam and Donatello, doubtful of the quality of such rages, startled that they exist. Hester, Miriam, Zenobia—these full-blooded free-acting women he might have been if it had seemed worth while thus to wreak character upon experience. It was doubtfully worth while to his skepticism. Those scenes where the great were destroyed, the meek anguished, the sinner exalted by his sin, where the moral will worked always to its own or another's confusion, seemed better to watch than to live in. His notebooks are one long confession of this weakness for a man, strength for an artist. Like his mother and sister in their solitary chambers, action, for him, was to brood, not to be.

And thus Hawthorne's books are a full measure of what he allowed himself to express; and indeed, if he had expressed more it would probably have been vague and of little value, like a great deal recorded in his "Journals." He was a good tight-lipped Yankee, in this as elsewhere, with plenty of common sense. Where he says too much it is never of the profundities, but rather of those picturesque but respectable commonplaces of life that his generation favored. There are many of Hawthorne's sketches and some of his more platitudinous stories that are not saved, even by his style. His children's stories are the professional hack work of a grave, poetic man who could always write. Even his best short stories savor a little of the bad fashions of gift book and popular magazine, which the poor recluse tried so hard to imitate in his struggle to get someone to publish and some to read.

And in spite of this timeserving, in essentials he is closer to the American mind than Melville, even though the latter was so much more modern in his psychology. For Hawthorne is the one man who handles the results of our long evangelism with insight and justice. The ethical and spiritual problems which concern him are precisely those raised by a Protestantism that probably reached its peak of influence in our national history. His skepticism plays over a morality that is exactly what America, north, south, east, west, has predominantly accepted. Only the new megalopolitanism of the great cities since the war, has made a difference. The stimulation and the warping of the will, the troubled perceptions of sex, the ever present conflict between old and new in a culture where change has been speeded as never before, the discomfort of conscience and free nature at war, above all, the acceptance of moral necessity as a major premise—all these factors are close to our social history, and the very fibre of Hawthorne's tales.

Recluses, it seems, are our best critics and best interpreters, and this recluse was, in a very real sense, crucified for us. That is why three generations of readers, in the decades of our most intense materialism and on into anti-romance and scientific naturalism, have never lost their respect for Hawthorne. He is old-fashioned, but he is like an ancestor—the strain is in us still.

II.

I RANK him high as a romancer, in spite of his dark lanterns and the plush hangings of German romance—much higher than do some modernists unsympathetic with his sense of moral responsibility. For romance is not to be appraised by its details—which often, as in Shakespeare and Wordsworth and Keats, are absurd—but by its total effect. And whatever change may come over our *mores*, "The Scarlet Letter" is sure to retain its hold upon every imagination not morally numb.

I rank him as a narrator far lower than did his contemporaries. He is often a bungler there, seldom sure of himself except in his great moments, always resorting to tricks and reticences, usually depending upon situation and scene to hold an interest that his rambling story cannot claim. Whole chapters of "The Marble Faun" are merely the stuffing of a guidebook, put in to meet a supposed demand of the public while he delays coming to grips with his story. "The House of Seven Gables" is repetitive, "The Scarlet Letter" drags through its middle portion, some of "The Twice-Told Tales" and "The Mosses" are only fables, others no more than pictures.

As a student of character I rank him very high indeed, but in a narrow field. His ordinary mortals are either attempted photographs, or done according to some literary convention. His drunkards, stagecoach agents, millers, etc., etc., are often hack work drawn from a painstaking diary, where the shrewdness is in the thought, not in the observant eye. Only when there is *character*, in its specific sense, and only when that character is under moral stress, does he rise to the height of his faculty. But even then one cannot praise the subtlety of the psychology. He is not interested in psychology as we understand it, for his concern is not with the apparent *is* but the probable *ought*. In this he is prescientific, and possibly postscientific also. Useless for behaviorism, his Hester is a prototype for the great soul in mortal strain. Nor is this slight praise. The bankruptcy of naturalism as an art is already manifest. When we begin to seek spiritual values interpreted in terms of character, we shall hurry back along the path where Hawthorne broods over souls tossed in moral conflict.

And indeed, in spite of his prim retreats into what we call Victorianism, in spite of his fripperies of Gothic romance, and in spite of his paddings of descriptive journalism, Hawthorne is certainly a major writer, and probably belongs among the enduring monuments of English literature. When one considers all that can be said against him, this is curious. Style is too easy an answer, for stylists do not make themselves by contemplating words, they are created by an urgency of the whole being that makes words its instrument. And Hawthorne would not unwillingly have omitted words altogether! His inner world was so rich that, if his circumstances had permitted, its inconclusions might well have kept him absorbed in contented brooding without putting pen to paper. "It is now sunset," he sets down in 1843, "and I must meditate till dark." He would gladly have meditated for a lifetime. But the recluse years in Salem stored up reflection that pressed upon utterance, and economic need in combination with a happy chance of association with writers unlocked, first a little gate and then the narrow door of his fortress. What came through he viewed skeptically with ironic depreciation— "these stupendous works of fiction which have since impressed the universe with wonderment"—and yet with an almost childish pleasure at what he had accomplished— "In this chamber fame was won."

No, his magnitude is not ultimately due to any suave and felicitous choice of words, but to some close correspondence between his imagination and that New England, whose spiritual history engrossed him, as its natural history engrossed Thoreau, a New England rich in those issues of the imagination which, like the clouds of a summer storm, take on the shapes of most significance only at the moment when change is in the air, and the forces that caused them are already discharged in the past.

For here, as I have said before, was a man who stood outside of the perspectives of his society, so that he viewed the old New England and the new on a single plane of human nature. He both denied and accepted the society into which he was born: denied its premises, which were the confused and conflicting ideas of a community in which a decadent Calvinism, an ethereal Transcendentalism, and an onward sweeping materialism were all at play and interplay at once; but accepted what might be called its conclusions—the men and women whose inner conflicts were determined by their spiritual histories. For him they are neither heroes nor villains, neither right nor wrong, although he tries to establish a right and a wrong by which the reader may judge them. They are types of the "moral being," in which the fourth dimension, time, has been given unusual extension, so that the sins of the fathers are part of the story of the third generation.

Our new Hawthornes have been brooding over futility, with the experience of a dozen years of postwar demoralization for their sources. These new moral psychologists in fiction (Aldous Huxley for an example) mix scientific theory, philosophy, and observation in their studies of character. The result is a physical, not a chemical, compound, and their novels do not make up by their acuteness for a lack of unity and orientation. Hawthorne's psychology seems childish to them; to him their reflections would lack significance because the by-products of industrialism that they describe—neurotics, erotics, exhibitionists, morons, futilitarians—would seem to him mere diseases not worth brooding upon. He would be not so much right as fortunate, in having had richer material for his studies. His position is more strategic than theirs because he came like Plutarch (and Hawthorne is the Plutarch of the Puritans) at the very end of a strong period in which one of the great experiments in moral progress and the good life had worked itself out into failure. He grasped his opportunity, and this is the main reason for his eminence in literature.

Hawthorne's New England, in which, in spite of his melancholy, he lived "in a righteous and heaven-blessed way of life," not always impatient with his failures, is as dead as the New England of the first Pyncheons and the White Old Maid was dead in his own day. It is gone, like Emerson's new world of hope beyond the Alleghenies, and Whitman's democracy. It lives only in those subtle strains of habit and thought which come to us by tradition, as blood and cell structure come from our physical heredity. But an age must die if it is to live again in art or philosophy, and my confidence in the enduring quality of Hawthorne's best is due to his power of creating representative aspects of his period that were perhaps never fully realized in actuality. Facts alone never can record such aspects, but only an imagination (like Chaucer's, Shakespeare's, Milton's) that reshapes the clay of ordinary experience into a form of clear significance. I do not rank Hawthorne with these greater artists, yet the New England of which he wrote had unique qualities, and his lesser genius was not devoid of that magic by which the written word becomes more real than the past which it seems to record.

CHAPTER SEVEN

Edgar Allan Poe

TO LEAVE the society of Emerson, Hawthorne, and Thoreau for the Philadelphia, the New York, the Richmond, of Poe is to pass from a quiet village of philosophic Greeks to an active, hustling present, from retirement out of space, and often out of time, to the more familiar world that lives in the moment. And to leave these men for Poe is to exchange elevation for intensity, and the study of man for the practice of art. There is not in the range of literature a wider dissimilarity than that which separates everything that Emerson and Thoreau were and could and wished to be, from this man Poe and his work.

The New Englanders were deeply religious—even Hawthorne; to Poe religion—except the religion of beauty—was meaningless. They were either philosophers, or ready with the least excuse to philosophize, and the goals they set themselves in art were philosophic or ethical—an understanding of the spiritual and moral nature was what they essentially sought. Poe's purpose in writing was to amuse, to interest, to impress, and to enlighten, which last is very different from seeking enlightenment. The others, even Hawthorne, and certainly Melville, were "seekers." Poe was a journalist. Poe the neurotic fits best and easiest into the familiar curves of modern living, Poe the writer is nearest to our norm; the New Englanders belonged to a culture so different from our megalopolitan civilization that they might well have come from that star which Poe was always seeking. Professionals in the life of the soul, they often seem amateurs—sometimes of genius —in the craft of writing. An amateur in scholarship and philosophy, and cursed with hot lunacies, Poe nevertheless, as a man of letters, was the true professional. He is more normal—as an artist—than Thoreau or Emerson or Melville.

2.

I SHALL return to this comparison, which is fundamental. Of Poe himself, the most poignant fact is that he was unfortunate. Unfortunate men who are touched with greatness become notorious, whether or not they achieve fame. They make legends for themselves, and legends are made for them that are colored or interpreted differently by each generation that follows. They are no more complex than happier men of genius, but they seem so, because, having contradictions in themselves, they induce contradictions in others. If, as with Poe, the misfortune is congenital, interpretation is confused between the man and his works. One, of course, explains the other, but in Poe's case the variety of contributory circumstances presents so many possible causes for so many extraordinary results that criticism runs this way and that. Every book on Poe has its thesis, and both his art and the man himself are lost in exegesis and argument.

We know, in fact, almost too much about Poe—or rather, too many Poes—for a clear picture of the man and an easy comprehension of his work. There is no mystery left in him except the supreme mystery of neuroticism and no mystery in his work except the mystery of art, and yet it is as a man of mystery that he is constantly presented. Contradictory, extraordinary, perverse, he certainly is, but not mysterious except in so far as the sources of beauty are always mysterious. Few writers have left more abundant evidence of the workings of their minds. Few writers have had the nature of their minds, with the impact of circumstances upon them, so elaborately analyzed and explained.

We know now, thanks especially to Mr. Hervey Allen's summaries,* the story of his relations with the Allan family in reasonable completeness, and can understand the frustrations of a boy who expected to combine the arrogant, chivalrous independence of a Southern gentleman with the pursuit of beauty, and found himself penniless and unclassed. We know enough of his adolescence to guess the effect upon his sex life of his foster father's infidelities. And if Mr. Krutch's theory † of sexual impotence (whether real or of the brain) with a consequent singularity in his relations with women, still awaits more knowledge of Poe's youth, it is sufficiently substantiated in his later life and work to serve as a handle for criticism. We know well enough now that Poe the drunkard and opium-taker was simply a psychic victim saving himself from a nervous crisis—that he drank as a woodchuck takes to his hole, from fear, and then irresistibly. We have rid ourselves of the superficial nonsense about artistic temperament and the immorality of genius. We have accepted—to the detriment of clear criticism, which suffers from the overemphasis, and yet very usefully—the modern ideas of complexes, inferiorities, egomanias, in Poe's case easily accounted for. We understand that Poe was a neurotic, and if we do not know what neuroticism is, we know how it works. We are aware not merely that Poe was abnormal, but why, and that knowledge had to be gained before his reputation could be cleared from the moral obsessions of those who discussed it, and his egregious vanities and incredible megalomanias assigned to cause.

* "Israfel: The Life and Times of Poe," by Hervey Allen.
† "Edgar Allan Poe," by Joseph Wood Krutch.

But no man can be restored to an approximation of what he was, or his work criticized as a whole and in its relation to the flow of literary history, solely by abnormalities. He eats, he is cared for by the pathetic Mrs. Clemm and her ever-emptying basket, he works for money, he nurses his ambitions, he is gentle, he is irritable, he is ill, he is mean. These familiar traits do not make him the man he is, unless they are all. Nor does the merely skilful in his work explain its genius, where there is genius to be explained. But these normalities of life and literature do constitute the representational elements of the picture. They define it in terms of normal human effort, and, so defining it, explain more than partisans are willing to admit. The design for the composition may depend upon something deeper—and if in Poe that depth is neurotic, in neuroticism may be found a key to his inspiration. Nevertheless, to see Poe not as he wished to be seen, or as the dark forces sometimes compelled him to become, but as he prevailingly was, it is essential to retreat from the psychic ground his recent critics have trod so confidently, and begin again with aspects of his life that may seem trivial to the psychological critic but which to him were all-important. For a first glimpse of Poe it is wisest to consider him as neither drunkard, neurotic, nor erratic genius, but as a hard-working journalist of the third and fourth decades of the American nineteenth century.

3.

INTELLECTUALLY and from the broadest view it was a curiously dual society. The thirties and forties were astir with spiritual and ethical unrest. Free land and freedom from restraint in a society rapidly democratizing were having their inevitable effect upon the tense sectarians who swarmed in America. The convalescence from Calvinism was well under way, and relaxed nerves tingled to every suggestion. Intelligence was keen and aroused, minds untrained, the country at large undisciplined. From New England westward it was all isms, and all but the deep South was speckled with strange cults. Philosophers went transcendental and scientists toyed with phrenology.*

Yet in the cities, and especially in Philadelphia and New York, the sophisticated, worldly life of urban Europe was being imitated with an ardor born of a consciousness of provincialism. Philadelphia in 1840 was in its wish psychology much more cosmopolitan and more cultivated than it is today. Journalism was rampantly active and especially literary journalism. From small beginnings, *Graham's* and *Godey's* attained a national circulation. *The Saturday Evening Post*, and especially *The Ladies' Home Journal*, were already present in the imagination, indeed they needed only better transportation, postal privileges, high-speed printing plants, and advertising to be there— more sentimental, more fastidious, more literary, but in the blend of uplift and interest much like what they actually became. Thoreau, printing his "Walden" as much from a sense of duty as from a hope of cash and reputation, was a century away from the American Grub Street where men's inventions were stimulated by expectation of immediate success. Thanks to the pirating of British and Continental books, the native author was heavily handicapped if he wished to publish a volume, but the timely magazine escaped this competition and was an ever widening field, unfailing, if never rich.

It is true that Poe's sole reality was his self, but this self was an ego of extraordinary magnitude and even greater sensitiveness, which demanded recognition. In the journalistic world of commercial writing he was as much at home as in Eblis, and with it and in it his normal

* See the dignified gravity of *The American Phrenological Review*, 1840-41.

CLASSIC AMERICANS

thoughts were so deeply engaged that in his waking moments it is as a journalist that he seems most intensely alive. In contrast with the New Englanders, always reluctant to leave their rural Parnassus, he was certainly happiest in the hurly-burly of production and consumption where professional literature is usually made. The contempt for the writing trade that Cooper expressed and Irving felt, was utterly foreign to his mind. He was an insider, and often by necessity, and not always unwillingly, a hack. He planned no more soul revolutions and retreats into nature than does the feature writer today. Instead, his inventiveness tirelessly wrought new methods of plot development, devised poems that would take with elocutionists, discovered journalistic genres like the detective story and the literary personality (which go on and on), perpetrated hoaxes in order to make the front page, guessed at the publicity value of personal attack, and set out directly, not hesitantly like Hawthorne, to amuse, to interest, to harrow, the reader.

He was, as is now well known, an excellent editor, and a study of his methods and results will make it abundantly clear that his editing was much more than a means of getting his own work published. He knew how to plan a magazine, he knew how to get contributions, he knew how to get new subscribers. His lifelong dream of a national magazine, literary in quality, general in interest, was sound, and except for his nervous disabilities, would certainly have been realized. We should have had a *Harper's* a quarter of a century before its time, nor would Poe's periodical have begun, like *Harper's*, in slavish dependence upon overseas. The neurotic upset whatever the inventive and executive faculty got under way, yet there is no question as to Poe's transcendent ability in journalism. Professionally speaking, he was an editor and journalist first and foremost, and the effect of his profession upon his enduring contributions to literature is of the highest critical importance.

He would, I think, have been a journalist under any conditions permitting journalism—most certainly so to-day. There is no mistaking the steady flow of interest from his college years onward to his death while on a last attempt to launch his own magazine. Poetry with him "was not a purpose but a passion" and the same in less measure might be said of scientific speculation. That poetry (with some dabbling in science perhaps) would have been "the field of my choice," as he says in the Preface to his '45 poems, would doubtless have been true, if Allan had left him the Southern gentleman of independent means that he expected to be. But that he would have kept away from journalism, never satisfied his craving for immediate returns of praise, never used his abundant invention to fool, perplex, terrify, and fascinate the public generally, must be incredible to anyone who follows through what was essentially a career of journalism. If he had got that government job, if he had taken to teaching, sooner or later he would have been back in Grub Street again, seeking for someone to finance his magazine!

No one is born a journalist. It is a profession made by teaching a quick and articulate mind to satisfy the curiosity of the public. Or rather by adapting the work of that mind to the public need, for the mind, the self, can, and in good journalists often does, stand contemptuously aloof. Poe's faculty of expression was perfectly adapted to journalism; indeed it was very largely conditioned by it. His tricks of puffery, his constant plagiarism from his own writing, his insistent bluffing, his powers of lucid exposition, his indefatigable invention (only a journalist could have invented the detective story), his complete freedom from intellectual conscience, his meticulous craftsmanship, are all attributes of the journalist, particularly the free-lance journalist. He had the short breath of the journalist, always ending this side of possible weariness. He had the wide and not too discriminating interests of the editorial type of mind. He differed from other literary journalists of eminence in the nineteenth century chiefly in that he had unusual powers of creation, wrote far worse than the average when he wrote badly, had such a sense of form as comes to only one or two in a generation, and was too vain to be able to distinguish with any consistency his fudge and bunkum from the efforts of his genius.

4.

It is often assumed that the trash Poe wrote was forced out of him by circumstance. I doubt it. The fudge was essentially Poe's, and Lowell was generous in his estimate of "Three fifths of him genius, and two fifths sheer fudge." * The same impulses that led him toward journalism account for much of his trash.

Perhaps two thirds of Poe's work is not worth reprinting at this distance of time, and of this two thirds not more than a half has any value whatsoever except as an instance of successful pioneering, or for its biographical reference. His fudge is of several sorts. There is the sheer hack work of most of his literary portraits, too many of his reviews, and pieces like "The Elk," which read as if they had been written for a school reader. The man had to live—but the pompous assurance of omniscience and omnipotence makes trash of this kind offensive to later generations. Read his "blurb" on Bayard Taylor, or the review of his admired Mrs. Osgood's poems, which descends from eulogy to this: "Regarding the loftier merits, I am forced to speak of her in more measured terms. She has occasional passages of true imagination—but scarcely the glowing, vigorous, and sustained ideality of Mrs.

* "Fable for Critics."

Maria Brooks, or even, in general, the less ethereal elevation of Mrs. Welby"! It was this series of highly personal criticisms, made up equally of fulsome praise and cutting satire that, before "The Raven," was the chief cause of Poe's notoriety. The flings skyward into general principle which have made his later critical reputation were little regarded, and are but moments in his flow of inconsequential writing relieved only by a pungent phrase or a restatement of a "principle" borrowed from himself.

Lamentable failures are all of Poe's humorous stories. Many of them, as Professor James Southall Wilson has shown, are burlesques of fashionable writing that deserved chastisement. But it is questionable whether they are not worse than their originals, and certainly now they are mirthless. It is sad to be devoid of a sense of humor, it is worse to think that you have humor and pity others for its lack, as Poe did, and then to practise as vile a brand as his. The jokes cackle like bad actors, incongruity and exaggeration in their most extreme forms alone appeal to him, and his parodies are as mirthless as a second-rate revue. Those who say that he reflected the humor of his America may have right on their side, but should remember Irving. All humor not of the first class stales with time, but Poe's humor crumbles and dusts. And yet no writer makes his characters more frequently and more extensively laugh in type. He will take three lines for his teehees.

Worst of all is his meretriciousness. The fake erudition with which he daubed his stories and essays, and even his poems, has often been analyzed, and never to Poe's credit, who was capable even of stealing his notes. Mr. Allen has suggested that much of this second-hand knowledge came from the English reviews, which Poe as a youth could have seen in his foster father's warehouse. Later, of course, in his various editorial offices, a wide variety of current books and magazines were always at hand. He used this borrowed learning as a boy uses all the tags he can remember for an examination paper, in the hope of impressing the reader. The materials were good, the use he makes of them often pertinent, but it is all a show-off, and is felt to be such.

I make a partial exception for science and mathematics, and a complete one for æsthetics. In science and mathematics he had better than an average good training (of which more later), and when he borrowed he really sought the truth. He tried to be honest, and did hard thinking on an insufficient basis of accurate knowledge. In æsthetics he had that native aptitude which is better than training, since it finds what it needs, and here his thinking bore fruit. And yet even in æsthetics his deficiencies are painful. The value of his "Rationale of Verse," with its clear statement of the principle of prevailing time, is seriously marred by his failure to see the accentual nature of English verse. He hits all around the bull's-eye, but never in the center, and winds up his essay by excluding French poetry from excellence altogether because it will not fit a theory that he has made without grasping essential linguistic differences! Or see him in his review of Horne's "Orion" pouring contempt upon those who prefer the great passages on hell in "Paradise Lost" to the extracts he chooses from his favorite of the moment. The fault here is not merely taste, which is always liable to defects in current consideration, but cocksureness and a desire to be emphatic at all costs.

And consider those extraordinary *tours de force*, "The Domain of Arnheim" and "Landor's Cottage." In the former, Elliston, the incredibly rich proprietor of the Domain, seeks that beauty which results from "a spiritual interference with nature," and which gives a point and an interest to landscape arrangement, and is only one step depressed from the great art of creation possible only to God. With this characteristically interesting theory Poe begins his description. But alas, the approach to the heart of the Domain is through a fervid landscape that mingles the rococo with the baroque; and the palace at the end of the vista, with its semi-Gothic, semi-Saracenic architecture suggests, and perhaps was suggested by (since we find it often repeated in Poe), the architecture that Mrs. Wharton celebrates as Hudson River Bracketed. "Landor's Cottage" is better controlled because the simpler—and how much needed!—idea of due proportion in home and garden architecture was less grandiose in principle and could be satisfied with less strain upon Poe's experience. His search in this sketch for a "proportionate strangeness" in environment was an evidence of his inventiveness in a period that had lost its sense of architectural proportion, but though his description of the tulip poplar is justly famous and should be more often read, the artificiality of the cottage and its surroundings tugs at the memory until one finds the crude original in a Currier & Ives print! Poe had the theory, but he lacked both taste and experience to carry it out. The proof is in his "Philosophy of Furniture" (and *seriatim* in his works)—its ideal room with two windows of crimson-tinted glass, and a wall paper of crimson with arabesques of silver and large pictures set thereon. One sees such rooms in the steel engravings of the Annuals! Poor fellow, he bluffed magnificently. But his inventive imagination was often like an expensive automobile carrying an ill-dressed, inexperienced provincial.

I do not call "The Domain" and "Landor's Cottage" fudge, yet in them as in most of his stories of the grotesque and arabesque there is a strong fudgean element. It is the show-off, that same trait which made him want to be a journalist, and as a professional journalist made him use every scrap, tittle, jot, and ounce of whatever he possessed or could lay his hands on. His invention raced ahead and he threw whatever was handy into the too often empty cars behind it. Thus "The Raven," whatever its inception, was undoubtedly tuned up for the show-off of elocution by precisely the methods described in "The Philosophy of Composition."

In a study published many years ago I traced the relationship between the obviously—and then modern—journalistic methods of Kipling in the short story and the early influence of Bret Harte, himself a writer trained in American journalism; but the relation, felt but not proved, between Harte and Poe, the originator of the American short story, puzzled me. It is quite evident when Poe is thought of, as he should be, as a magazine writer. Not only are his tales shaped and consciously fitted to the necessity of that quick impression that the magazine requires (since its success is conditioned by the existence of a public that is intelligent but too large to be literary) but his critical theory of the short story—still the best expressed—shows how directly his art was squared to the medium for which he wrote. Stories do not *have* to be written as he describes them in his famous review of Hawthorne's tales, unless they are written as the journalist writes for quick consumption by the many. We have already, outside of journalism, reverted to a looser type of story, capable of more character study, a fuller background, and a subtler dialogue. Nor do poems have to be short poems, unless the writer is a lyrist in talent, or a journalist who can find publication only for the brief. Poe's failures—his forced humor, his sham scholarship, his cocksure criticism, and frequent petulance—are due in large measure to the pressure of his profession of journalism upon his vanity, or the reverse, and his great successes also are deeply indebted to the virtuosity of a master journalist. Fudge and the fruits of genius were alike ripened for the magazine markets of Philadelphia and New York.

The amazing statement has often been made that Poe had no roots in American literary history, and derived nothing from the American tradition. It is a rash assertion to make *a priori*, of an American who after his school years in England fluttered like a spectral moth around the great publishing centres of New York and Philadelphia. His critics have been misled by his inner life, which indeed was of a brand different from the neuroticism of the Puritans and had its roots in universal human nature rather than in the local conditions of America. They have too little considered the circumstances of his Southern upbringing that were responsible for so many manifestations of thwarted pride and intolerant arrogance. They have generously overlooked the provincialism of his lesser work, which was entirely American in its character. But most of all they have failed to note that Poe as a professional writer was trained, his ambition shaped, his powers chiefly exercised, in a flourishing period of American journalism, the first magazine era, when the periodical was proving its admirable adaptiveness to the peculiar conditions of American life. To New England he owed nothing, to New York and the Knickerbocker school substantially nothing, but one can exclude him from the American tradition only by assuming that Thoreau or Irving was fully representative of American life, which is nonsense. His terror, as he said, was of the soul, but his technique was simply the best yet developed for that magazine literature which had already become an American specialty.

I propose no singularity in this description of Poe as a journalist, but only a new and juster view of him regarded as an American man of letters and as a master of a peculiar virtuosity. It is never safe to be snobbish in criticism, and to think of Poe in terms of world literature only is to generalize overmuch and to miss some of the flavor of his genius.

5.

POE's virtuosity, true to the aims of journalism, is a technique for catching the attention of the reader. It is not one trick but a handful. When the subject matter was beyond his narrow apprehensions, and few great writers have gone so often outside their powers as Poe (another trait of the journalist), the result is often what seems to us a failure, but in every instance there is some trick of plot that explains his current success. Poe had no humor and hence his rather dreary burlesques, "The Spectacles," and "The System of Dr. Tarr and Prof. Fether," were foredoomed to artistic failure; he had neither pathos nor sentiment, and therefore "The Oblong Box" was sure to be banal; and yet in each story there is a clever trick. The introspective Hawthorne would have recorded the themes of these stories in his notebook as: "A man to marry his own great-great-grandmother because of shortsightedness," "A houseful of lunatics to overpower their keepers and run the asylum according to their own ideas," "A coffin containing the body of a beloved wife to be mistaken for the case of a treasured painting—what might happen?" How Hawthornesque these themes are, how surely he would have made memorable if somewhat stuffy allegories of them! Poe's dreams fitted in none of them, and his logic found nothing it could work upon, but he could catch his audience with the trick in the plot.

Yet how brilliantly he succeeded with a trick when that which caught the attention was worthy of it! "The Purloined Letter" in its origin is exactly like these trashy stories. The theme, that it is characteristic of the human animal to overlook the obvious, is a tricky one. Dupin, the great original of detectives, is a symbol of logic and

observation personified, the Minister D——— is just as unreal as Poe's other characters, the background of the story
is conventional melodrama. But the trick by which Dupin
finds the missing letter lends itself to an exciting logical
analysis, and it is for this that one reads "The Purloined
Letter." There was no room, and no time, for Poe to go
wrong. The detective story, of which this is the prototype,
is, if you please, all fudge; but it is good fudge, and fudge
is what we read it for; not humor, not character, not truth
to typical life, but the application of logical principles to
a fabricated sensation or mystery. How delightful is "The
Gold-Bug" for the same reasons! The characters are conventions, the darky absurd, but the trick by which the
buried treasure is found is absorbing. And Poe's invention,
which throws off grotesque nonsense and banalities in
other trick stories, here settles down to work.

"The Fall of the House of Usher" is tricky in the same
sense, although in Poe's stories of terror other factors enter in that make the journalistic classification only partial.
Every one of his famous tales of mental pathology begins
with a problem, and concludes with a revelation that is
itself a kind of trick. In "Usher" it is the intensification
of the senses; in "Berenice," the diseased obsession with
a physical object, in "Eleonora," the transmigration of
souls, in "The Cask of Amontillado," a macabre practical
joke, in "The Black Cat," the invulnerability of the feline
kind. And each of these revelations is prepared for and
released with the utmost care for emphasis in the best
journalistic fashion.

And even in his poetry, where other and more important
considerations also enter, a technical trickery was responsible at least for his success in catching the attention of
his contemporaries. The theme of "The Raven" comes
from Poe's deepest experience, but its form—so accurately
described in "A Philosophy of Composition"—is technical

trickery so able that its artificiality now begins to offend.

So does the careful focus of Poe's stories, and the in-weaving of word and sentence in a pattern that in every stitch regards the end and all of the tale, and all crafts-manship that secures a single vivid impression from a brief narrative. These technical tricks have grown out of our fashion and liking because they begin to *seem* tricky. Ex-cellently useful in tales of artifice and supremely successful in Poe's best stories, they have nevertheless, and as I have already said, become a mould from which the modern short story has escaped as from a press.

Even Poe's criticism was shaped in its application by the needs of journalism, and his reviewing depends upon a trick that does not always come off. His practice when he was in good form was to set down a generalization (not necessarily or often a fresh one) so contradictory as to startle the reader into attention:

"It is often said, inconsiderately, that very original writers always fail in popularity, that such and such per-sons are too original to be comprehended by the mass. . . . It is, in fact, the excitable, undisciplined, and child-like popular mind which most keenly feels the original."

"The decline of the drama . . . The drama has *not de-clined*."

"I hold that a long poem does not exist. I maintain that the phrase, 'a long poem,' is simply a flat contradiction in terms."

"In America, we have refused to encourage satire—not because what we have had touches us too nearly—but be-cause it has been too pointless to touch us at all."

These are headlines demanding attention. Sometimes they are true and brilliant, sometimes brilliant and partly true, but always the extraordinary lucidity of the expo-sition that follows persuades the reader that Poe is omni-scient. The important contributions of Poe to criticism are taken from such introductory generalizations. They exhibit not only the audacity of the journalist who must make his killing quickly, but also his intuitive inventiveness, and indeed the further applications of his principles are seldom quotable, and seldom reliable beyond the second page. In the fields of the short story and in the æsthetics of poetry he was an expert and there his criticism is good to the end, but as a rule the actual discussion of contemporary books in Poe's reviews is distinguished only by an occasional brilliance of definition or attack from such average reviewing of the period as was practiced by, for example, Simms.

But these technical tricks which Poe mastered or invented in order to conquer the magazine rose to virtuosity when the subject matter was right. When the dark realms of his imagination through which his working mind had thrown roads for an almost scientific exploration were to be the scene of a story, his marvelously contrived order of composition could compress into a few thousands of words a speaking symbol of what was to him a cosmogony and an experience combined. When with a logical chain of reason he set out to discover the cause of murder, or the hidden place of treasure, as La Place had worked in pure mathematics or Newton in pursuit of a planet, his art of intense brevity could create suspense and rouse interest to the highest pitch. One has only to compare the ratiocination of "The Narrative of A. Gordon Pym" with the coiled intensity of the later "The Murders in the Rue Morgue" to see what this virtuosity, acquired for journalism, could accomplish.

6.

It is high irony that Poe should have invented the detective story, that stand-by for breadwinning of the hack writer, and yet half starved himself. Why did he leave to

Conan Doyle the capitalizing of his invention? For the Sherlock Holmes stories—good as they are—owe everything except the wide application of a formula to Poe, and Sherlock himself is only Dupin materialized a little further and fitted with a few more attributes. Essentially Holmes is a figure of romantic disillusion, a superbrain too contemptuous of his environment to play the usual games for success, who is roused only by a kind of misanthropy when his miserable fellow creatures exploit their viciousness too far. He is a solitary, he takes drugs to relieve his boredom, he is an artist, he lives exotically—he is Dupin revived, which is to say a self-dramatization of Poe.

It was certainly no literary scruple or fear of repetition that held back Poe from adding to his handful of great detective stories. He would have sold "The Gold-Bug" in ten different versions if he could, and have followed up any likely chance of publication if he had seen it. Of course he did use his famous method of ratiocination in many stories—such as "Pym"—and the interpreting of observation that is its central principle is woven through nearly all of his poetic tales of terror. But it was only in the detective story that it was realized as a story itself. I suppose that he failed to capitalize because he was too inventive, and, like many inventors, turned from one creation to another as the wind of interest blew. He thought that he could do anything, but he had little time except for the nearest task. When he was not a practicing editor he was for considerable periods sick from disease, from alcohol, or from opium, or psychically incapacitated with that mental illness which redoubles every physical pain. And the labors of a literary editor are endless. He has to read—endlessly. Poe read as a journalist reads, who knows that everything is grist for his mill and that the mill must be fed; he read like a man who knows that eventually he must write of everything he reads. And when he was his own man his megalomania led him to the immense and futile efforts of such work as "Eureka." His inner life was always a conflict. Like the Minister D—— he was both mathematician and poet. When he was well, his need and his ambition drew him into the endless routine of editing —when he was at home, in a leisure too often enforced by a breakdown, his sick soul and clear logical mind combated for his pen.

7.

THAT Poe was only a journalist, is, of course, a statement too absurd to rest upon. But I wish to make it clear that as a journalist he could be superb, and to emphasize that everything of importance that he wrote, with the exception of a few of his best poems, like "Israfel," was influenced, and often shaped, and frequently made possible in its existing mould, by the technique he acquired for his profession. Yet to account for the form of his work, unless it be in the detective story (which is, in a true sense, pure form) is by no means enough to account for Poe's place in our imagination. No American writer has sent wider circles of interest and influence across the reading world. I have seen a copy of Baudelaire's translation of Poe's stories open upon a firing platform in a trench in France. Much modern poetry and some modern fiction would never have been if Poe had not written. Leave then the journalist, and look at the man of letters, and the man. Not that the two were dissociated. Poe had a duality of character depending upon whether his nerves were in or out of control, but there is no duality here. What he wrote, he wrote with all of himself, and there is morbidity in "The Murders in the Rue Morgue," a pathologic luxury in "The Gold-Bug," and sheer journalism in "The Bells" and "Eleonora."

So far I have considered Poe's way of working rather

than the imagination with which he worked. If in so doing I have leant toward disparagement it is for the double reason that analysis of clever artifice is always disillusioning, and that unquestionably Poe's weaknesses even more than his strengths were exploited by the show-off of journalism. It is the result, not the thing itself, that endures in journalism. Thus in this study of Poe's inventiveness under pressure by the crowd I have viewed from one angle only those creations in which Poe transcended journalism while seldom ceasing to be journalistic. Let us turn then to aspects of the man that make for greatness rather than a great technique.

8.

THE type to which Poe approximates is familiar enough, increasingly familiar as our civilization grows more febrile. But it is, of course, rarely combined with a passion for beauty amounting to genius, and still more rarely with a powerful, logical intellect, completely articulate. Without attempting a scientific description, it may be said that two attributes go far toward defining the peculiar temperament that made Poe's inner life so fruitful for literature, and yet so calamitous for himself.

He was, in the first place, egoistic in the last degree and, like all his favorite characters, sensitive beyond ordinary comparison. This, of course, is a symptom of his neuroticism, but in literature as in life it was a curse. It is not too much to say that for Poe no one really existed except himself. No one except the unsexed Virginia, his caretaker, Mrs. Clemm, and the few women who touched him in his youth ever entered the realms of his deepest consciousness, and they only as dim shapes projected from the faint stirrings of the human in his otherwise purely intellectual desires. Such egoism is relieved only by triumphant creation. The I must be entirely successful or the anguish that results from the ordinary casualties of living—hopes

282

thwarted, affection unreturned, and all the slings and arrows of outrageous fortune—is rationalized in the familiar symptoms of paranoia and megalomania. Either the man flings back in suspicious anger at a world that will not adjust itself to him, or he rises above it in a diseased, uncertain assurance that he is greater than his enemies. Yet, granted exquisite sensibilities, the spur of fame desired, and the expressiveness of literary genius, and a tragedy common enough in lower orders becomes articulate and noteworthy. Poe's two characters, so often spoken of by his contemporaries—the gentle husband, so dependent upon love and cherishing, and the truculent, unscrupulous fighter, drunk or "mean"—are only two phases of a single temperament. Their exaggerated difference is due to the excessive sensitiveness of the patient. When his ego was soothed or weary, he was a lamb; when it was inflamed or injured, he was a beast in a corner, frenzied, wounded, smeared with blood and with dirt.

No such egoist can by any possibility have real humor, for a sense of proportion in human relationships is denied him. No such egoist can by any possibility comprehend with any real success the types of human nature that other writers interpret and dramatize but in which his interest is mathematical at best. They are figments for his thinking, aliens to his ego. His self-portraits may be of the utmost vividness, but his generalizations upon temperaments that are not essentially like his own will be platitudes or falsities. He knows only himself, and the temperamental qualities of his own ego will strictly limit his achievement.

This is negative criticism, for we do not ask of our men of letters that they shall all be Goethes or Shakespeares—or even Wordsworths and Hawthornes. Positively speaking, Poe's inner life was rich enough for a great literature, and his excessive egoism gave it an excessive importance

283

in his own eyes that he always carried over into his work, and sometimes with impressive success. It was the inner life of a neurotic, by which I mean here no more than that the waves of thought and emotion, which in self-communion or dreams stir in us all, were vehement in him and out of proportion to their external causes, and were often out of control and in violent odds with apparent reality. And Poe's neuroticism was not only intensified by his violent ego, it was also qualified and defined by a passionate love, inherent and congenital, of that wilder beauty than earth supplies, which he believed to be the origin of poetry. He speaks of "readers who, to hearts of maddening fervor, unite, in perfection, the sentiment of the beautiful, that sense which proves and which alone proves, God's existence" *—and so writing, wrote of himself.

The permanent possibility of neuroticism is a universal human attribute, and a great neurotic, such as Poe, has an obvious place in important literature. Alcohol and opium in alternation may have increased the fervor, or defined the sensory nature, of his sublimated dreams, but the drugs were the results, not the causes, of his neuroticism. It is not the "wilder beauty" for which they are responsible, but the excess of morbid sensation. That which made other men gross or fantastic could taint, but not create, the Aiden of Poe's imagination.

The subliminal world of Poe's poetical stories and of such poems as "Dream-Land" and "The City in the Sea," reached

> By a route obscure and lonely,
> Haunted by ill angels only,
> Where an Eidolon, named Night,
> On a black throne reigns upright, . . .
> Out of Space—out of Time,

owes little that is good to stimulants, but much to neu-

* Review of Horne's "Orion."

roticism. It is a region of supersensation where each sensory faculty trembles with expressiveness like the heartstrings of Israfel. That is its geography and its atmosphere. And in such a clime the perfervid and often irrational emotions of the Great Egoist can escape from the repressions of reality in an environment where every tortured suspicion, fear, or hope is realized with an intensity as great as itself. The mind brooding upon its own terrible propensities finds in these spectral regions its most hidden fears stalking. Sadism, incest, claustrophobia, perversion, paranoia, megalomania—these are but names for phases of the inflamed ego, beating against the cage of self-control, but in dream life they are not names, they are things of human attribute, realized in that air electric with vivid sensation. In "Eleonora," "The Masque of the Red Death," "Ligeia," "Morella," "Usher," Poe's neuroticism freed an ego whose morbidity was not so much abnormal as abnormally representative of the darker emotions. By a "wilder" beauty he meant precisely what he himself achieved—a beauty in which every intense emotion of the ego had validity and finds expression. The fears and cravings that the sane man puts down because they disturb or conflict with reality, were to Poe more real than external reality itself, because they were his, and so he made a life for them in a world of supersensation, where, like electrons in the physicist's laboratory, they could become tangible to other men.

9.

MANY a neurotic has created his own world—and written of it too—but few such worlds are fit for other minds to live in. Poe's dreams were made habitable by his powerful sense of order, and this instinct for form is closely related to his passion for science and the methods of science, which was second only to his love of æsthetic beauty, of which it was, of course, a part. The interest in science that he manifests from his youth up is, like his journalistic ambition, a link, one of the few links, between his inner life and the external world.

The thirties and forties were the romantic age of science in America, an age rich in premonition of all that science could do for a democratic society in a still new continent. Poe was as deeply enthralled by it as Emerson or Thoreau. His deep interest is displayed in the most unexpected places. Fully half of the tricks in his stories are derived from the discoveries—often the commonplaces—of physical science. Astronomy is never long out of reference, and if there is an opportunity to boast of being *au courant* with the latest researches in this science, or others, or a chance to expose error in his slipshod contemporaries, Poe never misses it. It has been assumed that his knowledge was superficial. That is not entirely true. Of all sciences he pretended to know something, and usually his knowledge is a journalist's, and a bluffing journalist's at that. The solemn nonsense of phrenology took him in completely. He made capital out of mesmerism, and was quite unscrupulous in using what he could pick up, from his abundant sources, of this and better defined sciences for his own literary purposes. But the methods of science he did understand, even if its end—the description and measurement of physical phenomena—was far too modest to appeal to him. Of mathematics and astronomy he had knowledge enough to make him, if not a scholar, at least a connoisseur. There was natural science in his reading at the University of Virginia, and social science in his courses. At West Point he studied advanced mathematics and natural philosophy, which must have embraced some astronomy. He stood seventeenth in his class in mathematics in a class of eighty-seven, and West Point, whatever its educational deficiencies, has never numbered mathematics among them.

At first he used his scientific knowledge chiefly in his stories of ratiocination, and in his hoaxes, of which the voyage to the moon is a good example, but steady reference in his criticism shows that he was thinking not only along the lines of his famous sonnet "To Science," in which he realizes ahead of most of his contemporaries the disillusion that might follow upon the scientific revolution, but also speculatively and philosophically upon the relation of science to a possible explanation of the universe. "Eureka," the book that he expected in his mounting egomania to sweep the country and establish his reputation as a cosmogonist, is the summary of many years of thought.[*] It is, of course, literary science. What interested Poe was never the experiment, but what could be done with the fruits of experiment to further the expansion of the imagination. Yet, unlike his contemporaries, he did not take his premises from metaphysical assumption, if he could possibly avoid it. He sought them, as best he could, in the latest discoveries of physical science. And to these he applied that mixture of intuition and logic which we call mathematics—a science based upon an art.

"Eureka" was a failure at publication, and has been called an absurdity ever since. To Mr. Krutch it is "only a wild fancy," which illustrates Poe's growing lack of control over his mental processes. Professor Stringham of the University of California contributed to Professor Woodberry's biography of the poet in 1885 an analysis of "Eureka" that not only points out many errors of fact, but ridicules the whole work as an attempt to combine materialism and Transcendentalism in an undigested mass. It is an attempt, one may say parenthetically, that we have been at ever since. He is severe upon Poe's identification of matter and force, upon the nonsense of explaining material phenomena in terms of the will of God,

[*] See for example the earlier "Mesmeric Revelation."

upon the assumption that space is "given," not created. Physics has moved ahead since Professor Stringham's day. We are not so sure now of the finality of the conservation of energy, or the materiality of the atom! And Poe has many successors and will have more in the attempt to call metaphysics to the aid of experiment. A careful reader of "Eureka" today, reasonably familiar with the complexities in which physics has enmeshed itself, must say, not that "Eureka" is the Great Explanation which Poe in his megalomania thought it, but certainly that it is an extraordinary monument of clear and logical thinking raised upon premises many of which are false, and involved, like every cosmogony, in self-contradiction. While futile as either science or philosophy, it does command respect, does involve the kind of thinking and the method of attack that modern scientific philosophers are beginning to employ. It is a return (as Stringham says disparagingly) to the method of the Greeks, and if Poe had more self-confidence than equipment this does not lessen the interest of his *tour de force*, which is probably as valuable for science as is that other *tour de force* of American logical thinking, Jonathan Edwards's "The Freedom of the Will," for psychology.

For "Eureka" is, as Poe specifically said, "a prose poem," a book offered "not in its character of truth-teller, but for the beauty that abounds in its truth." Incidentally it is a model of lucid exposition. The universe, he argues, is composed of atoms that have been radiated outward by a primal creative act of God, from a unified and homogeneous centre to the bounds of an almost infinite sphere. The act ceasing, reaction began, and the universe is now moving back toward its centre. This is the cause of gravity. When the shrinkage is accomplished both attraction and repulsion will cease in homogeneity, and since attraction plus repulsion is the definition of matter, there will be nothing. God himself is now extended in this creative act. And other gods in other universes may likewise be functioning. We and the inanimate are all parts of God. On the final reuniting He will be entire God again and may re-create. God's will, more specifically, is identified with the æther, a spiritual influence that keeps matter in heterogeneity. It is the separative, repulsive function, and heat, light, magnetism, are all due to æther. Matter exists solely to subserve its purposes, and thought and the animate are due to its influence, which is manifest only through heterogeneity. This theory Poe works out with an elaborate apparatus of mathematics, physics, astronomy, and sheer metaphysics, and he attempts to account in detail for the formation of planets in his universe, and the nature of life. His method, like Eddington's, resorts finally to intuition, which he maintains is an indispensable aid to formal logic in the searching of ultimate causes. He erects a theory by purging scientific fact of its inconsistencies, identifying a perfect consistency with truth; and indeed whatever else "Eureka" may be, it is an extraordinary anticipation of the modern criticism of the use of a purely factual science as a philosophy.

"Eureka," of course, is a poem, not a Newtonian or Einsteinian hypothesis, and suffers from its attempts to square imagination with the imperfect cosmogonies of science just as "Paradise Lost" suffers from its tie-up with an intractable theology. Done, like his "Mellonta Tauta," as pure fancy it would have been magnificent. But Poe was overweening. It was not enough to be poet, he must be the all-explainer, the scientist too!

And yet in a criticism of Poe, the evidence that "Eureka" affords of a power to bring into lucid order an extraordinary range of knowledge and to carry through a train of logical thinking that a practiced philosopher might envy, is surely important. His inaccuracies and his errors in metaphysics are less significant than the extraordinary force of mind displayed upon the whole. Undoubtedly it is true that the neurotic Poe, always trembling on the brink of insanity, did dramatize the logical faculties, and did erect in himself the fiction of the supreme logician, the superman of ratiocination from whom nothing was hid, to whom by the cold processes of inflexible reason the universe became subject as to God. Nevertheless, however absurd his monomania, he did possess in a high degree the faculty of logical analysis and that of scientific imagination. Far from being a wild fancy, "Eureka" is a startling indication of what Poe, with a different equipment and purposes differently directed, might have been able to accomplish in the realm of constructive thought. It is certain that the shams of current literary criticism were no more transparent to him than the crooked conventionality of average thinking. If he had been interested, like other American intellectuals of his time, in politics, in slavery, in morality, in religion, he would have been as radical in his way as Emerson or Thoreau. But he was not interested. A little rant upon the Abolitionists (in the attempt to score on Lowell), some lucid remarks about the fallacy of progress and the weakness of democracy, and other notes in passing, sum up his criticism in the area where the most serious American writing was being done. Formal religion touched his brooding soul so little that it no more occurred to him to attack it—than it does to most scientists. The Protestantism of his day was simply irrelevant to his quest for a stranger beauty than this planet affords. When he came back to earth from Aiden or Weir, it was to search for the one beauty which this earth contained for him—the beauty of order, form, of laws beautifully coöperating until they were seen as Law, and controlling that physical matter which he believed existed only to subserve the subtle spirit of the universe.

La Place, Descartes, Herschel, Newton, Faraday, spoke to him, when Plato, Christ, Kant, Emerson, were negative or meaningless. His hatred of the whole Transcendental school was surely not all due to his jealousy of Boston's prestige in American literature. He felt, I think, that the Transcendentalists were taking short cuts to omniscience, drowning logic in a sea of words, and using intuition not as an aid, but as a substitute for the lovely art of mathematical thought.*

Poe the neurotic was also Poe the logician and analyst, and if his sensitive imagination projected lurid worlds of emotion more darkly terrible than the dreams of his fellow romanticists, in less abandoned hours he could subdue his mind to the rigorous processes of the intellect, follow the direction of scientific thinking, or put plan, order, and form into the supersensitive world of his overcharged fancy. Amid "the gorgeous and fantastic draperies, in the solemn carvings of Egypt, in the wild cornices and furniture, in the Bedlam patterns of the carpets of tufted gold," where his hero "a bounden slave in the trammels of opium" pursues his desperate, perverted love, there are laws of human nature, profoundly illustrated by the spectral figures of his plot, which are reasoned as logically as

* These quotations from "Eureka" are interesting with reference to the paragraphs above.

"The human brain has obviously a leaning to the 'Infinite,' and fondles the phantom of the idea. . . . What is general among the whole race of Man of course no individual of that race can be warranted in considering abnormal; nevertheless there *may* be a class of superior intelligences, to whom the human bias alluded to may wear all the character of monomania."

"The pleasure which we derive from any display of human ingenuity is the ratio of *the approach* to this species of reciprocity [of adaptation]. In the construction of *plot*, for example, in fictitious literature, we should aim at so arranging the incidents that we shall not be able to determine, of any of them, whether it depends from any one other or upholds it. In this sense, of course, *perfection* of plot is really, or practically, unattainable—but only because it is a finite intelligence that constructs. The plots of God are perfect. The Universe is a plot of God."

the plot itself. The tossing seas and fiery depths of neuroticism were charted by the same faculty that dared, in "Eureka," to force consistency upon the universe. Nor is it without interest to note that when the physical and the moral man were on the verge of final shipwreck, and when, as his last letters show, his tragic fortitude was breaking down into self-pity, it was then that his now uncontrollable egomania raised this intellectual faculty to its height of confidence and display. With it he could order everything but himself, and this is natural, since Poe's self was God, and more than the universe.

And indeed the persuasive beauty of Poe's best work is due not to its subject matter—which is valid only when he projects his own morbidity, and then of a nature that has commanded more interest than liking—but to a subtle relationship between idea and form that gives quality to the childish excitements of "The Gold-Bug" and to the perverted madness of "Usher" alike. It is this feeling for the rhythm of a consistent principle which makes the *aperçus* of his criticism invaluable, and his guesses in science at least remarkable.

10.

BUT Poe suffered as do all who live inwardly and seek absolute beauty (even Shelley and certainly Coleridge) from a failure to assimilate the external world. Such men are so unsure in external reality as to be very dependent upon circumstance, and may remain entirely in the abstract and so fail to be artists, or resort uncritically (like Poe's contemporary, Chivers) to images unworthy of their conceptions. In his best stories of ratiocination, Poe escaped entirely from this disaster, thanks, perhaps, to the artificiality of his medium. He arranged his story as the scientist arranges his experiment in the laboratory, and restricting himself to bare incident, uncolored by his own experience, built up the pure form of his chain of reasoning. But even in these stories, and much more when the beauty he sought to capture was of an idea or an emotion rather than of an exercise in logic, he was dependent upon the furniture of an outside world in which he was well read but little experienced. A Rue Morgue could be described, but for Ligeia, Morella, Berenice, and Eleonora, complete habitations had to be created in which, no matter how fantastically, they might live. For his shapes of beauty he needed a *décor*—and thanks to the provincialism of America in the thirties and forties, and to a life that when not spent in dreams or in routine work was lived almost exclusively in books, Poe's prose and much of his poetry is full of descriptive terms that are second-hand to a degree unusual in genius. This is the cause of the distaste amounting almost to disgust with which even the most appreciative read too much of Poe at a sitting. The stifling luxury, and the parvenu profusion of his backgrounds, are phases of the same taste that makes the plushy eloquence and tawdry erudition of his prose style in description. Since his own room was bare he lived in his reading, and from his reading he borrowed his stage sets, which are like the furnishings of a de luxe hotel apartment, where everything has just come from somewhere else with the price tags still attached.

This bad bookishness, which, much more than his morbidity, is offensive in both the poetry and prose of Poe, was tragically inevitable. The strange beauty he grasped in exquisite form with an imagination that kept its sense of order even when the dreams seemed maddest, was pathetically dependent for expression upon images that had to be drawn from experience. And Poe's experience outside of his own soul was so largely verbal! Words he knew, knew too well, for in his constant playing with their powers of suggestion he became, like his modernist successors, too often uncritical of what they meant. He pillaged words from his abundant reading and used them for effects precisely as the architects of his period reared their "Saracenic-Gothic" piles out of any column, cornice, or parapet that took their fancy. The backgrounds of his stories come from the pictures that his mind made when he read: it is not Rome or Paris but Bulwer and Moore that he remembers when he needs a scene. Even nature—which was already a specialty in America—he could not see directly, with such rare exceptions as the tulip-tree in "Landor's Cottage," but assembled his descriptions from a half-remembered lumber of reading in his head, into which his genius struck fire only when the scene was on the road that leads to the underworld. Sincere for himself alone, and essentially unrelated to the life about him, it was through words only that Poe made his contacts. No wonder then that he helped himself so freely to quotation, reference, description, wherever he found them, and in matters of taste was dependent in everything but pure literature upon what he read in his books. Books were his chief school and almost his entire external experience. The art of securing great effects with his borrowed furnishings was of course his own, and so was the genius by which in his best work they are transmuted into new and intensely original shapes of pure beauty. He had, indeed, the methods and the conscience of a journalist, combined with the intuitive sense for *ultimate* beauty of a great artist. He could be a great poet and a skilful and unscrupulous and pretentious magazinist, both in the same sketch and almost at the same time.

II.

SOME writers are capable of a comprehensive, an exalted, and an unshakable unity. They approximate culture itself, and apply to whatever passes through the mint of their genius an intellect and an imagination that are always of the first rank and which always function with magnitude and nearly always with success. Goethe was such a writer. Another order of writers also works in a unity of genius or talent. They are single, not myriad, minded, but the singleness if narrow is consistent and intense. They do one thing well, and are content to be one thing. Such a writer was Tennyson, and Hawthorne was another. But still others are comprehensive in their powers and ambitions, willing and wishing to grasp the universe, yet cursed with a tendency to split upon tension, and hence uneven in a high degree. They have the scope of the broad genius, the intensity of the narrow one, but lack the ability of one and the steadiness of both. Such a writer was Poe, who had the pretensions of a Leonardo, but, like Shakespeare's Antony, could not hold his shape, except in a combination of circumstances exactly right for him. As his character split apart under nervous pressure, so did his work. His reach was infinite, his grasp uncertain except in fortunate moments, but then, tight.

In poetry, the condition that permitted success seems to have been an equal balance and happy correspondence between inspiration and technique. When the dark loveliness of the images that haunted Poe's imagination yielded their beauty to sounds and rhythms exquisitely artificial and yet profoundly expressive, then he wrote that "pure poetry" which was so deeply to intrigue the nineteenth century:

> Banners yellow, glorious, golden,
>   On its roof did float and flow
> (This—all this—was in the olden
>   Time long ago),
> And every gentle air that dallied,
>   In that sweet day,
> Along the ramparts plumed and pallid
>   A wingèd odor went away.

Or:

> Resignedly beneath the sky
> The melancholy waters lie.
> So blend the turrets and shadows there
> That all seem pendulous in air,
> While from a proud tower in the town
> Death looks gigantically down.

Or:

> Come, let the burial rite be read—the funeral song be sung:
> An anthem for the queenliest dead that ever died so young,
> A dirge for her the doubly dead in that she died so young.

Or:

> In Heaven a spirit doth dwell
> Whose heart-strings are a lute;
> None sing so wildly well
> As the angel Israfel.

Or:

> And all my days are trances,
> And all my nightly dreams
> Are where thy gray eye glances
> And where thy footstep gleams—
> In what ethereal dances,
> By what eternal streams.

In these poems the tricks (if you wish to call them so) of repetition and alliteration are only the more obvious touches of a structure of sound that rises in intellectual response to the poetic idea.

But in "The Raven" and in "The Bells" the artificer has overworked his metal, adding ornament when the inspiration was cold.

> On the cushion's velvet lining that the lamp-light gloated o'er,
> But whose velvet violet lining with the lamp-light gloating o'er
> *She* shall press, ah, nevermore!

and:

> How the danger sinks and swells,—
> By the sinking or the swelling in the anger of the bells,
> Of the bells,

EDGAR ALLAN POE

> Of the bells, bells, bells, bells,
>   Bells, bells, bells—
> In the clamor and the clangor of the bells!

Here the journalist has exploited the poet.

In his prose success was even more arbitrary. His technical skill seldom failed but his taste betrayed him often. The effort in his satirical and humorous pieces is painful. They are shrill. And so with his works of pseudo-knowledge, his imitations of voyages, his personalities in criticism, and his set pieces of description. Like his God in "Eureka," he was extended over the universe of literary effort, and he could not concentrate power enough upon these crystallizations. He did them with his left hand, which only his long habit of skill guided.

Thus in his stories the whole man functioned only in two sets of circumstances—and those very different. When his oversensitized dreams sprang from deep intuitions of a human tendency magnified by the abnormality of his ego, then his shapes of beauty had meaning for others. When these dreams crystallized about an idea in an order prepared by his logical mind, then his ever ready eloquence of prose flowed into the pattern.

The popular taste has been right, I think, in preferring "The Fall of the House of Usher" as the best of these achievements. Here the blending is complete. The neurotic's intuition is dressed in the folds of macabre but intelligible romance. The idea of tendency is dominant, the images of sensitiveness vivid, the symbolism of soul destruction powerful, the relevance to the dark universals of humanity in nervous tension true with that poetic truth which outlasts apparent fact. And the artifice of style and consummate skill of plot elaboration is such as Poe himself described in the lines from "Eureka" quoted above, and is indispensable if this heavy charge of imagination is to be sublimated by a creative act.

"About the whole mansion and domain there hung an atmosphere peculiar to themselves and their immediate vicinity: an atmosphere which had no affinity with the air of heaven, but which had reeked up from the decayed trees, and the gray wall, and the silent tarn: a pestilent and mystic vapor, dull, sluggish, faintly discernible, and leaden-hued. . . . Perhaps the eye of a scrutinizing observer might have discovered a barely perceptible fissure, which, extending from the roof of the building in front, made its way down the wall in a zigzag direction, until it became lost in the sullen waters of the tarn."

These stories were difficult feats of coördination by a brain grappling with nothing less than the secrets of the universe. But Poe was equally fortunate in lesser but equally original exercises of logic and intuition performed in a more mundane air, when the mystic vapors rising from his inner life were for the moment quiescent. In his tales of ratiocination, his constructive faculties worked in paths cleared by logic, following ideas of the pure intellect unclouded by emotion. And freed for the moment of neuroticism, his clear brain had a task the ease of which is reflected in the perfect narrative sequence and simple, lucid style of the best of these stories. In "The Purloined Letter" as in "The Fall of the House of Usher" he was Poe complete, in a self-unity, even though the dominants and recessives of his temperament differed sharply in the two stories. Effort and idea were exactly balanced.

And this was true also in the best of his criticism, where his subject was the nature of beauty or a device of art, like the tale or the short poem, where he was a familiar. Under such circumstances his intuition is keen, his style lucid, his judgment sound. Let opposition thwart him, a jealousy irritate his ego, or the journalistic challenge of the moment set him to making copy, and he shoots off in exhibitionism, or flounders in pretense, with only a keen sentence here and there for the profit of the reader. But see him on the short story:

"A skilful literary artist has constructed a tale. If wise, he has not fashioned his thoughts to accommodate his incidents; but having conceived, with deliberate care, a certain unique or single *effect* to be wrought out, he then invents such incidents—he then combines such events as may best aid him in establishing this preconceived effect. If his very initial sentence tend not to the outbringing of this effect, then he has failed in his first step. In the whole composition there should be no word written, of which the tendency, direct or indirect, is not to the one pre-established design." *

It is true that this description of *the* short story is really the description of *a* kind of short story, although a very effective one, true also that it much more accurately defines Poe's own work than Hawthorne's, to which it was applied. Nevertheless it is one of the classic analyses—or self-analyses—of critical literature.

But even when the nice adjustment between an oversensitive ego and his ambition was complete, some evidence of split, or at least of tension, is nearly always visible in Poe's writing, and to this no exception can be made except for a few poems and perhaps one or two criticisms. It is always present in his stories, usually in style. That his first great literary reputation was made in France is really not at all surprising. It was, paradoxically, easier for the French than for English readers to apprehend his essential genius. They were not thrown off by the meretricious and the impure in his style, because, like Poe himself, but for a different reason, they were concerned only with the beauty of words. Poe's tawdriness and his dependence upon the second-hand were not evident to them, since they got only the sound and the simple meaning of

* Review of Hawthorne's "Twice-Told Tales."

the words, the connotations, as usual, escaping aliens to the tongue. And for those who read in French, which means of course practically all Frenchmen, it is not too much to say that Poe's prose narrative is usually better for them in French than for us in the original. It is refined and purified by a taste better than his own. As for his best poetry, which made, of course, a particular appeal to perfecters of the beautiful in image and sound, like Baudelaire, the beauty of word sounds and the exquisite art of their arrangement is his peculiar triumph, and if such poems as his cannot be translated, they can at least be far better apprehended by alien readers (as with Virgil and Homer) than poetry less dependent upon verbal music. But Poe's poetry needs no defense. At its best it is the best of its kind, and flawless.

12.

I HAVE praised Poe as a great journalist. His merits in pure literature are not so easy to rank, and cannot be allowed to rest only upon a happy coincidence of virtuosity with an appropriate subject.

His passion, well rationalized, for beauty as an end in itself, was not original, of course, with him, indeed, as a philosophy was no more than an ardent adaption, from Coleridge and others, of a principle exactly suited to his own cravings. But since he was an American bred and nourished within the confines of an ethical tradition, his convinced æstheticism gave him a freedom such as no other contemporary man of letters of anything like his power enjoyed. Calvinistic Protestantism had left a sense of duty to the moral principle that was as strong in the South as in the North. This obligation, which Emerson sublimated into a religion, which weighed upon Thoreau, and was the irritant of Hawthorne's genius, the trade of Longfellow, and the obsession of Melville, Poe utterly escaped. He not only did not believe in it; he did not even for an instant feel it. Beside him the antimoralists of our own day are in comparison perverted missionaries. Only Keats in England shared his passionate, unqualified devotion to beauty as such and without a question.

And this beauty which he served was a "wilder"beauty than earth knew. He was like the spirit of his "Al Aaraaf" who sought another star, and if he too was driven back, he never ceased to renew his wanderings. It is a romanticist's beauty, transcending normal earthly experience, and seeking forms of expression that suggest the unearthly. Whether his neuroticism was the cause or the result of this passion is hard to say. It was probably both, and more specifically it was the psychical circumstance that conditioned his search. The waves of mental and physical distress that dashed through his sensitive spirit, the exaltations and abasements, were transmuted in his self-centered ego into shapes of grandeur and escape which, though out of space, out of time, were the very fabric for a dream world that could be made precise in art. Nor is this a phenomenon of the romantic movement and to be dismissed as such. The instinct to create forms of beauty free from earthly inconsistency and patterned out of desire, is inevitable at certain arcs of the evolutionary curve. Romanticism, and particularly the dominance of a romantic literature, favor it of course, but the great poets all know it. Poe's distinction is not that he gave a new though late intensity to romanticism, but that the concentration of his life within the ego created a geography so lurid and baleful, so utterly determined by factors of diversity in beauty itself, and projected from the fires of his inner consciousness with such immediacy, and yet with such control, that no saner writer has been able to produce, no insane writer able to master, its like.

I say no saner writer, implying a relative insanity in

Poe, yet his world of Weir, while murky with the mists of neuroticism and therefore consonant with visions of that irrationality which lurks in the sanest, was nevertheless and profoundly a world of order. For the visions of Poe differ from the visions of irrational dreamers because they have order. They have form because form was implicit in Poe's imagination, and (as I have already said) they invariably mean something in human experience. If that experience is in the dream stories invariably morbid, that is because in the morbid the wall of reality wears thin, and because, for Poe, morbidity was an inevitable accompaniment of emotional excitement.

And this order, which leads him to explore the mathematics of the universe for symbols, is no accidental attribute of beauty. It is a beauty itself, and clearly Poe belongs with those philosophers who find the ultimate reality to be only man's perception, or imposition, of form in chaos. The science that Poe brings to his aid may be inaccurate, the decorations of his pieces may be stale, but the intuitive perception that only by form is beauty realized is more profound than many an æstheticism more consistently practiced than his.

This beauty, wild yet ordered, pressed upon expression with a vehemence in proportion to its unconventionality. And this is the reason why Poe, in variance from all journalistic practice, wrote and rewrote, both poetry and prose, ever trying phrases in new contexts, or rephrasing with new words. In poetry especially he persisted until the intangibles of ethereal beauty are realized not so much in statement as by sound and rhythm and a subtle play of verbal light and shade.

And furthermore, the intensity of Poe's own ego made this ordered world of strange beauty to seem of dominant importance. His contempt for realism he adequately expressed, but the realism he despised was the realism of supposed fact. Reality for him lay only in the perception of order, because only through order did his insulated soul make contact with the universe. Yet if the universe was important, his own soul was even more so. He made his discoveries with the self-assurance of a God who draws back the veil of the probable and commonplace, to show behind it the livid realms where disordered fancy tortures its victims, then declares that these too are a part of the order of the universe. It was the antithesis of that calm reliance in material comfort upheld by science which his generation was so rapidly acquiring. And if Poe is often shrill and exaggerated it may well be because there was only defeat for him in the new philosophy of efficient and strenuous normalism, and because an aggressive egoism was indispensable in a writer who in such an environment was determined to be heard.

13.

THERE was, as I have tried to indicate on earlier pages of this book, a summary quality in the settled civilization of the Atlantic seaboard in the decades before the great cataclysm of the Civil War and the re-creative processes of industrial development and the opening of the West that followed in the later nineteenth century. This static condition was most notable in the South and New England, but it was discoverable in New York and Philadelphia also, although partly obscured by the rush of a new economic life. The chief product of the South was character, and the South was really articulate only in oratory. But New England was both intellectual and articulate. A type of mind was developed there as a fruit of a long ripening that in America, and perhaps in Western civilization, was an end-product. There are no more Emersons. That serene and yet intensely practical orienting of life toward ideal ends, in which energy and contemplation were reconciled, was an effort that has left its impress upon the mental, and indeed upon the political and social, life of every American, but the creative act is finished. A Thoreau is quite as incredible here and now as the English find Gandhi, although his like may reappear in the future. We are not that kind of man any longer. He states our problem, but we turn from his solution, not because it is impossible, but because it seems impossible to us. The will of God that he, like unbroken generations of Protestants before him, tried to interpret is no longer a reality for us, not even in the monistic form in which he saw it. We belong to a different dispensation, if indeed in our momentary sense of power over physical circumstance we are aware of the necessity for any dispensation. Our prophets are as yet unborn.

Emerson and Thoreau and Hawthorne, in their ideals are further away from us than the humorous, worldly elegance of Irving, or even the romantic simplicities of Cooper. Their ideas are burningly alive, but only as stimulants for new thinking. Melville, too, is an extinct species. However modern his sense of the dark recesses of the human spirit, his ideology can be interpreted but not absorbed by a modern. We in our time will never repeat his desperate Transcendentalism, nor let our imaginations expand into shapes of grandeur symbolizing powers of good and evil that we now permit neither to man nor to God. Instead of God's experiment in New England, instead of Penn's woods where the inner light was to guide a civilization, instead of Brook Farms and Harmonys and Shaker villages, and the pioneer theocracy of Deseret, it was our destiny to carry on (first, if not finally) with Ford factories, Chicago, and New York. They were, it proved, the first order of business for the mature American, although not until after the Civil War did we wholeheartedly realize it. The Emersons and the rest were premature in the history of the United States, but not in the history of the human mind, where they have their place and have borne their fruit.

Poe was not premature, nor does he represent the end-product of a civilization. He belongs in any urban, sophisticated culture. Discount his freight of stale romanticism and he slips into modern life like a hand into a glove. Born in and living in Europe, he would have been the same Poe, with an absorption of a sounder, less provincial culture, and a readier market perhaps for his wares, but without the strong stimulus of American journalism that both permitted and commanded him to make his dreams and ratiocinations lucid and impressive for the general reader.* Under fortunate conditions he might, indeed, have written far more poetry, with quicker and more adequate recognition, but Poe fortunate would not have been Poe. Indeed, in a like social and economic condition he would have drifted toward the underworld far more quickly. Mrs. Clemm's basket would have been oftener empty. His pride and vanity would have been oftener hurt. In England the great age of romanticism had definitely passed. The Moores and the Bulwers would have been his guides. And in Europe he would have lacked one pitiful success that meant much to his egoism. Abroad he would not have found a naïve community that he could impress with his scientific learning and literary erudition and surprise by cutting criticisms in a press that was accustomed to be ignorant, tolerant, and good-humored in questions of art. Nor would he have found a quick intelligence among the populace that could be flattered by writing which was always lucid yet well over their heads.

* "But the simple truth is that the writer who aims at impressing the people is always wrong when he fails in forcing the people to receive the impression." Review of Hawthorne's "Twice-Told Tales." Poe would scarcely have learned this in literary Europe.

These successes, which made life tolerable for him, would have been far harder to come at abroad. The cultured there were more cultured than he was, the uncultured were unintelligent.

I am arguing that Poe was not misplaced in America, in spite of his immense detachment from everything American except journalism, nor premature in spite of his seeming discrepancy with later industrialism. For Poe is in the truest sense a prototype of the modern intellectual who himself is both product and antithesis of industrialism.

He has the complete detachment from those questions of welfare and progress for the mass that would make him at home among the intellectuals of what has aptly been called our North Atlantic civilization, and uneasy in the Y.M.C.A. or a Methodist church. He has their devotion to abstract idea, whether called beauty or logic. He has the modern desire for publicity, which is the intellectual's method of living off a crowd that he despises. Most of all, his intense sensitiveness and congenital morbidity gave him, nearly a century ahead of his successors, that power of acute registration of the life of the nerves which is so entirely characteristic of our modern rebels against the mechanizing of industrialism. Poe's morphine was just such an excitant as the roar and racket, the speed and recurrent stimulation, of New York. He was congenitally febrile and we have become so. He is one of us, as we recognize. And the beauty he attains is the fragile beauty of artifice: exquisite, penetrating, unhealthy, perfect in form, unsubstantial in substance, sincere only in its effects, subtle, but profound only in its dependence upon the subconsciousness. It is the beauty of Proust, of Virginia Woolf, of Cabell, of the modern metaphysical poets.

A Poe in the forties of our literary history was as inevitable as an Emerson or a Hawthorne. He was phenomenal only in his pathology, which made his nervosity abnormal in his time, and of course in his genius, which I believe was essentially a genius for form. Regarded as an American he is essentially a journalist, regarded as a poet he is at his best as a lyricist of unearthly beauty, regarded as a man of letters he is the most articulate of neurotics, and at the same time a cool craftsman, intuitive, inventive, and in full control of the logic of related ideas.

Poor fellow, with his worn, humorless face, and the look of one who expects an affront, what a man he might have been if he could have turned those analytic powers of his upon his own inflamed ego, and seen that a feverish life-long show-off was not the way to convince Philadelphia and New York of his genius! But that, as I have tried to say in these pages, would have been not to have been Poe. I am not much impressed by the arguments that poverty, or impotence, or youthful conditioning made Poe what he was. They had their part no doubt, but the thing that made him was that same psychic tension which kept him from ever once heartily laughing. One laugh, and we might have had not our Poe, but Poe fulfilled as the universal mind he sought to be. He could not laugh, and that was his tragedy—if indeed a world-wide reputation for beauty wrested from the macabre and an exquisiteness of rhythm such as English poetry has rarely elsewhere shown, can be called a tragedy at this space of time from his miseries and frustrations!

CHAPTER EIGHT

Walt Whitman

THE reviewers of the slim and anonymous "Leaves of Grass" of 1855 were the first to feel the challenge, the impertinence, the disturbance, of Walt Whitman. They responded, especially the English (for Walt had spread his copies widely), with excited pages of criticism where denunciation was mingled with respect.* It was a freak they were reviewing, if not a monstrosity, and yet they were not quite sure—it seemed to be safest, for the English at least, to take their cue from the reference in the first poem to Walt Whitman, an American, and to say that here probably the American (not popular at the moment in England) showed himself as in all his raucousness he really was. One critic, looking at the frontispiece of a wistful figure, the dreamy face belying the felt hat set akimbo and the undershirt buttoned workmanwise above his open shirt collar, said that here was the Yankee in all his assurance; another fastened with whoops upon the line "an American, one of the roughs" † as a full explanation. The American reviewers were less impressed by the native audacity of the poems, and more violently shocked by the rough coarseness of many lines. Nothing less than the lash for such a violation of decency was solicited by the *Boston Intelligencer!* There was some-

* An interesting selection was published by Whitman himself in the second edition.

† In the poem afterward called "Song of Myself" this phrase appears only in the first edition.

thing in this Western apparition to disturb, to anger, to excite, every reader.

The numerous pages of Traubel's "Walt Whitman in Camden" do not explain this electric quality. The old man was tied by the leg when his Boswell began to record him, his exuberance was sunk into a rather platitudinous philosophy, and his hearty coarseness reduced to "damns" and "ain'ts." But the man in his vigorous prime is completely self-dramatized in that "Song of Myself" which so particularly irked his first readers. Rereading it and them, it is clear that their distress was not mainly due to the poet's "barbaric yawp" (his phrase is an excellent transcription of the exuberant scream of the night hawk * wheeling and flashing above the roofs of the city), nor to his coarseness, but to the man's intolerable assurance. Here was a poet who boasted of being common, average, and was so except that the candid vulgarity of those who live close to their instincts was in him intensified and made articulate, a poet who talked as carpenters and fishermen talk, of genitals, procreation, and the smells of the body, in their plain language; a poet who believed as every common man does that commonness and vulgarity are reality, and yet in an undeniable eloquence of strange verse forced cultivated readers to read his identification of spirituality with what they had been accustomed to consider grossness, soul with sweat. From a self-erected pulpit he flaunted his rank red † undershirt and maintained that it was the banner of a full life, of democracy, of religion, of what all Americans were supposed to believe in. This presumption was too much for his reviewers—and has been too much for genteel critics ever since.

* The night hawk, cousin of the whippoorwill, is of course not a true hawk, and does live in cities, nesting on flat roofs.

† I have no evidence except my own conviction that the visible undershirt was red.

What the reviewers encountered upon their first reading was the official Walt Whitman, who was, however, only one phase of this least typical and most representative of all Americans. The Walt of the "Song of Myself" and of all the "arrogant poems" of the "Leaves of Grass" was a Whitman on duty, and about what he regarded as his Master's business. He was the Puritan Whitman, crying out like a voice in "Pilgrim's Progress," "Are you saved?" He was the self-dramatized Whitman who felt himself to be a "kosmos," a representative being, with a Way by which men and women might find salvation in this life and afterward. In his old age Whitman (so Traubel records) was puzzled in considering whether the "Leaves of Grass" was not really autobiography. It was, indeed, the autobiography of the cosmos individualized that the poet called "Walt Whitman" in his poems, a literary figure, a symbol standing to the man himself in somewhat the same relation as Brand to Ibsen.

The man himself, or at least that phase of him which friends knew, was certainly less aggressive and less impudent than the American of his first poem. He had the exuberance of his "eidólon" and the faith, but in person he seems to have expressed himself best through his genius for comradeship. It is difficult to reconcile the Walt Whitman of a thousand hospital bedsides in Washington of the Civil War, who gave love to the living and comfort to the dying, with the preacher and boaster of the more raucous poems. They need not be reconciled. The American rough was only Walt in armor, out to reform the world. Cocky he must always have been (you can see his cockiness in the "Pete Doyle picture" of 1889) but there are other photographs of the sixties that fit the poet of "Drum-Taps" and the author of "Specimen Days": in them are the breathing affection, the quick sympathy with everything genuine, and the evident joy in living that must have

WALT WHITMAN

been his attributes.* He offended the virtuous, meaning precisely what Falstaff meant by the word, but not those big of mind and heart. I like the story of his Camden days, not hitherto, I think, published, how visiting in Philadelphia he would occupy the sole bathroom for hours, chanting cheerfully while the family suffered. Here you get a glimpse of the living man.

He posed often, if not always, in public, seemed a clever old faker to the Philadelphia reporters, was extravagantly solicitous for the reputation of his work, took whatever cash tribute came his way like a Hindu temple god, was in his youth more sensual probably than even the rationalizations of his poetry admitted,† was both heterosexual and, in the psychological sense, homosexual—the latter the stronger and the more important passion in his work— never got beyond the self-made in his culture, judged his contemporaries by their attitude toward "Leaves of Grass"—had in fact all the failings of genius except meanness. But unlike most literary geniuses he practiced what he preached, and most emphatically, and with hundreds, *was* the Great Personality he celebrated in his work.

2.

THE religious and moral preoccupations of early mid-century America were sure to find, sooner or later, an outlet in æsthetics. When the pressure of Calvinism abated, the enthusiasms sprung from introspection fizzed and fumed until they gave rise to a hundred American religions in the thirties, forties, and fifties. In New England, and the provinces of New England, the Emersons and Hawthornes relieved for their generation the perilous emotions that rise on the line of tension where conduct encounters beauty. But Emerson, as Whitman said, was too

* In Traubel's "Walt Whitman in Camden," Vol. I, p. 390; Vol. II, p. 454.
† See "Of Many a Smutch'd Deed Reminiscent."

311

dandified to speak for the whole people. He held the key to that identification of energy and the soul which best suited a successful race of pioneers, but it was left for Whitman to turn the key.

To call Whitman a pagan because he was of the earth earthy is misleading, to call him a natural man is misleading; he was more than either when most that "kosmos," which he called Walt Whitman. He was more religious than either implies, yet the compound made him better able than anyone else then alive to give expression in an art form to the spiritual turbulence of decades when inspiration became democratic and every region had its prophet. His paganism, his unsophistication, and the sources of his spirituality all were close to the people.

Yet on the intellectual side he was nearer to the Quakers than to the hearty vulgar. He was a half Quaker, with part of that half converted to Emersonism. Compare him to a man carrying a burning coal that he turns this way and that to see which wind will best fan it, and where is the tinder which it will ignite. Walt's personality was a glowing coal, and already in his youth his Quaker environment had taught him to look into his heart for the breath that came from God. His idea that the average man is an ideal temple of God because any excess above the average obscures the inner light,* was Quaker also; and the assurance with which Walt Whitman, as a plain American, spoke to powers and principalities and, what was more courageous, to his conventional and orthodox fellow countrymen, was Quaker in its inspiration, if pagan in its audacity, and democratic in its nature. They will, said Charles Lamb of the Quakers, endure no tyranny. And when the bright radiance of Emerson's moral idealism reached to Paumanok and seemed to answer his desire for

* Robert Barclay, as cited before on page 30, defines it as an inspiration which, though not Christ himself, is the spirit of Christ.

a lofty spirituality common to all men, Whitman became the perfect channel through which a high potentiality of blended religious and physical emotions could be transformed into the concrete terms of an art. All of which means simply that the hearty pagan in Whitman first became Quaker, and then philosophical idealist and moralist, without losing its original apprehension of physical life. Keeping the enthusiasm of the religious emotions of the period of his youth, Whitman translated them into a religion for democracy that was pagan in its sensuousness, self-reliant in its spirituality, moral in its purpose, and above all idealistic, and this is the basis of his art. In no other country of the world could spiritual enthusiasm, a gusto for living, equalitarianism, a moral end, and absolute self-sufficiency in religious inspiration, have been so naturally and hence so successfully brought together and focused through one man's personality.

3.

HE MADE also a religion of democracy. The spirit of American democracy was made articulate by the French Revolution, but actually it was more pioneer and Puritan than French. It was a democracy rich in inconsistencies and contradictions, equalitarian in the words it used to describe itself but more interested in opportunity than equality. Before it became a national philosophy it was only the inevitable result of pioneering in a new land, where every man began life anew, and recognized the right of every one of his own race to do the same, if not now, then later, if not here, then further west. The cardinal difference in outlook of a land without a white peasantry or a stable aristocracy was recognized long before the Revolution. It became a creed with Jefferson and a national policy when the common people made Jackson their symbol.

Democracy of this American type had abundant outlets into oratory but substantially none into literature. There is no democratic literature of merit before Whitman precisely because American democracy was essentially a creation of the frontier. It was crudest where it was most alive, too crude to be effectively articulate in its own language, and hence dependent upon conventional literary moulds that were quite unfitted to its essential spirit. The school "Readers" of the early century are full of democratic themes expressed in the stale diction of what Whitman would have called feudalism. Rhetoric of the spread-eagle variety was the emotional outlet for democracy. Its prophets borrowed their language from Rome and the Old Testament because their own tongue, like the primitive Romance tongues of Europe, was incapable. The rotundities of the Great Age of American oratory do not move us now. Emerson and Thoreau still speak, but Calhoun and even Webster are silent. The democratic idea had critics, expounders, refiners, but no natural voice. Whitman wished to be that voice. And yet as he had democratized religion, extending its affirmation of the sacredness of the common man, so now he spiritualized democracy so that the "en masse" of his republic should become a double comradeship in "muscle and pluck," and in spiritual significance:

Know you, solely to drop in the earth the germs of a greater religion,
The following chants each for its kind I sing.
My comrade!
For you to share with me two greatnesses, and a third one rising inclusive and more resplendent,
The greatness of Love and Democracy, and the greatness of Religion. . . .
And I will not make a poem or the least part of a poem but has reference to the soul,
Because having look'd at the objects of the universe, I find there is no one nor any particle of one but has reference to the soul.*

* "Starting from Paumanok."

WALT WHITMAN

This rather metaphysical conception of democracy made it impossible for him to be a voice intelligible to the masses of which he wrote, the more particularly since, although he was largely unaware of it even up to his death, they were already embarked on the great and sordid adventure of industrialism that was to swing them further and further from spiritual fervors toward the materialism of prosperity. His celebration of the body electric, his insistence upon the ideal of comradeship, his identification of soul and sense, were all inevitable in him, but by no means inevitable in his American democracy, in which they were at most inherent possibilities, and seemed scarcely that. He was one of the en masse, the average, genuinely. He lived their life, and thought their thoughts, as well as his own, and felt keenly and truly with their instincts; but he had been bred in the mystic self-reliance of a Peculiar People, as the Quakers called themselves, and had also come under the influence of the highly uncommon philosophy of Transcendentalism. He could speak the language of democrats and make literature of it, but his spiritual insights were much closer to that seventeenth century when the Quaker sought equality to secure not the rights of man so much as the rights of God within every common man. Whitman spoke for the people and of the people, but to suppose that his idealism was governed by the mass desires of the people he celebrated, would be to misunderstand him utterly.

Nevertheless, in a world sense, he is rightly regarded as the representative of this common man, who never reads him, because he never recognizes himself in Whitman's heroes of the broad-ax and the soul. And rightly indeed, for he was the first to give ordinary, vulgar, vital man a ranking with the captains and the kings, as one whose daily life and intuitive processes were of infinite importance and worthy of expression as well as of description.

And the ideal democracy of his poems, while it is always ideal, has deep roots in history. "First class literature," Whitman wrote in "A Backward Glance," "grows by circumstances. . . . It does not shine by its own luminosity." The "circumstances" of the United States in the fifties were rich and varied for the poet of democracy. It was an age of exuberance of which Walt's own exuberant personality is a proper fruit, an age of confident energy in an America politically and economically emancipated, where a growing materialism was scarcely to be distinguished from spiritual and intellectual endeavor, since all three went hand in hand. Its records are abundant in memoirs and letters and social histories. Its monuments are the "Song of Joys," "The Song of the Broad-Axe," and "Pioneers! O Pioneers!" "Strong shapes and attributes of strong shapes, masculine trades, sights and sounds," were common. "The beauty of all adventurous and daring persons" was common, and "the glad clear sound of one's own voice, the merry song, the natural life of the woods, the strong day's work." It was easy then to say that "the roughness of the earth and of man encloses as much as the delicatesse of earth and man," because in the brimming energy of those decades that was true. It was a community still essentially agrarian that he celebrated, yet focusing in great villages, like his beloved Mannahatta. By comparison with Europe there was little opportunity for development in pure intellect or in art, less probably than in Federalist times, but for the faculties shared by all men and requiring no excess of refinement for their development, opportunity was never anywhere greater. Upon men who set out to make "far more arrogant republics" economics weighed lightly, for if they failed they could always move west. Few precedents bound them, government did not trouble them, with all their faults, they had

The beauty of independence, departure, actions that rely on them-
 selves,
The American contempt for statutes and ceremonies, the boundless
 impatience of restraint,
The loose drift of character, the inkling through random types, the
 solidification; . . .
The power of personality, just or unjust. . . .
Muscle and pluck forever! *

Thus the swinging picture poems of Whitman's—and
he is a great maker of pictures—had plenty of basis in fact.
In Whitman's time there were many to say of this apple-
shaped earth, "I do not know what it is except that it is
grand, and that it is happiness," many more, less philosophic or less fortunate, to enter heartily upon sweat,
labor, fighting, carousing, loving, and hoping, in a country
where you could always expect to make good, where the
men who did the work, slaves and the new mill hands excepted, were still very largely the men who owned the
work. There is nothing false in the heartiness of Whitman's pictures of the American democracy. Even the
Civil War, which shocked his mystical adoration of the
Union to its heart's core, comforted by its innumerable
proofs of the heroism of ordinary humanity, even from the
corrupted and sophisticated cities. "Wisdom," he said,
"is the certainty of the reality and the immortality of
things," and this his Americans had. Poe, who lived temporally in Whitman's New York, but spiritually on another
planet, seemed to him "morbid," because (I believe) he
could not feel this heartiness and this hope. He criticized
Thoreau for his disdain of Tom, Dick, and Harry, Emerson for distrusting the earthy in man. With all its panics
and boom-bustings, with the malaria and the degeneracy
of frontier life, with violence and corruption in the cities,
and religious crankiness in the rural districts, America,
North and South, in Whitman's day, did present the spec-

* "Song of the Broad-Axe."

317

tacle of a vigor and a hope not altogether physical, in which more men and women shared than elsewhere on the globe. If it was not always, or often, a place for a gentleman or a scholar (as Poe found), it was a paradise for one who could say even of his poems,

> Camerado, this is no book,
> Who touches this touches a man.*

4.

NOR was it unnatural that a poet so favorably cast by temperament and experience for comprehending such a moment of time and such a revelation of human nature, should put on the mantle of the prophet and, describing truly what he knew, build upon it a spiritual democracy of the future.

As a prophet, in the restricted modern sense of the word, he was wrong, wrong at least for America, and wrong for world democracy as far as we have gone with it; but in the truer sense of seer and diviner he was not wrong. For however true to the "circumstances" of his exuberant age are the descriptions in the "Leaves of Grass," the democracy there is the democracy of a Utopia and known by Whitman to be such. He knew the America from which he drew his types far better than his critics, and he himself is not uncritical. He knew corruption, misery, greed, sordidness, and the negation of progress. The society of the "Leaves" is realistic, but it is prophetic and Utopian also. It is not like earlier Utopias. These he brushed aside because they left out precisely what he found in his United States—

> I heard what was said of the universe,
> Heard it and heard it of several thousand years;
> It is middling well as far as it goes—but is that all? †

* "So Long."
† "Song of Myself."

Utopias had been aristocratic; there was no place in them for sweat, exuberance, libidinous desires, for the passion of virility, equality in spirit among camerados, hearty mirth, for something the common man had that Plato had lost. But he never regarded America as a Utopia here and now, nor the American democracy as an ideal. It was, at most, a basis for triumphant prophecy.

By 1870 he could say in the after-war disillusionment of "Democratic Vistas," what is implicit in all the confident urging of his earlier work: "I say that our New World Democracy, however great a success in uplifting the masses out of their slough, in materialistic development, products, and a certain high-deceptive superficial popular intellectuality, is, so far, an almost complete failure in its social aspects, and in really grand religious, moral, literary, and æsthetic results." And further on in a footnote he adds "the absence, or perhaps the singular abeyance of moral conscientious fibre all through American society." And yet on sweeps his pæan of the ideal ensemble.

This religion of the future (for that is its best description) of the "Leaves of Grass" was drawn like all religion from experience that was physical and spiritual both. It was close to the reality of circumstance, and deeply colored by Whitman's own personality. Indeed, it began when Whitman first felt:

> I am larger, better than I thought,
> I did not know I held so much goodness.*

It was shaped by the Emersonian idea of acceptance, congenial to a man of Whitman's temperament, and hence readily carried to a logical conclusion where the celebrant no longer dallies with the mysteries of good and evil, but presses on to complete self-development—

Let others deprecate, let others weep for sin, remorse, humiliation.†

* "Song of the Open Road." † "Passage to India."

Accepting vice with virtue, the prostitute and the faithful mother, death as well as life, he idealizes his own experience with common man in exuberant America. And here his Quaker training supplies a further rationalization of his faith in humanity. The individual is sacred because he is, if he wills, a receptacle for the inner light. Democracy realized will be spirituality also. But the Quakers stopped short of happiness through complete self-possession. They distrusted the body. Emerson saw that the body too must be accepted, but Whitman went further. He was so intensely aware of his body that the slightest neglect of its most secret desires was unthinkable because impossible to his thrilling nerves. One sees him vacillating between the chant of the body electric in the "Song of Myself"—where he is God, God he, he is the earth, the earth he, and all a part of bodily sensation—and less sensual ideals of universal comradeship through spiritual communion.* The logical result was his defiant assertion that he was a "kosmos," which so amused his early reviewers. He meant just that. The representative man was in himself neither flesh nor spirit alone, but cosmos, and Whitman, as poet, was the representative man. In his idealized republic no heroes will be needed, for all will be heroic, all will be Walt Whitman, not the man Walter, but the aspiring prophetic poet, Walt. It will be a democracy of Walt Whitmans, with everyone in happy self-possession of *all* his faculties, potentially a man, a woman, and a cosmos.

And thus in his old age he came back willingly enough in his conversations with Traubel to the idea that the "Leaves" was an autobiography, which, by recording the

---

* Mss. lines for the "Song of Myself" not used include:

In all of them and all existing creeds grows not
   so much of God as I grow in my moustache;
I am myself waiting my time to be a God.

experience of a representative man, had given "that entire faith and acceptance which is the foundation of moral America" * sinews, glands, heart, and soul.

Whitman's democracy is thus a heroic presentation of what he actually saw and felt in his own America. But every line that describes it is transformed into the shining idealism of prophecy by his unwavering belief that all experience recorded man's rushing on toward, or his holding back from, absorption in the nature (not the will) of God. A nation of "athletes," eager to live and love and have comrades, believing in life, not afraid of it, trusting their own intuitions as to good and evil, accepting blindly no precepts or conventions, respecting their own souls, making no distinctions between body and spirit, anxious to realize themselves and aware that this could happen only among those that they loved and that loved them—this was Whitman's democratic Utopia, in which even God was most accessible to the most typical man. You will get his best commentary upon it by reading, first, "A Song for Occupations," and then "Passage to India."

5.

No AMERICAN can read of Whitman's democracy without moods of sadness, and an unwillingness to accept it all as illusion. His own knowledge, his own memories, almost defiantly pick out aspects of undeniable truth. Yet regarded as a society upon which the future might be built it is only Walt Whitman's personal adaptation of that world dream of Quakerism which touched his imagination in youth. The Society of Friends hoped, no, expected, to make all the world friends. Men, they believed, had a common access to the inspiration toward good. When the mind was cleared of vanity, when the way was open for the inner light to shine, there was no one not

* "A Backward Glance."

capable of friendliness, no one unable to recognize in the humblest man his brother. Who will flatly say and prove that under the happiest of conditions, with the strongest of religious impulses, this might not, for a while, even with human nature what it is, prove to be true! But Whitman's universal comradeship is more difficult than the spiritual Utopia of the Friends. Where the Quaker denied, he proposed to accept. He would have no bloodless salvation but a world of camerados who would eschew vanity but taste every draught offered by experience. He would make bodies friends as well as minds and souls, and trust to love to emerge from the rough and tumble of a society in which all should be of the "letting-it-go-kind," as he described himself—all concerned for the welfare of each.

It was illusion of course, and yet in that hearty age of America when the "Leaves" were born, there was more sense in it than seems possible at the high curve of the machine age when conformity to the rules of a complex mechanical organism is the price of success. His vision of a country economically and socially free to an extraordinary extent, turbulent, joyful, potential, believing in itself with an intensity that no one born after 1890, perhaps after 1850, can understand, is one of the great assets of the American imagination. It was permissible to expect that such a country might become anything. It was easy to mistake, as did Whitman in "Salut au Monde," rapture with living in such an environment for a mission to lead Europe toward the recognition of a democratic God. Even the sedate Emerson let himself go when he looked across the Alleghenies; how much the greater the intoxication of one who could "sing and laugh and deny nothing," who was

Pleas'd with the native and pleas'd with the foreign, pleas'd with new
   and old,
Pleas'd with the homely woman as well as the handsome,

Pleas'd with the quakeress as she puts off her bonnet and talks melo-
diously,
Pleas'd with the tune of the choir of the whitewash'd church,
Pleas'd with the earnest words of the sweating Methodist preacher, . . .
Hot toward one I hate, ready in my madness to knife him,
Solitary at midnight in my backyard, my thoughts gone from me a
long while,
Walking the old hills of Judæa with the beautiful gentle God by my
side, . . .
Storming, enjoying, planning, loving, cautioning . . .
I tread day and night such woods.*

And he believed, and for millions it was true, that

We must march my darlings, we must bear the brunt of danger,
We the youthful sinewy races, all the rest on us depend,
Pioneers! O pioneers!

And his ideal democracy has exactly the validity of
every good ideal, including the reign of peace of the
Friends from whose quiet city of the spirit he came self-
exiled to his brawling Mannahatta. It remains a permanent possibility for man, if not a prophecy for the future.
To his credit he saw that this democracy would have to
be all-accepting, all-using, unrefined, powerful, una-
shamed, or it could never begin. And he was ideally right
in unsettling theory by his claims that every experience
possible to man must be part of the ideal state.

6.

THE Quakers and Emerson between them may be said
to have lifted Whitman's zeal into a poetic philosophy.

Whitman of the "Song of Myself" is still a braggart
and a sensationalist, breaking up the conventional moulds
of expression and breaking through the Victorian reticences out of sheer restlessness of blood as much as by
principle, and determined to speak nature without check
and energy without qualification in an abandon that un-

* "Song of Myself."

regulated would have made him a source book rather than a master. But the Whitman of the "Leaves" as a whole (and including the "Song") is seen to be a far more important person, who revels in experience for the joy of telling it, but lifts, coördinates, directs every item of it toward some larger harmony in which meaning has a place. He began as an expressionist, and if he had not been an expressionist he would not have been Whitman. But it was his vision of a "Passage to India," which for him meant a relationship between his delights and fervors and the world soul, that made him an artist on the grand scale. His philosophy is often questionable, but it gave form to his intentions and a structure upon which his imagination could build.

It is difficult to write of Whitman's philosophy because it was more a faith than a philosophy, and more consistent in its reiterations than logical in its development. If to the Quaker's confidence that God's spirit was in every man it be said that Whitman added a man's confidence that he was a part of God, a beginning is made of definition. Acceptance of everything in experience therefore became easily a part of his creed, for every function was of God, "All is Truth, There are no lies"; but this acceptance was not to be passive, it must be, as it was in Whitman, a passion for living. Live hard enough, and love while you are living, and all will be well. There are negatives, but not the usual ones. Not sin, not error, is what his creed denies, but whatever cramps or checks the flow of life. Manners, castes, conventions, fears, reticences, inhibitions of every kind, these are the items in the "Good Lord, deliver us" of his ritual. It is a philosophy based upon the psychological necessity for self-expression, rationalized by the belief that every motion comes from God.

And yet Whitman does not expect or demand perfectibility. All men shall love each other, *as they are.*

It was a philosophy that exalted the common man, because in him life moves with the least artifice. But the common man of Whitman was neither the primitive of Rousseau nor the peasant of Europe. He was a man civilized by Europe but freed from the weight of convention by a change in environment, and relieved of his inhibitions by becoming his own master in a country where self-reliance and initiative brought an almost sure reward. The common man of Whitman's philosophy was the "independent American citizen" of nineteenth century oratory.

Neither a servant nor a master I,
I take no sooner a large price than a small price, I will have my own whoever enjoys me,
I will be even with you and you shall be even with me.*

And this common man, as one finds him in the "Leaves," has Whitman's uncommon intensity of living.

Whitman's deity is manifested in life itself, and best manifested in love. He is not personal in the Calvinist or the Catholic sense, but he is indwelling in the soul and personality is a part of him. I doubt whether it is possible to be more precise as to Whitman's theology. It is pantheistic, monistic, and yet these terms are too abstract to define the intensity of Whitman's faith in an indwelling spirit that was life and love and also the tabernacle in which it joyously flamed. Hence the paradox of his hearty delight in the "conquest of nature"—forests falling, prairies ploughed, factory smoke rising, successful labor clipping its vines and breeding children to share in a plethora of abundance—that same conquest of nature which was to bring in an age of crass materialism. It was a paradox, for he hated and was incapable of materialism. But in his philosophy these gains were spiritual, for body was spirit, and the happy laborer was gaining freedom to live and

---

* "A Song for Occupations."

to love. And so he would—in Utopia. In fact this philosophy of Whitman's belongs unquestionably among the
phenomena of expansionist romanticism; but it is a unique
romance, which is happy only with the attributes of what
to others would be realism, and often most unpleasant
realism.

Such a philosophy could come only from a new and
successful country. It could be held only by a convinced
individualist. It is sound only if one admits the capacity
of everyone to love, denies original sin, and believes that
self-expression and salvation are identical. This Whitman
believed. Love, like the inner light, needed only in his
estimation a release in every soul and body. And the release came from rushing upon life. If he erred, the psychological researches of the last decade have at least proved
that his uncritical faith was not without sound elements
of practical truth.

This was Whitman's Way, and before it is jibed at by
the too easy cynicism of an age of religious anarchy, let it
be remembered that he held to it through the darkness of
the Civil War, where his experience of evil was intense,
and which for him represented a major overturning of
every theory of comradeship in a United America in which
he had believed. Let it be remembered also that he kept
his faith through the meanness and corruption of the seventies and eighties, of which he was vividly aware. And
our contemporary society has apparently accepted in
practice his freedom in experience (especially sexual experience), and freedom from convention, without the love
that he regarded as indispensable. An ethical humanism
should be more severe with us than with him.

It is an extravagant philosophy, which finds little support in the recorded history of human nature, and must
be regarded as arbitrary in its assumption that the man
who lets go is more admirable than the man who holds

back, quite as arbitrary as the opposite opinion; but it is a philosophy of aspiration, a prophetic philosophy, a defiant philosophy, with certainly truth enough in it to make it dangerous to stiffened creeds, and so the very stuff for poetry.

7.

I HAVE written enough already to indicate that Whitman must be regarded as one of the major influences upon the modern imagination. You cannot touch him without being drawn into a discussion of nations and philosophies. He believed himself that his "Leaves" were seminal, creating a new type of human, and he addressed Christ as a brother and an equal—

My spirit to yours dear brother,
. . . we make our ineffaceable mark upon time and the diverse eras,
Till we saturate time and eras, that the men and women of races, ages
    to come, may prove brethren and lovers as we are.*

He *was*, and he *is* seminal, and it is not necessary to admit his lifelong pugnacious contention that his "Leaves" were the utterance of a major prophet, or to subscribe to his prophecy, in order to believe that one of the immortals walked in Camden. Why then has he failed of complete recognition, and wherein did he come short of his expected stature?

I do not refer, of course, to a recognition by the camerados of the so-called working classes that he so loved to celebrate. Walt never wrote for classes; the idea of a world proletariat based on economic grounds would have been repugnant to him. He wrote for individuals, and the ideal democracy of spiritualized sweat that he presented to them required the expensive simplicity of a rather complete education to understand. Longfellow's moral sentimentality was far easier of comprehension by the masses,

* "To Him That Was Crucified."

who would have been merely puzzled by the spectacle of one who called himself their comrade becoming undisguised and naked on a bank to feel the delicious contacts of outdoors, and outraged to find him injecting into their hearty coarseness an incomprehensible mysticism. Nor was the great poet of the democracy fool enough to seek his praises upon the deck of a Brooklyn ferryboat. He wrote of powerful uneducated people, for he felt life pulsing from the masses, but he wrote *for* powerful educated people, and saw that they got complimentary copies of his books. They were sharp enough to recognize vigor and truth in what would have been to the uneducated only words. I think that Whitman would have preferred to call himself the interpreter and prophet of democracy rather than its bard.

Nevertheless, it cannot be denied that his failure to be read by the masses, or at least to get to them as Shakespeare got to them, is a qualification of his program. He proposed, as he says with such reiterance in "Democratic Vistas," to prepare a new literature to supply imaginative ideals for a democracy, a literature that was to give an archetype for the common man. But this Whitman did not do. In breaking away from tradition he broke away from the only symbol that common men understood. The mystic realism of Whitman's portraits could mean nothing to them. They would have recognized their own *mores* but these heroic trampers of roads and sailers of seas did not touch their imagination because, though like them in manners, they were too unlike them in spirit, and there was no familiar bridge of myth or story over which they could cross. Our culture is international and when Whitman tried to substitute for it a transcript of American customs, he became, paradoxical as it may seem at first, unintelligible to the masses. He had, in fact, created a new mythology of democracy, which only the educated could understand. Furthermore there was too much Whitman in his archetypes. His heroes were all prophets. They told the democracy in recitative what to do and be, but they never were what the American democracy could by any stretch of the imagination hope or expect to become. His archetypes were themselves characters in Utopia; and, indeed, American literature has never yet been able to make characters (at least of the magnitude and imaginative power which Whitman desired) in which the actual American democracy could see its aspirations humanized, as Elizabethan England saw its thoughts and emotions in the plays of Shakespeare. We have Babbitts and Silas Laphams and petty failures and frustrations, but no American Hamlet, Macbeth, or Cleopatra.

He failed of direct contact with his camerados, but has been impressively successful in touching the imagination of the thinkers and the dreamers and hence cannot be said to lack an indirect success. If he did not convert America, he left a race of prophets behind him. But even by those who make literary reputations and for whom all literature not strictly popular is written, Whitman has never been received without qualification. For a major force in modern literature, as he indubitably is, his readers are still not numerous, his place in fame is still undetermined. For this, I think, three things are chiefly responsible—the form of his poetry, his dealings with sex, and an egoism that is the secret of his weakness as well as his strength.

8.

IN DISCUSSING the oft-discussed form of Whitman's poetry, his inflexible determination to escape from literature as such must be remembered. He was resolved to break away from moulds of expression made conventional by their success in expressing the emotions of the old-world society. He assumed a far wider cultural divergence from

his new world than in fact existed and this was the prime
cause of his failure to communicate with his camerados,
but he rightly felt that life in America had been conditioned by experiences so different from the European that
an indigenous literature must show a difference in form if
it were to express an inevitable difference in content.
There is a fiery passage on the nature of poetry in his
Preface to the first and 1855 issue of the then slender
"Leaves of Grass," which should be read again and again
by lovers of poetry and lovers of Whitman. This preface
does not explain the form of his poetry, but it does explain
what he believed that he was doing. The poet and the
poem, he says, are identical:

"The poetic quality is not marshal'd in rhyme or uniformity, or abstract addresses to things, nor in melancholy complaints or good precepts, but is the life of these
and much else, and is in the soul. . . . All beauty comes
from beautiful blood and a beautiful brain. If the greatnesses are in conjunction in a man or woman, it is enough
—the fact will prevail through the universe; but the gaggery and gilt of a million years will not prevail. Who
troubles himself about his ornaments or fluency is lost.
This is what you shall do; Love the earth and sun and the
animals . . . dismiss whatever insults your own soul;
and your very flesh shall be a great poem. . . . The greatest poet . . . scorns intervals. . . . The art of art, the
glory of expression and the sunshine of the light of letters,
is simplicity. Nothing is better than simplicity—nothing
can make up for excess, or for the lack of definiteness. To
carry on the heave of impulse and pierce intellectual
depths and give all subjects their articulations, are powers
neither common nor very uncommon. But to speak in literature with the perfect rectitude and insouciance of the
movements of animals, and the unimpeachableness of the
sentiment of trees in the woods and grass by the roadside,

is the flawless triumph of art. If you have looked on him who has achiev'd it you have look'd on one of the masters of the artists of all nations and times. You shall not contemplate the flight of the gray gull over the bay, or the mettlesome action of the blood horse, or the tall leaning of sunflowers on their stalk, or the appearance of the sun journeying through heaven, or the appearance of the moon afterward, with any more satisfaction than you shall contemplate him. The great poet has less a mark'd style, and is more the channel of thoughts and things without increase or diminution, and is the free channel of himself. He swears to his art, I will not be meddlesome. . . . What I experience or portray shall go from my composition without a shred of my composition. You shall stand by my side and look in the mirror with me. . . . A heroic person walks at his ease through and out of that custom or precedent or authority that suits him not. . . . Nothing is finer than silent defiance advancing from new free forms. . . . The cleanest expression is that which finds no sphere worthy of itself, and makes one."

Here again appears that Quaker theory that Whitman absorbed so deeply, but this time blended with Carlyle and Emerson and transferred to æsthetics. Most of all, however, it is Quaker, the tenacious Quaker idea that man must be a free channel for the passage of spirit; that ornaments and fluency, gaggery and gilt, are interruptions, barriers; that customs, precedents, authorities, must, if they are in the way, be swept aside. So it was with Whitman's poetry sprung of the love of sun, earth, and animals. It, too, must have no barriers. With a few changes in language, the passage I have quoted might be applied to either form of spiritual release.

If this parallelism is granted, and I think it must be granted, the analogy may be pushed further. As the Quaker's obstinate freedom from convention led to a drab monotony of dress and custom, so Whitman's determined avoidance of artifice resulted in a monotony of verse forms. In both, the medium of expression, through very formlessness, lost the variety of form. Indeed the Quaker succeeded better than the poet, for he made a code of his simplicity with a ritual dignity all its own, whereas Whitman's diction remained like a too wet clay that will mould instantly but will not hold its shape. Even his prose, which, in the passage I have just quoted, is so terse and pointed, fell into tags and parentheses and loose additions in his later writing.

Monotony is Whitman's chief fault as a poet. He took the rhythmic freedom of prose for his "Leaves" and unwittingly took with it prose's limitations. He made the oracular style in free verse his own so emphatically that a line of quotation taken anywhere reveals the author, and yet in form never got beyond what he called "my recitatives." The "Leaves" were not poems in the conventional sense. They were self-expressions, oracular, prophetic, descriptive, to be recited as the Bible is recited. Ossian was a factor in their making, for Whitman read Macpherson young. English speakers well read in the Bible have always been powerfully affected by the kindred but more romantic lines of the Gaelic maker of poetic prose. Miss Constance Rourke * is doubtless right in believing that the rhapsodic "boasts" of the frontiersman in liquor or about to fight had their influence upon Walt's long strings of eloquent assertions. And the resemblance between the "Leaves" and the apparently free structure of Italian opera has been noted. Indeed the parallel between Whitman's style and music deserves careful consideration. Unlike his contemporaries in American literature, who were either tone-deaf like Emerson, or childish in their knowledge, Whitman was at least a good amateur of

* In "American Humor," 1931, pp. 172-74.

music, and especially of the opera. His poetry often and quite evidently moves with the memory of music behind it, notably such poems as "Out of the Cradle Endlessly Rocking," but it is not, of course, based upon a musical structure. His verse forms flow with the rise and fall, the expansion and contraction, of music, as one appreciative who is not an expert hears music. It was not opera in words that he wrote, but words that moved as the opera sounded to him. In refusing a recurrent rhythmic structure, in insisting upon absolute freedom, he of course denied the principles of musical art. But I am not here concerned with the sources of Whitman's style so much as with its results. Let us add that Emerson and Carlyle, but most of all the oracular, ejaculatory Carlyle, must be reckoned with as prime sources for his diction, and go on with the discussion.

His "Leaves" were to be poetry, were bound to be at their best, for no one can doubt the lyric inspiration of the man who could write "The Last Invocation," or "Out of the Cradle Endlessly Rocking," yet not such poetry as had served for the dandies, the scholars, and the aristocrats. His poetry must echo exuberant acceptance; must speak naturally for all the commonplace things that literary people thought unpoetical—the material achievements of science, the instincts of everyday man, the rattle, dirt, and restlessness of Mannahatta, the broad-ax, procreation, loafing, the en masse. And yet it must be heroic as his subject as a whole was heroic, and oracular as his message was an oracle, and eloquent with the eloquence of the Great Person speaking to the populace. It must be a language that all men could speak and understand ("By God! I will accept nothing which all cannot have their counterpart of on the same terms"),* and yet it must

* "Song of Myself."

transcend their speaking, transcend art literature by going beyond it into religion.

Now it cannot be denied that the unrhymed unmetrical medium he created was excellently suited to description. Whitman has never been sufficiently praised for his word pictures. They are vivid, loving, and of an extraordinary range; and they have the quality of caught motion, so that they quiver with immediacy. The secret lies in his power over metaphor. The simile must have seemed artificial to him, or perhaps a comparison took his eye off his beloved environment and called for a parallel from the past, or from the literature of the past, which he was trying to escape. Certainly he will not be diverted from the direct phrase and prefers the cumulative effect of a catalogue to the balance of this and that. He prefers words flashing, not from the far-away, but from the scene itself—"The proud black ships of Manhattan." Hence the packed quality of his phrases ("I hear the wheeze of the slave-coffle"), and hence too the diffuseness of his descriptive poems, built up as they are of vivid detail and never concentrated by an appeal to the literary memory.

It is a democracy of diction where, as in "A Song for Occupations," no atom of experience is greater than another, and hence everything, from flour-works to hog-hooks and the unseen soul must have its equal celebration—

Strange and hard that paradox true I give,
Objects gross and the unseen soul are one.

Often we weary of such shotgun methods. The details of American experience drop like rain upon the imagination, which grows cold beneath their impact. The theory that all must be told confuses the artist in him, and indeed there was an obstinate self-confidence in Walt that was definitely not artistic at all, but rather a prophet's egoism that gives an almost mystic value to everything seen by him and said. Nevertheless, it needs only a judicious selection from Whitman (and, far more than Wordsworth, he needs an Arnold to edit him) in order to reveal his extraordinary descriptive power. A social history of the United States should be sewn thickly with quotations from "Leaves of Grass." It is curious that in accounts of the Civil War, the brilliant phrases of his "Drum-Taps" have not been more often used. For word pictures his free rhythmic style is excellently suited.

And yet these innumerable and excellent descriptions rise into poetry less often than they should. When Whitman argued that the modern world of science and the common man and the new world of American experience had not been put into poetry, he was, generally speaking, right, but the democratic diction he created to convey his imaginative perceptions was no guarantee that they would become poetical. If Whitman had really been scientific, as scientific even as Thoreau, his Quaker logic would have led him to a simple and lucid prose for at least half of his work. But for all his talk of "exact demonstration" and the approaching millennium of science, he was much more of an amateur in science than in music. It meant to him just a new and powerful function of the common man, and his romantic doctrine of uncritical acceptance of everything vital led him inevitably to a compromise, where he chose as his sole medium what is essentially a rhythmic prose that slides into poetry and out of it with equal ease. In the furnace of his temperament, the soaring hawk, the scented herbiage of the breast, the wet caresses of ocean, or John Brown on the scaffold, take on aspects of eternity, and are then fitted into a rhythm of recitative, presumably that which his own speech would fall into when he was moved. That is, he gave them style; and that Whitman has a style of his own, marked, characteristic, unmistakable, no one can ever question. But style is not the same as poetry, although he clearly thought it was, as the passage already quoted proves. Style is the imprint of personality upon adequate expression, and for Whitman's own purpose his expression was always adequate. It is never the form, but the substance, of his poems that in his rare moments of self-doubt he distrusts.

Poetry, however, is selective. It cannot absorb the new until the new has reached the right emotional intensity— one might add, with some fear of being misunderstood, the right emotional refinement. With a ground-breaker, a pioneer, a prophet, like Whitman, all he does may have the quality of literature, but poetry is reserved for the fortunate moments. He rises into poetry, not by a change in style or by the handling of his rhythms, but only when he reaches the intensity that poetry requires, and can stamp that intensity on the form of his verse. It happens so frequently in Whitman that without reference to his theories or to his most characteristic literary achievements he must be reckoned a major poet. It happens most frequently when he leaves the prophetic and grows lyrical:

I am he that walks with the tender and growing night,
I call to the earth and sea half-held by the night.
Press close bare-bosom'd night—press close magnetic nourishing night!
Night of south winds—night of the large few stars!
Still nodding night—mad naked summer night.*

It would, I am persuaded, have happened oftener if Whitman had not bound himself to the slavery of free verse. This is not to say, if he had not been Whitman. His choice was free, although whether his power was great enough to have been Whitman in metre no one of course can say. He chose what, if he was to be a *representative* poet, was unquestionably the right path. The exuberant

* "Song of Myself."

WALT WHITMAN

America of the mid-century, the expansiveness of democracy, and a hearty acceptance of everything, could scarcely have found a more expressive medium than the heroic realism of a style that moved with no incongruity from the commonplace to the sublime, linking God and the workman in the rhythms of emotional speech. The very adjectives which best describe that strange compound of enthusiasm and brutality, energy and animalism, aspiration and individualism, religion and greed, new beauty and new ugliness, which was America, could be fittingly applied to the qualities of the style and diction of "Leaves of Grass." Whitman, as a poet, discharged his debt to his Americanos.

But poetry is another matter. Inclusiveness is not its virtue, nor does it gain greatness merely by being representative. It must reach complete expression of what is finally most worth saying, and in this the emotional effect of rhythm must blend with the effect of the words. A democratic diction, resembling in its looseness what all men might use, will never do for this. Nor even a style as perfected as Whitman's. There must be restraint as well as release, or the poet runs away from his task. Regularity has no virtue in itself; it is the possible variation within a fixed form that releases the poet but holds him to his pattern of sound and makes necessary the blend of sound and sense. Whitman's free verse is not really free at all. He is bound to the broad rhythmic effects of his style, but he has no guidance for the line or the poetic phrase. Because he is free to write as he pleases provided it sounds like Whitman, he repeats again and again the same rhythms, with variations so unsubtle as quickly to become monotonous. And there is no foil, no prevailing time for the ear to check against, except the vague stylistic pattern of the whole. A tremendous task is thus imposed upon the writer. He must make his poem flow with the thought,

337

and yet is in the position of a dancer without steps who must improvise as she goes. Whitman does this sometimes with resounding success, especially when he has the memory of a musical ebb and flow for pattern. "Out of the Cradle Endlessly Rocking" is an instance, although even here the analogy is closest with the stylistic but unconstructed song of the mocking bird that the poem purports to describe. Yet in a heavy majority of poems in the "Leaves" you can hear the poet falter after the first few lines. The Whitman style is held, but the poem becomes shapeless. Its lines bunch or sprawl. They have style, but not position in the poem. The phrases slip through the fingers or gather others that are expressive but not indispensable. That unity of movement which is quite as important for expressiveness in poetry as unity of emotion or thought can, theoretically, be achieved as readily in free rhythms as in formal metres, but actually it is lost a hundred times for once that it is kept with gain.

And the curious result follows, that when Whitman is compared with a good poet (it is useless to compare him with any other), such as Keats or Milton, his verse seems monotonous. There is more subtlety of adaptation of expression to the thing expressed in the "Ode to the Nightingale" than in ten times as many lines from Whitman. There is more true variety in "Lycidas" than in all the "Leaves of Grass."

That Whitman should have written like Keats or Milton is a hundred miles from what I mean. In his "Song of Myself" he struck his blow for a new medium in which his expansive ego and his exuberant country could say their say as soul and as flesh. That barbaric yawp was a challenge to poetry. It had the defects and the merits of all exaggerations, but also the strength, as I have tried to show, of deliberate effort based upon a philosophy as well as upon emotion. The "Song of Myself" is his most char-

acteristic work, but it has a double charge of his temperament and only large hints of the broader interests and less
eccentric enthusiasms of his later life. Unfortunately, the
attacks upon his first editions touched the vanity of the
prophet in Whitman. He changed from the doctrine of his
first preface, that poem and man must be identical, to a
theory that these poems, and the methods of verse writing
first adopted, were utterly and irrevocably him. And the
philosophy of Quaker freedom from artifice that had rationalized his system of writing hardened (as it did with
the Quakers) into a rule. Thus he committed the cardinal
error of crystallizing too early, and perhaps the advanced
age (for a poet) of thirty-seven at which he got his first
significant publication, was partly responsible.

I see him, therefore, not free, but shut off by resolve
from experiment. By the time "Drum-Taps" had been
written it was probably too late for him to learn anything
else. And thus we must regard the free verse of Whitman
as a noble experiment, amply justified by its literary bene-
fits, but become for the man himself a chain about the
neck of style.

The monotony, the diffuseness, the turgidity, the frequent raucousness, of Whitman's verse is one of the
reasons why, so far, he has reached only the intellectuals.
Judicious editing will carry him further, but nothing can
make up for his own belief that whatever he said and however he said it was *right*—not right æsthetically, for he believed, with some reason, that trying to be right æsthetically has been the ruin of much honest speaking, but right
as the oracles are right. It was a dominance by theory
combined with the familiar obstinacies of the self-educated man, which kept him from realizing that æsthetics
may be calamitous for the weak but is the ladder upon
which the strong climb upward. He would never have
written conventional poetry, in spite of the flat conven-

tionalism of his early prose, but he might have escaped from monotony, and while still being Whitman, still red-shirted, hairy, democratic, exuberant, have lifted more of his recitative into poetry, and got the wider hearing that he always expected would come when the world went democratic. It was not camerados he needed for a wider reading so much as more art.

9.

I AM speaking of the limitations of a great man, but it is questionable whether the word should be used in the plural. Few men have achieved a unity of personality, intellect, and achievement so complete, and his faults, like his virtues, radiate from the centre. Often they are but different aspects of the same quality. Thus, for example, his principle of free verse-forms expressing a free man has for its logical corollary that the man should also be free to put into poetry whatever concerns the body primarily as well as whatever concerns first the mind or the soul—

I will effuse egotism and show it underlying all, and I will be the bard
    of personality,
And I will show of male and female that either is but the equal of the
    other,
And sexual organs and acts! do you concentrate in me. . . .*

And here the bard of Camden did fire a shot heard round the world, in reverberations more lasting than the minute guns of Concord. Modern literature, Continental as well as English, echoes with his influence. To say that he made the first breach in the wall of Victorian reticence would be measurably true, but far too simple to represent all the truth. To charge to him the quite Puritanic ardor with which our generation of anti-Puritans has attacked the conventions of prudery, flaunting what used to be called

* "Starting from Paumanok."

340

indecencies in an ecstatic fanaticism, would have a measure of truth in it too. Legitimate, or illegitimate, they are
his children. But such statements generalize too much.
The Victorian castle would have been breached without
Whitman, and D. H. Lawrence would have feverishly
preached salvation through sensuality if the "Song of
Myself" had never (as well might have happened) been
printed.

Whitman's early and favorable reception by English
intellectuals such as John Addington Symonds was due
(I think) much more to his daring than to his democracy.
His outspokenness seemed and was inevitable. It was part
of his program, it was implicit in his personality, it was a
corollary to his religion. Once his Quaker principle of
spiritual democracy expanded to include his instinctive
belief in the unity of nature, man, and God, an utter
frankness of self-expression logically followed. Full-
blooded, amorous, with many a "smutch'd deed" in his
memory, Whitman's frankness would have wreaked itself
on sex, even if there had been no Victorian taboo to make
him see red and charge at reticence. The divine principle,
he believed, was in every man, but that principle was
more than an inner light, it was the man himself, every
organ, every emotion, evil as well as good. All that was
human was of inescapable importance, and it was better
(so he thought) not to consider too carefully whether evil
was thwarted good, or some other mystery, but to concentrate upon the immense lovableness of life. There the
poetlings, lacking gusto and stature, had failed.* They had
tried to segregate the virtues, see beauty only in roses,
praise the clothed man but turn from the naked. Wrong,
all wrong, for man was the mightiest of themes, and hence
his most secret functions were, rightly considered, to be

* Traubel quotes his remarks on Howells and Aldrich: "They run a few tem-
porary errands but they are not out for immortal service."

accepted as part of the "kosmos" that he was, and especially whatever concerned procreation or love. As feudal poetry had neglected the common man, so polite poetry had passed over the common functions of the body, as noble as any because common to man. He would celebrate them, not to shock the priggish, but to inform and to praise and to make of his poem a whole. And who but Walt Whitman, great lover, great liver, great dreamer, was better able!

"And sexual organs and acts! do you concentrate in me, for I am determin'd to tell you with courageous clear voice to prove you illustrious. . . ." Such ideas he repeats again and again in his poems.

Thus the "Leaves" became propaganda for whatever had life and especially the heart of life in sex; so that to curb their frankness, as Emerson wished him to do, seemed impossible without stultification. The homosexuality of "Calamus," the heterosexuality of "Children of Adam," were as inevitably a part of the complete "Leaves" as democracy or religion. Euphemism or omission in the delicacies of love was an insult to the archetype he was creating. All, or nothing, must be said. And in justice to him it must be remarked that while his descriptions of physical love and the acts of procreation are franker and bolder in their realism than any others in English, he is never "suggestive," by which I mean that he never stimulates lewdness; and indeed, how could he?—for although he often offended art by his literalness, he felt always in the most secret or the most lustful act the presence of spirit as he understood it, the share of God. Blending, as he liked to do, the truth of paganism with the truth of more spiritual religions, he accepted everything vital to his case for man.

That he should shock the prudish was inevitable, and the disfavor in which he was long held, the tradition of a disreputable old loafer that persists, the long delay in his admittance to the respectability of the Hall of Fame, where many an American of not one quarter his calibre had preceded him, must be charged in the main to the priggish. They kept him out, they talked down his reputation, they distrusted him because he had broken a taboo. No such taboo upon frankness in sexual matters now exists, as even the courts are beginning to recognize, but even yet it is hard for respectable, unliterary readers to understand that the "Leaves of Grass," in its honest exaltation of the physical as inseparable from the intellectual and the spiritual, offered the fairest and most direct challenge to the unprecedented absurdities of Victorian reticence. It was possible to question the soundness of the morality of this book, but not to call it immoral. It was possible to question Whitman's definition of decency, but not to call his book indecent for the sake of sensation.

And yet many not priggish were and are shocked by Whitman. Some challenge his gospel of tolerance, which by gradations of acceptance finally becomes a kind of sensual Deism in which every act that runs with the blood and not against it is deserving of sympathy if not of approbation. The answer to them is that Whitman's philosophy and his ethics both break down when he or anyone else tries to erect them into a system. He was a poet and a prophet, creative, not critical, whipping with his imagination the laggard body to assert its rights. Those who read him for inspiration to good living must read him with the critical sense wide awake. He said what deeply needed to be said, but neither in ethics, nor in religion, nor in philosophy has he the final word. His call to the open road is clarion, but he did not too carefully consider where if followed to the end it might lead—did not know, and was honest enough to say so and say it often.

Others dispute his taste, and they, so it seems to me, are on better ground. Men and women of taste, who are as little afraid of love as Whitman himself, but whose conception of beauty differs from his, are troubled by the crude literalness, especially of his earlier and most characteristic poems. Not the ideas but the words shock them, and not the words in what they denote, but their connotations in the verse. The sexual functions, in poetry, can be made either lewd; or sacred, joyful, and beautiful; or they can be described in an ardent sincerity but with no concern for what the description may suggest. That was Whitman's method, and it was in complete consistence with his avoidance of the calculated, and the artificial. He disdained to use art in a process where art was necessary; probably he was temperamentally incapable, and lacking in skill as well as desire. Hence his fervid accounts of the actions of men and women sensually moved, or of the physiology of the sexual act, are disturbing, not as indecency or immorality, but because of the unpleasant nature of the images they often suggest. They tremble always upon the edge of humor and often plop over to the accompaniment not of libidinous snickers, but disgusted guffaws. I will not quote in illustration, for to take his phallic metaphors out of their context is to make them rawer than they are, but for confirmation read "Spontaneous Me," in many other respects a fine poem.

These are offenses against manners rather than against morals and art. They are sins of omission as much as of commission, sins that come from not knowing how to lift the phrase by imagination until subject and object blend. Whitman could lift the phrase, indeed in his celebration of the body electric he is more successful in glorifying the nerves and muscles of sex than any writer before or after, but his uncritical acceptance of whatever he mightily wished to say misled him often enough to explain why the least prim are sometimes upset by a dose of "Leaves of Grass."

Is it all due to lack of a sense of humor? I fear not. Whitman does lack humor, but that explanation is too simple. It was not a lack so much as an overplus that accounts for his faults. Every member of his body shone and tingled with a light that he regarded as spiritual. Egomania and megalomania dazzled him.

I hear and behold God in every object, yet, understand God not in the
　　least,
Nor do I understand who there can be more wonderful than myself.*

Whether blood or spirit predominated, what he was moved to say, became oracle by his saying it. He was a mouthpiece; and the mouthpiece takes no account of the susceptibilities of its audience.

10.

Last of his limitations is his unbridled egoism. This criticism is fundamental. The I, Walt Whitman, who "walks the States with a barb'd tongue, questioning everyone I meet," the self-appointed Great Person, declaiming against "grace, elegance, civilization, delicatesse," boasting of his least experiences as if they were of world importance, scorning the past, bragging of his own particular present, patting the world on the back, shouting his love affairs from the fence tops—this flaunting egoist, who is one aspect of Walt Whitman, wearies the reader. And yet it is the same egoism that made Walt Whitman of "Drum-Taps" without reserve or shame the father and mother of the wounded; it is the egoism that broke through the crusted reticence of the Victorians; it is the egoism that made possible his discovery of God in the common man.

You cannot attack the results of this egoism by an appeal to any philosophy of life, for it is infra-philosophical —it is in the temperament of the man himself. The criti-

* "Song of Myself."

cism of the classicists—that here is a prime example of the romantic expansionist, freed from every inner check and accepting everything because he likes it—is not so much wrong as wrongly directed. Walt's philosophy was expansive because he himself was expansive as was no other man of the nineteenth century, because his exuberance was fed by the exuberance of his United States and justified by his religion of the inner light. As a philosophy this egoism run loose is childish in its metaphysics and dangerous in its ultimate implications. But it is not a philosophy, it is something more fundamental than a doctrine, it is a fact, a reality. It exists in such a plenary measure, it radiates such power and light, it exercises such sway upon the imagination, that to sweep it aside as an error is as silly as to brush aside the tears of a woman. We do not ask, Was he often or finally right? we ask, What has he said that such vitality flows from it?

To use an old distinction, it is his faith, not his theology, that convinces, that swept away taboos and lifted the ideal of comradeship in a democracy to a level where religion and poetry could work upon it. And those who condemn rightly the blatancy and self-assurance of the yawper over the roofs of the world, forget that his self-assurance was an act of courage and that when his faith wavered self-doubts oppressed him:

O baffled, balk'd, bent to the very earth,
Oppress'd with myself that I have dared to open my mouth,
Aware now that amid all that blab whose echoes recoil upon me I have
    not once had the least idea who or what I am,
But that before all my arrogant poems the real Me stands yet un-
    touch'd, untold, altogether unreach'd,
Withdrawn far, mocking me with mock-congratulatory signs and bows,
With peals of distant ironical laughter at every word I have written,
Pointing in silence to these songs, and then to the sand beneath.
I perceive I have not really understood any thing, not a single object,
    and that no man ever can,

Nature here in sight of the sea taking advantage of me to dart upon
    me and sting me,
Because I have dared to open my mouth to sing at all.*

They forget the Whitman who, seeing all the sorrows of
the world, and all oppression and shame, all meanness and
agony without end—

           I sitting look out upon,
           See, hear, and am silent.†

They forget, in reading the "arrogant poems," the frequent humility of the poet who knew that "the hands of
the sisters Death and Night incessantly softly wash again,
and ever again, this soil'd world," and kept his high-
hearted courage with more knowledge of the grosser aspects of reality than most poets possess.

No, the passionate heart of Whitman cannot be told to
cease its beating by metaphysicians and philosophers, no
matter how logical. He is elemental, and, like all elemental
things, is sometimes extra- and sometimes infra-human,
and always needs, and often lacks, the discipline of
thought. If he is censurable, it is not because his ego expanding to a "kosmos" felt the divine possibilities of comradeship among common men, or proposed the solution of
life by yielding to it. It is rather the old Puritan in him
that leads him astray. He must make the "Leaves of
Grass" a Bible for new believers; he must be expansionist
à l'outrance, as Thoreau was protestant à l'outrance; he
must be arrogant in his claims, must shout his barbaric
yawp, must translate his own discovery that the body was
spirit also into a doctrine. Walt Whitman the preacher in-
vites the criticism of the judicious and deserves it. In his
philosophy, as in his art, he throws off old shackles only
to embrace passionately the dogmatic, the didactic, the

* "As I Ebb'd with the Ocean of Life."
† "I Sit and Look Out."

doctrinaire, and frees his ego only to let it rant. Nevertheless there was a rightness in his egoism, no matter how wrongly he used it, and how often he turned the loudspeaker too high. He was a great man, with something at least resembling a cosmos in him—just as he thought.

II.

THERE are some writers who disintegrate under criticism, leaving at the last only a talent, slender if persuasive, by which their hold upon our memory can be explained and justified. Irving is at the end only a graceful style and an abiding humor, Cooper a teller of excellent stories transfused with a hearty idealism. But Whitman is a far more satisfactory subject for the explorer of genius—both in his depths and in the careless tossing foam of his extravagance. He grows beneath destructive criticism. Subtract whatever you can for enthusiasms uncontrolled, for ideas run riot, for art abused, and there is always as much genius left.

He cannot certainly be ranked among the greatest poets. There is a lack of co-ordination between his hopes and despairs that is quite different from the perplexity of an Æschylus before the spectacle of fate, and more resembles the shifting enthusiasms of the young.* Philosophically he never grew up. "Do I contradict myself? Very well then I contradict myself (I am large, I contain multitudes)," † has the bravado of a youth just past adolescence. Nor will his defects in form permit him the attribute of greatest. In poetic technique he remained, to the end, the gifted but dogmatic amateur, striking magnificent chords only when the fingers fell right. His perfect passages are not uncommon, but are always unsure. One holds one's breath lest he spoil them before they are said. Most dangerous of all to the supremacy of his art was his rôle of prophet self-

* Both death and God he left unanalyzed.   † "Song of Myself."

imposed in which, with Carlyle and Emerson at his back, and an ever-present fondness for exhibitionism, he too often got out of hand.

Nor can he ever be ranked among the lesser men. He is a great poet, and a great man, when you have said your worst. Great because he shares the plenary inspiration that great poets must have. I do not refer to some reservoir of inner light to be tapped by the worthy, although Whitman would have liked that explanation. I mean rather a sense for the significance of the human in that blend of temporal and timeless which makes an age or an epoch. The great poets have this, and whether they are greatest depends upon the use they make of it. Such a sense is utterly denied to a Longfellow, for all his skill. He "ran errands" for the culture of his America (which is not to disparage him), but he could not feel the heartbeats of the society of which he was a part. Whitman had it. He had specifically the vision of ideal equalitarianism. Perhaps there never was and never will be even an approximate equalitarianism. What does it matter! Such a term is only a name that never indicates a perfected state but only a tendency, a permanent possibility of the human race. The possibility of perfect comradeship, the possibility that faculties common to all men might be exalted, the possibility of democracy in a blend of the physical and the spiritual, the possibility that nothing human would be alien to the soul of emancipated man—that was Whitman's vision. His inspiration came from that; he speaks for that, enriching his words from a lifetime of intense experience, precisely as Shakespeare spoke for the aristocratic virtues and Milton for ineffable righteousness. Right or wrong—and it is yet to be proved that any devoted thinker has been utterly right or utterly wrong in the history of the world—he raised his vision into an art, which, since it had its roots in human aspirations and human experience, is valid and vital, whatever its faults in æsthetics and philosophy.

Rough, vigorous old fellow, stretched on his bed at Camden, endlessly talking over his past, or wandering about looking for some letter or clipping that would prove that the world had begun to believe in his gospel, always posing as the good gray patriarch, the cosmos made flesh; and yet within, to the end, the boy of Paumanok, ecstatic, crying with unsatisfied love, and the youth of Brooklyn throbbing with love and pride and life! Poet who disdained to be just a poet and so fell something short of his powers, voice of the exuberance of democratic industrialism putting the earth under by ax and plough and steam, he belongs now in that Platonic world where republics never realized keep their power to enrich the imagination and kindle faith and hope. Politically he is dead, for this age at least, and his joyous individualism has no part in the program of those who in Russia now exalt the common man in a proletariat whose end is that equality of opportunity with which Whitman began. Æsthetically his favorite doctrines have been tried and outmoded. But the man and his poetry are inextinguishable. "Poets to come," he said, "you must justify me." They have had other business to attend to, little of it as important as Walt Whitman's, but it is no matter, for whatever happens to his beloved country and its literature, he justified himself. There was truth in his magnificent boast in "Songs of Parting":

O book, O chants! must all then amount to but this?
Must we barely arrive at this beginning of us?—and yet it is enough,
    O soul;
O soul, we have positively appear'd—that is enough.

12.

WHITMAN, the great modernist as we have been accustomed to call him, was nevertheless at the end of a period, long prepared for. Although he lived to our own day, although I myself believe that I have seen his white beard among the flower-sellers of Market Street in Philadelphia, he remembered things impossible for us, impossible but intelligible, and which will become unintelligible at our peril. His soil was the fecund earth of antebellum America, in the age of exuberance. Mark Twain, the next great American, came also from that soil, but too late. He could go back to it only in memories of childhood, and only "Huckleberry Finn" belongs among the American classics I have been discussing, and even that book is written with an irony which belongs to the gilded age. American culture is continuous but its spiritual exuberance ended with the sixties. The problems become economic, social. Classic American literature turns conventional, materialism brings realism with it, and the reactions toward romance are soft with sentiment. There had to be a breaking down of moulds and an immense airing of the imagination before anything like greatness could again come into literature. In technology we may be close to our peak of accomplishment, but imagination has not yet had, in any thoroughgoing sense, its second incarnation in American literature.

Thus the next age after Whitman must be studied as transition and preparation, not as achievement. But the classic Americans are not dead. Beneath the show of an utterly different world, they are still intelligible, though potential rather than active. We cannot go back to their era, yet without a full consciousness of their spiritual and æsthetic significance we shall never profit by an inheritance that has possibilities still but half realized. The American tradition is best read in them.

A Selective Bibliography

Additional references will be found in the notes.

General Works on American Literature and on its Historical Background

ADAMS, HENRY. History of the United States of America. New York, 1890-1909.

ADAMS, J. T. The Founding of New England. Boston, 1921.

—— Provincial Society, 1690-1763. New York, 1927.

—— Revolutionary New England: 1691-1776. Boston, 1923.

ANGOFF, CHARLES. A Literary History of the American People [from 1607 to 1815]. 2 vols. New York, 1931.

BEARD, CHARLES A. and MARY R. The Rise of American Civilization. 2 vols. New York, 1927.

BROWNELL, W. C. American Prose Masters. New York, 1909.

Cambridge History of American Literature. 4 vols. New York, 1917-1921.

CANBY, H. S. American Estimates. New York, 1929.

—— Definitions: First and Second Series. New York, 1922, 1924.

—— The Short Story in English. New York, 1909.

COOKE, G. W. Unitarianism in America. Boston, 1902.

The Dictionary of American Biography. New York, 1928- .

FOERSTER, NORMAN. American Criticism: Studies in Literary Theory from Poe to the Present. Boston, 1928.

—— Nature in American Literature. New York, 1923.

—— and Others. The Reinterpretation of American Literature. New York, 1928.

GATES, LEWIS E. Studies and Appreciations. Boston, 1900.

GODDARD, H. C. Studies in New England Transcendentalism. New York, 1908.

HAZARD, LUCY L. The Frontier in American Literature. New York, 1927.

HOWE, M. A. DE WOLFE. Memories of a Hostess. Boston, 1922.

HOWELLS, W. D. Literary Friends and Acquaintance. New York, 1901.

KITTREDGE, GEORGE LYMAN. Witchcraft in Old and New England. Cambridge, 1929.

A SELECTIVE BIBLIOGRAPHY

LAWRENCE, D. H. Studies in Classic American Literature. New York, 1923.

LEISY, E. E. The American Historical Novel before 1860 (on American Themes). Urbana, 1926.

MUMFORD, LEWIS. The Golden Day. New York, 1926.

—— Sticks and Stones. New York, 1926.

PARRINGTON, V. L. Main Currents in American Thought. 3 vols. New York, 1927, 1930.

PATTEE, F. L. The Development of the American Short Story. New York, 1923.

—— A History of American Literature Since 1870. New York, 1915.

PERRY, BLISS. The American Spirit in Literature. New Haven, 1918.

QUINN, A. H. A History of the American Drama: from the Beginning to the Civil War. New York, 1923.

RILEY, W. American Thought from Puritanism to Pragmatism. New York, 1915.

SCHLESINGER, A. M. Political and Social History in the United States, 1829-1925. New York, 1925.

SHERMAN, S. P. Americans. New York, 1922.

—— The Genius of America. New York, 1923.

STEDMAN, E. C. Poets of America. New York, 1885.

TYLER, M. C. A History of American Literature, 1607-1765. 2 vols. New York, 1878.

—— The Literary History of the American Revolution. 2 vols. New York, 1897.

UNTERMEYER, LOUIS. American Poetry from the Beginning to Whitman. New York, 1931.

VAN DOREN, CARL. The American Novel. New York, 1921.

VAN TYNE, C. H. The Causes of the War of Independence. Boston, 1922.

WEIRICK, B. From Whitman to Sandburg in American Poetry. New York, 1924.

WENDELL, BARRETT. A Literary History of America. New York, 1900.

WILLIAMS, S. T. The American Spirit in Letters. New Haven, 1926.

—— and ADKINS, N. F. Courses of Reading in American Literature with Bibliographies. New York, 1930.

WRIGHT, T. G. Literary Culture in Early New England, 1620-1730. New York, 1920.

354

A SELECTIVE BIBLIOGRAPHY

The Colonial Period and the First Decades of the Republic

ALLEN, A. V. G. Jonathan Edwards. Boston, 1889.

BASSETT, J. S., editor. Selections from the Federalist. New York, 1921.

BEERS, H. A. The Connecticut Wits, and Other Essays. New Haven, 1920.

BOAS, RALPH and LOUISE. Cotton Mather: Keeper of the Puritan Conscience. New York, 1928.

BOWERS, CLAUDE G. Jefferson and Hamilton. Boston, 1925.

CRÈVECŒUR, ST. JOHN DE. Letters from an American Farmer, edited by W. P. Trent and Ludwig Lewisohn. New York, 1904.

—— Crèvecœur, Sketches of Eighteenth Century America, edited by H. L. Bourdin, R. H. Gabriel, and S. T. Williams. New Haven, 1925.

EDWARDS, JONATHAN. Works. 4 vols. New York, 1881.

FAŸ, BERNARD. Franklin, the Apostle of Modern Times. Boston, 1929.

FRANKLIN, BENJAMIN. Autobiography, edited by Percy H. Boynton. New York, 1926.

—— Benjamin Franklin, Writings, with Life and Introduction by A. H. Smyth. 10 vols. New York, 1905-1907.

GUMMERE, A. M., editor. The Journals and Essays of John Woolman. Philadelphia, 1922.

LODGE, H. C. Alexander Hamilton. Boston, 1882.

MATHER, COTTON. Magnalia Christi Americana. 2 vols. Hartford, 1853.

MATHER, INCREASE. Remarkable Providences Illustrative of the Earlier Days of American Colonization, edited by George Offor. London, 1890.

MURDOCK, K. B., editor. Selections from Cotton Mather. New York, 1926.

—— Increase Mather. Cambridge, 1925.

MUZZEY, DAVID S. Thomas Jefferson. New York, 1918.

PARKES, H. B. Jonathan Edwards, the Fiery Puritan. New York, 1930.

PARRINGTON, V. L., editor. The Connecticut Wits. New York, 1926.

VAN DOREN, CARL, editor. Benjamin Franklin and Jonathan Edwards: Selections from their Writings. New York, 1920.

WENDELL, BARRETT. Cotton Mather, the Puritan Priest. New York, 1891.

A SELECTIVE BIBLIOGRAPHY

Washington Irving

ADKINS, N. F. Fitz-Greene Halleck. New Haven, 1930.

HELLMAN, G. S. Washington Irving, Esquire, Ambassador at Large. New York, 1925.

IRVING, P. M. The Life and Letters of Washington Irving. 4 vols. New York, 1862-1864.

IRVING, WASHINGTON. Works. New Knickerbocker Edition. 40 vols. New York, 1897.

—— Diedrich Knickerbocker's A History of New York, edited by S. T. Williams and T. McDowell. New York, 1927.

—— The Journal of Washington Irving, 1823-1824, edited by S. T. Williams. Cambridge, 1931.

—— Letters of Washington Irving to Henry Brevoort, edited by G. S. Hellman. 2 vols. New York, 1915.

—— Letters of Henry Brevoort to Washington Irving, edited by G. S. Hellman. 2 vols. New York, 1916.

——Letters from Sunnyside and Spain, edited by S. T. Williams. New Haven, 1928.

—— Notes While Preparing Sketch Book, &c., edited by S. T. Williams. New Haven, 1925.

—— Tour in Scotland, 1817, and Other Manuscript Notes, edited by S. T. Williams. New Haven, 1927.

WARNER, C. D. Washington Irving. Boston, 1881.

James Fenimore Cooper

BOYNTON, H. W. James Fenimore Cooper. New York, 1931.

COOPER, JAMES FENIMORE. Works. Household Edition. Edited by S. F. Cooper. 32 vols. Boston, 1884-1890.

—— The Correspondence of James Fenimore Cooper, edited by his grandson, James Fenimore Cooper. 2 vols. New Haven, 1922.

—— Gleanings in Europe (France), edited by Robert E. Spiller. New York, 1928.

—— Gleanings in Europe (England), edited by Robert E. Spiller. New York, 1930.

LEISY, E. E., The Early Novels of J. F. Cooper (1821-31). Urbana, 1926.

LOUNSBURY, T. R. James Fenimore Cooper. Boston, 1882.

A SELECTIVE BIBLIOGRAPHY

Ralph Waldo Emerson

BEERS, H. A. Four Americans: Roosevelt, Hawthorne, Emerson, Whitman. New Haven, 1919.

BROOKS, VAN WYCK. Emerson and Others. New York, 1927.

CABOT, J. E. A Memoir of Ralph Waldo Emerson. 2 vols. Boston, 1887.

CARPENTER, FREDERIC IVES. Emerson and Asia. Cambridge, 1930.

CONWAY, M. D. Emerson at Home and Abroad. Boston, 1882.

COOKE, G. W. A Bibliography of Ralph Waldo Emerson. Boston, 1908.

CROTHERS, S. M. Ralph Waldo Emerson: How to Know Him. Indianapolis, 1921.

EMERSON, RALPH WALDO. Complete Works. Riverside Edition. 12 vols. Boston, 1883-1893.

—— Uncollected Writings. New York, 1912.

—— Journals, edited by E. W. Emerson and W. E. Forbes. 10 vols. Boston, 1909-1914.

—— The Heart of Emerson's Journals, edited by Bliss Perry. Boston, 1926.

—— The Correspondence of Thomas Carlyle and Ralph Waldo Emerson, 1834-1872, edited by C. E. Norton. 2 vols. Boston, 1883.

FIRKINS, O. W. Ralph Waldo Emerson. Boston, 1915.

GARNETT, RICHARD. Life of Ralph Waldo Emerson. London, 1888.

HARRISON, J. S. The Teachers of Emerson. New York, 1910.

HOLMES, O. W. Ralph Waldo Emerson. Boston, 1885.

MICHAUD, REGIS. Autour d'Emerson. Paris, 1924.

—— Emerson, the Enraptured Yankee, translated from the French by George Boas. New York, 1930.

RUSSELL, P. Emerson, the Wisest American. New York, 1929.

WOODBERRY, G. E. Ralph Waldo Emerson. New York, 1907.

Henry David Thoreau

ALLEN, F. H. A Bibliography of Henry David Thoreau. Boston, 1908.

ATKINSON, J. B. Henry Thoreau, the Cosmic Yankee. New York, 1927.

BAZALGETTE, L. Henry Thoreau, Bachelor of Nature, translated by Van Wyck Brooks. New York, 1924.

CHANNING, W. E. Thoreau the Poet-Naturalist. Boston, 1873.

SANBORN, F. B. The Life of Henry David Thoreau. Boston, 1917.

—— Recollections of Seventy Years. 2 vols. Boston, 1909.

SHEPARD, ODELL. The Heart of Thoreau's Journals. Boston, 1927.

A SELECTIVE BIBLIOGRAPHY

THOREAU, HENRY DAVID. Writings. Walden Edition. 20 vols. Boston, 1906.
—— Familiar Letters of Henry David Thoreau, edited by F. B. Sanborn. Boston, 1894.
VAN DOREN, MARK. Henry David Thoreau: A Critical Study. Boston, 1916.

Nathaniel Hawthorne

ARVIN, NEWTON. Hawthorne. Boston, 1929.
—— The Heart of Hawthorne's Journals. Boston, 1929.
BRIDGE, HORATIO. Personal Recollections of Nathaniel Hawthorne. New York, 1893.
BROWNE, NINA E. A Bibliography of Nathaniel Hawthorne. Boston, 1905.
CONWAY, M. D. Life of Nathaniel Hawthorne. New York, 1890.
COOKE, G. W., editor. Early Letters of George W. Curtis to John S. Dwight, Brook Farm and Concord. New York, 1898.
DHALEINE L. Hawthorne, sa vie et son œuvre. Paris, 1905.
DWIGHT, M. Letters from Brook Farm, 1844-1847, edited by A. L. Reed. Poughkeepsie, 1928.
FIELDS, J. T. Yesterdays with Authors. Boston, 1871.
GORMAN, HERBERT S. Hawthorne; A Study in Solitude. New York, 1927.
HAWTHORNE, JULIAN. Hawthorne and His Circle. New York, 1903.
—— Nathaniel Hawthorne and His Wife. 2 vols. Boston, 1885.
HAWTHORNE, NATHANIEL. Complete Works, edited by G. P. Lathrop. Riverside Edition. 13 vols. Boston, 1883.
JAMES, HENRY. Hawthorne. London, 1879.
LATHROP, G. P. A Study of Hawthorne. Boston, 1876.
LATHROP, ROSE HAWTHORNE. Memories of Hawthorne. Boston, 1897.
LONGFELLOW, SAMUEL. Life of Henry Wadsworth Longfellow. 2 vols. Boston, 1886.
—— Final Memorials of Henry Wadsworth Longfellow. Boston, 1887.
MORRIS, LLOYD. The Rebellious Puritan: Portrait of Mr. Hawthorne. New York, 1927.
SANBORN, F. B. Hawthorne and His Friends. Cedar Rapids, Ia., 1908.
SWIFT, LINDSAY. Brook Farm: Its Members, Scholars, and Visitors. New York, 1900.
TICKNOR, CAROLINE. Hawthorne and His Publishers. Boston, 1913.
WOODBERRY, G. E. Nathaniel Hawthorne. Boston, 1902.

358

A SELECTIVE BIBLIOGRAPHY

Herman Melville

FREEMAN, JOHN. Herman Melville. New York, 1926.

MELVILLE, HERMAN. Works. Standard Edition. 16 vols. London, 1922-1924.

—— The Apple-tree Table and Other Sketches, edited by Henry Chapin. Princeton, 1922.

—— Pierre; or, the Ambiguities, edited by Robert S. Forsythe. New York, 1930.

—— Shorter Novels, edited by R. M. Weaver. New York, 1928.

MINNIGERODE, M. Some Personal Letters of Herman Melville and a Bibliography. New York, 1922.

MUMFORD, LEWIS. Herman Melville. New York, 1929.

WEAVER, R. M. Herman Melville, Mariner and Mystic. New York, 1921.

Edgar Allan Poe

ALLEN, HERVEY. Israfel. 2 vols. New York, 1926.

CAMBIAIRE, CELESTIN PIERRE. The Influence of Edgar Allan Poe in France. New York, 1927.

KRUTCH, JOSEPH WOOD, Edgar Allan Poe: A Study in Genius. New York, 1926.

PHILLIPS, M. E. Edgar Allan Poe, the Man. 2 vols. Chicago, 1926.

POE, EDGAR ALLAN. Complete Works, edited by J. A. Harrison. Virginia Edition. 17 vols. New York, 1902.

—— Poems, edited by Killis Campbell. Boston, 1917.

—— Poe's Short Stories, edited by Killis Campbell. New York, 1926.

WHITMAN, S. H. Edgar Poe and His Critics. New York, 1860.

WOODBERRY, G. E. The Life of Edgar Allan Poe. 2 vols. Boston, 1909.

Walt Whitman

BAILEY, J. Walt Whitman. New York, 1926.

BARRUS, CLARA. Whitman and Burroughs, Comrades. Boston, 1931.

BAZALGETTE, LEON. Walt Whitman, the Man and His Work, translated by Ellen Fitz Gerald. Garden City, N. Y., 1920.

BURROUGHS, JOHN. Whitman: A Study. Boston, 1896.

DE SELINCOURT, BASIL. Walt Whitman; A Critical Study. London, 1914.

A SELECTIVE BIBLIOGRAPHY

Furness, Clifton Joseph. Walt Whitman's Workshop: A Collection of Unpublished Manuscripts. Cambridge, 1928.

Ellis, Havelock. The New Spirit. London, 1926.

Holloway, E. Whitman: An Interpretation in Narrative. New York, 1926.

Perry, Bliss. Walt Whitman. Boston, 1906.

Symonds, J. A. Walt Whitman. London, 1893.

Traubel, H. With Walt Whitman in Camden. 3 vols. Boston and New York, 1906-14.

Wells, C. and Goldsmith, A. F. A Concise Bibliography of the Works of Walt Whitman. Boston, 1922.

Whitman, Walt. Complete Prose Works. Boston, 1898.

—— Gathering of the Forces. 2 vols. New York, 1920.

—— Leaves of Grass. Inclusive Edition, edited by E. Holloway. Garden City, N. Y., 1924.

—— Two Prefaces by Walt Whitman. The Original Preface to Leaves of Grass, 1855, and A Backward Glance o'er Travel'd Roads, with an Introductory Note by Christopher Morley. Garden City, N. Y., 1926.

—— The Uncollected Poetry and Prose of Walt Whitman, edited by E. Holloway. 2 vols. Garden City, N. Y., 1921.

Index

Abolitionists, 31
Action, in Hawthorne, 228, 229
Adams, Henry, xv, 44; on Boston, 159-160; on European travelers in America, 70
Adams, John, 84, 94; on the Revolution, 50
Adams, Samuel, 50
Adirondacks, 99
Adventurers, 200
Ahab, Captain, 251, 252, 253
Alcott, Bronson, 27, 154, 190, 242
Allan family, 265, 269
Allen, A. V. G., 12
Allen, Hervey, 265, 271
Allston, Washington, 76
America, 68, 81, 94; Cooper's criticism, 121; Emerson's, 181; Thoreau's feeling for, 222; Whitman and, 317
American literature, v, xi, xv, 138, 351; colonial, 34, 65; dawn of the republic, 60; European influence, xv; false dawn, 60; Federalist and anti-Federalist states of mind, 58; histories of, xii; misunderstanding, xi; most remarkable books, 187; Puritanism and, 22; Revolution and, 52, 54; value, xiv
American tradition, 351; Poe, 275
Americanism, 60; Cooper's, 100, 108, 139, 140; Emerson's, 150
Americans, 8, 47; Irving type, 94, 95
Andrews, C. F., 185
Anglicanism, Cooper's, 116
Angoff, Charles, 9, 50
Animals, 330, 331
Annapolis, Md., 34
Apothegms in Emerson, 168-169
Architecture, 273
Aristocracy, 54, 55, 117, 123; Thoreau, 225
Arminianism, 16, 18
Arnold, Matthew, 178
Arvin, Newton, 227
Astronomy, 286
Audubon, J. J., 49, 59, 221

Aurelius, Marcus, 177
Austen, Jane, 88, 172

Babbitt, 206
Ballet, 243
Barbarism, 37, 137
Barclay, Robert, 30, 312
Barlow, Joel, 61, 68, 70
Bartram, John, 49, 59
Baudelaire, C. P., 281, 300
Beauty, 284, 290, 330; Emerson and, 149-150, 172, 174; New England Puritanism and, 22, 23; Poe, 300, 301, 302
Beers, Henry A., 61, 165
Belianis, 128
Belles lettres, 3, 9; colonial, 4, 34, 35; Revolution and, 50
Bibliography, 353-360
Birch, Harvey, 128, 134, 137
Blackbirds, 175
Blake, Harrison, 194
Boasting, 64
Body, 309, 315, 320, 325, 340
Boone, Daniel, 94
Boston, 9, 22, 26, 34, 291; Emerson and, 146; Old North Meeting House, 24; Revolution and, 53; Unitarianism and, 159-160
Bourdin, H. Q., 46
Boynton, H. W., 101
Brackenridge, H. H., 55, 59
Brahma, 170, 253
Bread and Cheese Club, 107
Brevoort, Mr., 67, 72, 73, 75, 79, 85, 86
Brook Farm, 229, 231
Brotherhood of man, 30
Brown, Charles Brockden, 60, 67, 70; works, 68
Brown, John, 186, 208
Bryant, W. C., xiii, 93; on Irving, 92-93
Buckminster, Joseph, 27
Buffon, Comte de, 69
Bumppo, Natty, 112, 113, 115, 134; Quaker morality, 114, 116

INDEX

Bundling, 12
Burns, Robert, 34
Burr, Aaron, 94
Burroughs, John, 196, 220; on Thoreau, 213
Business, 58, 80, 81, 230

Calhoun, J. C., 314
Calvinism, 5, 10, 19, 23; Hawthorne and, 230, 232, 235
Calvinists, 8, 20
Camden, 309, 311
Carlyle, Thomas, 175, 178, 247; Thoreau on, 196, 216
Channing, W. E., 27
Character, 236, 259
Charleston, S. C., 20, 22, 34
Chase, the, in Cooper, 135, 140
Chingachgook, 123, 130, 131, 132
Christ, 327
Christian Science, 155
Christmas, 88
City life, 223, 224
Civil disobedience, 184, 185
Civil War, 78, 303, 304; Whitman and, 310, 317, 326
Civilization, American, 181, 224; New England, 20
Clark, H. H., 159
Classic Americans, 351
Clemens, S. L. *See* Twain, Mark
Clemm, Mrs., 266, 282, 305
Coffin, Long Tom, 112, 133
Colleges, 51
Colonial background, 3
Colonial literature, 65
Colonies, 5
Colonists, degeneracy, 37
Columbus, Christopher, 3
Commercialism, 59, 69; Irving and, 80
Common man, 325, 328, 342
Common sense, 35, 40, 44
Communism, 208, 229
Concord, Mass., 144, 157, 184; Thoreau and, 185, 186, 187
Conduct, 164, 179; Thoreau and, 188
Connecticut, 62
Conscience, 198, 239
Constitution, 77
Contemplation, 192, 198
Control, 202, 205, 206

Conventions, 324, 325, 326, 331
Cooper, J. F., vi, xiii, 27, 29, 75, 76, 91, 94, 95; amateurishness, 124, 125; Americanism, 100, 108, 139, 140; Anglicanism, 116; aristocracy, 117, 123; biography, 101; books, 101, 102; borrowings, 128; career, 127; the chase, 135, 140; courtship, 104; "Crater," 112, 117, 127; criticism and, 126; "Deerslayer," 124, 125, 141; education, 103; England, opinion of, 119; European literature and, 100; family, 101, 102; greatness, 136, 140; happiness, 107; hatred of mass rule, 118; history, 132; importance, 97; inconsistencies, 121; Indians, 130, 132; Irving compared with, 100; ladies in his works, 129; "Last of the Mohicans," 131, 133, 134, 136; "Leatherstocking Tales," 113, 123; manliness, 102, 104; his mother, 111; movement, 125, 135; Naïfs, 134; personality, 102, 111; "Pilot," 102, 105, 137; "Pioneers," 102, 103, 105, 113, 138; plots, 133, 138; politics, contradictions, 118, 119; popularity, 97, 100, 133; "Prairie," 136; "Precaution," 105; profit from books, 106; Quakerism, 109, 111; Quakerism in his books, 112, 114, 115; republicanism, 109, 118, 119, 120, 121; reputation, 127, 133; romance, 98, 134; scolding, 106, 109, 110; Scott and, 99; sea stories, 137; serious works, 127; "Spy," 102, 105, 137; style, 125; success of his writings, 107–108; "Travelling Bachelor," 118, 122; Unknowns, 133–134; writing, 104–105, 106, 124
Cooper, Judge, 103, 111
Cooperstown, 102, 103, 130, 134; character, 117
Country life, 223, 224
Crabbedness, 22, 23
Crèvecœur, M. G. St. Jean de, 32, 45, 95; "Letters from an American Farmer," 5, 46, 47; optimism, 47, 48; "Sketches of Eighteenth Century America," 46
Criticism, Cooper and, 126; Poe on the short story, 299

362

INDEX

INDEX

INDEX

Hell-fire sermons, 12, 13, 19
Hellman, G. S., 74
Henry, Patrick, 55
Herbert, George, 32
Herrick, Robert, 197
Hessian officers, 37
Hester Prynne, 232, 233, 239, 240, 243, 248, 253, 256, 259
Hilda, 233, 238, 239, 240, 243
Hindu nationalists, 185
Historians, American, 95
History, Irving and, 71, 73, 87
Hoffman, Matilda, 74
Homosexuality, 342
Hone, Philip, 79
Howells, W. D., vi
"Huckleberry Finn," 351
"Hudibras," 55, 64
Hudson, W. H., 196, 197, 220
Huguenots, 20
Humanitarianism, 29, 31; Hawthorne, 235
Humanity, Whitman's faith in, 320
Humbleness, 255
Humor, 126, 172; Poe's, 271; Thoreau and, 212
Huxley, Aldous, 261

Idealism, 182, 254; New England, 178, 179
Ideas, 153
Imagination, 351
Imitations, 60, 63, 99, 140; Cooper's, 128
Immigrants, 46, 47; Normans, 48
Immigration, 45
Immorality, 81
Immortals, 180
Indecency, 343
Independence, 50, 52, 55. *See* Revolution, American
Indians, 32, 114, 123, 200; Cooper's, 130, 132; Irving's stories, 90; Thoreau and, 221
Individualism, 155, 158, 181, 208
Individualists, 182, 183; New England, 225
Industrial revolution, 187, 201, 230
Industrial world, Melville and, 250
Industrialism, 205, 206, 208; Hawthorne and, 235
Inhibitions, 324, 325

Injustice, 207
Inner light, 29, 30, 110, 114, 115; Emerson and, 155; Whitman and, 312, 321
Intellectuals, early American, 6, 7
Introduction, xi
Intuition, 289; Thoreau, 214; Whitman, 321
Investigation, 162, 164
Irving, Peter, 85
Irving, Pierre, 70, 74, 75, 76, 77, 87
Irving, Washington, xii, xiii, 27, 54, 60; "Alhambra," 71, 72, 73, 81, 88, 90; "belles lettres writer," 67; "Bracebridge Hall," 72, 73, 81, 90; depression and melancholy, 75, 76; England and, 83, 88, 92; English reputation, 69, 70; essays and sketches, 87; estimates to be altered, 91; Federalism, 77, 80, 83; financial affairs, 74; histories, 73, 87; humor, 91; Indian stories, 90; influence on successors, 93; intellect, 67; Knickerbocker's "History of New York," 54, 71, 73, 80, 81, 85, 86; "Legend of Sleepy Hollow," 88; politics, 77, 78, 79; Rip Van Winkle, 72, 73, 81, 88, 89; romantic movement and, 83; significance, 96; "Sketch Book," 87, 88, 89, 93; style, 68, 70, 89, 92; "Tales of a Traveller," 90; temperament, 72; works, 71, 72
Isaiah, 177

Jackson, Andrew, 54, 79, 94
James, Henry, vi
Jay, Peter, 119
Jefferson, Thomas, 4, 50, 51, 54, 55; ideas, 56; significance, 55; writings, 56
Jeffersonian democracy, 56
Jeffersonians, literary, 58
Johnson, Samuel (1696–1772), 13, 16
Johnson, Dr. Samuel (1709–1784), 11, 37, 69
Johnston, Mary, "To Have and to Hold," 7
Journalism, 57, 269; Philadelphia, 267; Poe, 263, 266, 267, 268, 269, 274, 275
Justice, 208

INDEX

INDEX

INDEX

Sandys's Ovid, 34
Satire, 64, 181; Irving, 86
Satyagraha, 184, 185
"Scarlet Letter," 187, 232, 233, 237, 238, 244, 250, 253, 258, 259
Schneider, H. W., 19
School readers, 314
Schöpf, J. D., 59
Science, 153, 286; Emerson and, 159, 160, 161, 162; Franklin and, 41, 42, 44; Thoreau and, 191, 213, 214, 215
Scott, Sir Walter, 84, 89; Cooper and, 99, 128, 132, 134, 139, 140
Sea, in Cooper, 137, 139
Seabury, Samuel, 50
Self-development, 163, 180
Self-educated man, 254
Self-reliance, 189
Self-respect, 38
Senses, 197
Sentimentalists, 158
Sermons, 167
Servants, 36, 38
Settlement, 6; literature of, 3
Settlers, 6; intellectual force, 6; New England, 7
Sex, 341, 342, 343; functions, in poetry, 344; immorality, 239; organs, 340, 342; Thoreau and, 194, 195; Whitman and, 326, 329
Shakespeare, xiii, 128, 129, 173, 177, 329, 349
Sherlock Holmes stories, 280
Short story, xv, 274, 278; Poe on, 299
Sidney, Sir Philip, 197
Simms, W. G., 279
Simplicity, 330, 332; Cooper, 115
Sin, 18, 19, 23, 27, 230, 233, 240, 242, 245, 248; women's, 239
Skepticism, 237; Hawthorne, 233, 234, 235, 236, 253, 256; Melville, 234, 252, 253
Slavery, 31; Thoreau and, 188, 207
Smith, Captain John, "True Relation," 3
Smyth, A. H., 40
Social history, 36, 45, 95
Socialism, 208
Society, Thoreau and, 194, 195, 198, 200, 208
Solitude, 195, 226, 227, 229
Sophocles, 173, 177

Soul, 217, 236
South, 303
Spengler, Oswald, 158, 164
Spiller, R. E., 101
Spirit, problems of the, 145
Spiritual conflict, 254
Spiritual failures, 230, 233
Spiritual welfare, 148
State and individual, 207, 208
State papers, 51, 69
Stevenson, R. L., on Thoreau, 204
Stewart, Randall, vii
Stockbridge Indians, 17
Stringham, Irving, 287
Style, 60, 71; Cooper, 125; Edwards, 21; Emerson, 149, 167, 168, 182; Franklin, 43, 44; Hawthorne, 246; Irving, 68, 70, 89, 92; Thoreau, 216, 217; Whitman, 332, 335
Stylists, 259
Symonds, J. A., 341

Tammany Hall, 79
Taste, 343, 344
Taxation, 207
Taylor, Bayard, 270
Taylor, Jeremy, 32
Temple, Judge, 103, 111, 112
Tennyson, Alfred, 295
Theocracy, 11
Theology, 11; Edwards, 10, 12
Thoreau, H. D., vi, xiv, 24, 27, 49, 161, 304; American environment, feeling for, 222; appearance, 184; aristocracy, 225; books mislabeled, 220; character, 187; city and country, 223; "Civil Disobedience," 184, 185, 187, 202, 207, 220; Concord and, 185, 186, 187; criticism of literature and life, 219; dualism in his nature, 193; Emerson compared with, 187; epigrams, 193, 220; fight against society, 198, 200; greatness, 209; happiness, 209; "Higher Laws," 194; humor and wit, 212; intuitions, 192, 214; Journals, 189, 190, 193, 198, 199, 203, 217, 219; "Life Without Principle," 207, 217; living, 185, 186, 195, 202; love and friendship, 194, 195; "Maine Woods," 213, 220, 221; nature and, 189, 190, 195, 221; negative Tho-

INDEX

poetlings, 341; "Out of the Cradle Endlessly Rocking," 333, 338; paganism, 312, 313; "Passage to India," 319, 321, 324; personality, 312, 313; philosophy, 324, 325, 326; picture poems, 317; "Pioneers! O Pioneers!" 316; place in fame, 329; poems, form of, 329, 330, 331; his poetry, 336; prophecy, 318, 319; Quakerism, 312, 321; religion, 313; representative man, 320; "Salut du Monde," 322; sex, dealings with, 329, 341, 342; "Song for Occupations," 321, 325, 334; "Song of Myself," 308, 309, 310, 318, 320, 323, 333, 336, 338, 341, 345, 348; "Song of the Broad-Axe," 316, 317; "Song of the Open Road," 319; "Song of Joys," 316; "Songs of Parting," 350; soul and sense, identification, 309, 315, 325; "Spontaneous Me," 344; "Starting from Paumanok," 314, 340; style, 332, 335; taste, 343; theology, 325; Transcendentalism and, 315; Utopia, 318, 321, 326, 329; vision, 322, 349; Way, 326; word pictures, 334, 335; working classes and, 327, 328

Whittier, J. G., xiii, 29

Wilderness, 137, 196, 201; Cooper, 98, 105, 108; New England, 174, 175; philosophy, 116

Will, 18, 19, 20, 178, 179, 233; **strong will and good will**, 28

Williams, Roger, 10

Williams, Stanley, 46, 74

Williamsburg, Va., 34

Willis, N. P., 217

Wilson, J. S., 271

Wilson, Woodrow, 51, 57, 58

Wilstach, Paul, 50

Wine, 247

Wits, Hartford, 61, 63, 64

Women, Cooper's, 129; sexual sin, 239; Thoreau and, 194

Woolman, John, 45, 115; Edwards compared with, 30; "Journal," 4, 29, 30, 31; Quakers and, 28

Words, 259, 260, 293

Wordsworth, William, 174, 175

Workingmen, 36, 38

Wright, T. G., 10

Writing, 180

Wyalusing, 30

Yale University, 65; Cooper and, 103; Edwards and, 13, 14, 16; Hartford wits, 61, 64

Yankees, 24, 39, 46, 80, 85, 91, 166; Thoreau as an example, 189

Zenobia, 253, 256